The Furnace of Affliction

THE FURNACE OF

Affliction

Prisons & Religion in Antebellum America

JENNIFER GRABER

The University of North Carolina Press
Chapel Hill

© 2011 THE UNIVERSITY OF NORTH CAROLINA PRESS
All rights reserved. Set in Minion Pro by Rebecca Evans.
Manufactured in the United States of America

The paper in this book meets the guidelines for permanence and durability
of the Committee on Production Guidelines for Book Longevity of the Council
on Library Resources. The University of North Carolina Press has been a
member of the Green Press Initiative since 2003.

Library of Congress Cataloging-in-Publication Data
Graber, Jennifer, 1973–
The furnace of affliction : prisons and religion
in antebellum America / Jennifer Graber.
p. cm.
Includes bibliographical references (p.   ) and index.
ISBN 978-0-8078-3457-2 (alk. paper)
1. Religious work with prisoners—United States—History—19th century.
2. Corrections—United States—History—19th century.
3. Prisoners—United States—Religious life—History—19th century.
4. Protestantism—United States—History—19th century. I. Title.
HV8865.G73 2011
365′.665097309034—dc22
2010034641

A portion of this book previously appeared, in somewhat different form,
as "'When Friends Had the Management It Was Entirely Different': Quakers and
Calvinists in the Making of New York Prison Discipline," *Quaker History 97*,
no. 2 (Fall 2008): 19–40. Used by permission.

15 14 13 12 11   5 4 3 2 1

MIX
Paper from
responsible sources
FSC® C013483

In loving memory of
ROBERT MICHAEL WOODS

Contents

Illustrations

Acknowledgments

When a book takes more than five years to write, there are lots of people to thank. First, let me mention those who made it possible—materially—to write this book. For their financial assistance, I thank the Gilder Lehrman Institute of American History, the Duke University History Department, the Center for the Study of Philanthropy and Voluntarism at the Terry Sanford Institute of Public Policy at Duke University, the Graduate School of Duke University, and the Faculty Development Fund and the Luce Fund for Distinguished Scholarship at the College of Wooster.

Librarians from the following institutions shared sources and information through mail, email, and phone conversations or provided assistance during research visits: American Bible Society, New York; American Tract Society, Garland, Texas; Methodist Library at Drew University, Madison, New Jersey; Asbury Theological Seminary Library, Wilmore, Kentucky; Texas Baptist Historical Collection, Dallas, Texas; Archives of the Episcopal Diocese of New York; Union College, Schenectady, New York; Union Theological Seminary, Richmond, Virginia; New York State Library, Albany; New York State Archives, Albany; Science, Industry, and Business Library of the New York Public Library, New York; Burke Library at Union Theological Seminary, New York; Bobst Library at New York University; Presbyterian Historical Society, Philadelphia; American Antiquarian Society, Worcester, Massachusetts; Library Company of Philadelphia; Cayuga Museum of History and Art, Auburn, New York; and Special Collections at Duke University, Durham, North Carolina. Thank you also to interlibrary loan staff at Duke University and the College of Wooster.

In addition, the following libraries granted permission to quote from materials I found in their archival collections: Manuscripts Department of the New-York Historical Society Library, Manuscripts and Archives Division of the New York Public Library, Friends Historical Library at Swarthmore College, Rare Book and Manuscript Library at Columbia University, and Southern Historical Collection at the Wilson Library of the University of North Carolina at Chapel Hill.

I must also thank the people who provided the intellectual stimulation and social support that made this book possible. Elaine Maisner, my wonderful editor at UNC Press, and my anonymous outside reader offered helpful suggestions. I owe a great debt to my second outside reviewer, Michael Meranze, who carefully read the manuscript and asked the tough questions that helped this book become what it is. Thanks to all my critical readers along the way, especially Julie Byrne, Philip Gura, Seth Dowland, Jennifer Connerly, Brendan Pietsch, Kathryn Lofton, Theron Schlabach, Kip Kosek, and Heather Curtis. My colleagues at the College of Wooster, Mark Graham and Diana Springer, provided essential support in the book's final stages. My mentors Stanley Hauerwas and Thomas Tweed have played an invaluable role in my growth as a scholar. I have also received endless guidance and support from Grant Wacker. I will always be grateful for my experience as his student.

My final thanks go to my family: to my husband, Stacy, who read drafts and watched babies to make this happen; to my daughter, Sasha, who let me run away to the computer periodically during the first two years of her life; and to my son, Martin. As a baby, he napped in the archives of the New-York Historical Society. He will be six when we see the book in print. He has been there all the way. I wrote this book because we live in a country where so many mothers' sons are behind bars. I hope this story will prompt readers to question whether prisons are the right and best place for them.

The Furnace of Affliction

Introduction

Americans incarcerate. Though the United States has less than 5 percent of the world's population, it has almost a quarter of its prisoners. More than two million Americans live behind bars. That is one out of every one hundred adults. The United States imprisons a higher percentage of its citizens than any other industrialized country. The economic cost of maintaining prisons threatens to overwhelm the population. In 2010 California officials considered releasing thousands of inmates in order to balance the budget. The human cost—counted in broken families and decimated communities—can hardly be calculated.[1]

The nation's high incarceration rate prompts impassioned debate. Politicians and activists, editorialists and community leaders consider a range of issues. They discuss the severity of drug crime sentencing, the ethics of for-profit prisons, and the inordinate number of racial minorities behind bars. The focus on these admittedly important issues, however, has obscured the ongoing discussion about what prisons should do. For more than two hundred years, Americans have debated the prison's purpose. Should it be retributive or reformative? Do we put people in prison to punish them or to rehabilitate them? Or is it a little of both?

Since the 1970s, American prisons have had a decidedly retributive tone. Sentences are long. Institutions are bleak. Politicians stake their careers on being tough on crime. The public, though ignoring the prisons around them, eagerly consumes television shows and movies depicting harsh prison conditions. This tough approach to lawbreakers obscures two things: it over-shadows current work to enact reformative prison programs; and it causes us to forget that, throughout most of American history, citizens believed that the prison's primary purpose was inmate reformation. Though they agreed that lawbreakers needed to be punished for their crimes, citizens assumed that a democratic nation supported institutions aimed at reform, not punitive regimes better suited to despotic governments. Most of these people also assumed that religion was vital to inmate reformation.[2]

But creating reformative prisons that rely on religion can be difficult to do without imposing particular religious traditions on inmates. For instance, in 2006 Iowa judge Robert Pratt declared that the InnerChange Freedom Initiative (IFI), a Christian residential program inside a state prison, violated the Constitution. His decision noted that the program had the purportedly secular goal of reducing recidivism. Judge Pratt also observed that IFI welcomed inmates of any religious persuasion, or none at all, into its program. Nevertheless, he found that the program's message and methods amounted to the state's support of a Protestant prison unit. IFI's explicitly evangelical program was the only option available to inmates seeking rehabilitative support. Iowa taxpayers were footing the bill for Friday night revivals and therapeutic sessions delivering messages about sin and grace. The IFI's presence in a state prison, the judge concluded, constituted the government establishment of religion.[3]

The Protestant evangelicals involved in IFI and its parent organization, Prison Fellowship Ministries, disagreed. They believe not only that religion reforms inmates but also that public institutions such as prisons are natural platforms for Protestant expression. Legal scholar and historian of American religion Winnifred Sullivan offers an explanation for Protestant evangelical activity in places like prisons. Historically, she explains, Protestants have been skeptical of ecclesiastical power. Faith imposed by clerics is no faith at all. However, evangelicals have been less reluctant to use government power to impose morality in the larger culture. Considering the organization behind IFI, Sullivan writes, "Operating in a prison allows Prison Fellowship to rely on state structures of authority to enforce discipline of their utopian Christian community." Where churches have failed to secure citizens' disciplined living, government steps in to help. She compares the IFI to nineteenth-century public school campaigns, in which reformers promoted a nominally nondenominational program of Protestant Christianity deemed appropriate for every American child. While Protestant evangelicals deny particular forms of church authority, Sullivan asserts, they have embraced alternate formats for Protestant authority in places ranging from schools and the military to prisons and the marketplace.[4]

Sullivan makes an apt comparison between contemporary Protestant evangelical public activity and the antebellum public school campaigns. Some historians of the early nineteenth century argue that the public school controversy is one among many examples of Protestant Christianity's power and pervasiveness. In the nineteenth century, Protestants effectively positioned themselves to have their texts and their prayers placed in every American classroom. Other examples of their power abound. Revivals swelled the ranks of church members. Bible and tract societies blanketed the country in scripture and admonitions to be saved. Christian voluntary associations waged massive campaigns to improve conditions for orphans and prostitutes, sailors and slaves. At one point, the moneys available to these agencies combined to dwarf the federal budget. Through revival and reform, Protestants sought to secure moral lives and a moral nation. Their successful efforts, some historians argue, reveal the extent of their power and influence in antebellum life.[5]

Other historians, however, claim that dramatic revival campaigns and associations organized to enforce morality reveal antebellum Protestants' deep anxieties. In these readings, the public school campaigns expose Protestant fears about immigrant Catholics, free blacks, and other marginal groups taking their place in American democracy. Despite revival successes and reform achievements, prominent Protestants—especially the clergy— wondered how they could continue to shape the culture, especially in light of religious disestablishment.[6]

The first American prisons serve as a site for exploring these rival interpretations of antebellum Protestant public activity. The prison story reveals that citizens participated in revival and reform's optimistic fervor while they simultaneously struggled to negotiate government partnerships and relate to marginal social groups. As with the recent Iowa case, the first prisons sparked debate over the degree and character of religion's impact on public life. The prison's first decades show that just as the nation began to reform its criminal justice system and build institutions for reformative incarceration, citizens had no clear sense of how religious actors might contribute to the process.

The struggle over religion's place in the antebellum prison can be hard to see because so many observers at the time insisted on religion's vital role in reformatory incarceration. Though they disagreed on many other points, most partisans affirmed religion's central importance. For instance, the American prison experiment was only a few decades old when two Frenchmen, Alexis de Tocqueville and Gustave de Beaumont, came over to study it. They toured the United States for nearly a year, visiting prisons, jails, and reformatories from Massachusetts to Louisiana. They approved of the new American system's rehabilitative emphasis, a dramatic shift from the old system of steep fines and bodily punishments. They praised the disciplinary routines, which included various forms of isolation and labor. They commended programs supporting basic inmate education and physical health. Like so many of their observations about American life, Tocqueville and Beaumont also noted the key role religion played in the prisons. "In America," they wrote, "the progress of the reform of prisons has been of a character essentially religious. Men, prompted by religious feelings, have conceived and accomplished everything which has been undertaken. . . . It is [religion's] influence alone which produces complete reformation." The French visitors presumed that religion worked for good, not only in inmates' lives but also as a guiding force for American citizens and institutions.[7]

Argument and Approach

This book uses Tocqueville and Beaumont's observations about religion's role in reformative incarceration to ask broader questions about antebellum public life. Focused on the first prisons, it asks just how "religious" criminal justice reform was. How did religion influence reformers and their prison agendas? How did religion contribute to conceptions of inmate reformation? To answer these questions, this historical study of antebellum New York institutions investigates how religion affected developing prison disciplines. Concerning the place of religion in American public life, it considers the prison debates as a key site for understanding the ambiguities of American religious disestablishment.[8]

Three historical claims lay the groundwork for exploring these questions. First, Protestant reformers and ministers involved in New York penal reform argued that inmate reformation constituted the prison's primary purpose. This network included Quakers and Congregationalists, Presbyterians and Baptists, Methodists and the newly formed Christians, or Disciples of Christ. Despite their theological differences, they all claimed that a Christian nation demanded penal institutions with humane practices and reformative disciplines. They affirmed that criminals could and should be redeemed. Second, Protestant reformers played an influential role in early prison experiments around the turn of the nineteenth century. In New York, Quakers led the way in lobbying for, designing, and administering the state's first prison. Their experience, especially the difficulties they encountered with both state officials and inmates, leads to the third claim. Over the course of the antebellum period, Protestant reformers struggled to shape prison disciplines to their liking and found themselves increasingly marginalized from arenas in which policy decisions were made.

The experience of Protestant prison reformers reveals the early national period's great paradox. It was a society marked by both the disestablishment of religion and the citizenry's commitment to the nation's Christian character. While no denomination enjoyed particular, state-sponsored privileges, many Americans employed rhetoric about America's Christian identity. Debates about religion's role in the prison, then, spoke to conflicts over the reach and the limits of Protestants' public power. The early national prisons show the obstacles to integrating the language of Protestant piety into a public discourse of republican ideals. They expose the problems created as reformers attempted to merge the vocabulary of evangelical religious experience and ethics with their concern for governmental institutions and citizens on the margins. Contrary to Tocqueville and Beaumont's assessment, the Protestant reformers' experiences reveal the deep disagreements over religion's place in the prisons and the wider public sphere.[9]

This book focuses on the role of religion—in this case, the varieties of evangelical Protestantism that dominated early national American life— in debates about the antebellum prison. In order to secure a place in the prison experiment, Protestants articulated a united front about religion's contribution to reformative incarceration. They argued that religion played a crucial role in inmate reformation and in guiding the development of penal institutions. If and when they were welcomed into prisons, however, they struggled. The reformers and ministers offered recognizably Protestant notions of suffering and redemption. They provided a particularly Protestant version of what literary theorist Caleb Smith has called the "narrative of death and resurrection" that made the prison cell the scene of a "new political ritual." State officials and inmates, however, usually resisted the reformers' promotions of Protestant piety. These rejections created a new problem. If the Protestant reformers could not control religion's content, a new set of negotiations was necessary. In response, politicians and prison officials, along with some of the Protestant prison activists, articulated a religiosity of citizenship focused on ethical behavior and obedience to secular authority. Or, as theorist of religion John Lardas Modern has observed, they "shifted their referents" from Christian creeds to living daily life. The results surprised them. While the Protestant reformers supported a furnace of affliction to transform inmates, they found their own religion remade inside the nation's prisons.[10]

The Protestant reformers viewed these concessions as a loss. They had not managed to impart to inmates their cherished patterns of religious life. The prisons did not result in large-scale Christian conversion. The reformers frowned on the negotiations necessary to be in the prisons and stay politically relevant. They usually concluded that their prison efforts had failed. Their sense of failure, however much it troubled these tireless Christian activists, signaled the contested place of religion in American public life. As an institution developed by citizens committed to religion's centrality, but simultaneously in significant disagreement about religion's content, the antebellum prison is a primary site for exploring Americans' complicated commitments to religion in the public sphere.

Organization and Sources

The book's chapters detail the programs of Protestant piety offered by reformers, along with an analysis of how prison partisans debated these religious contributions. The reformers and ministers trusted that Protestant Christianity offered ways to address lawbreakers in need of change and systems of justice in need of reform. The first chapter focuses on the early republic, where mostly Quaker activists imagined incarceration as a response to the colonial era's severe corporal punishments and steep fines. The prison was to be a garden that rehabilitated, indeed reformed, those who had suffered from poverty and ignorance that resulted in criminal acts. These prison experiments quickly faltered. The second and third chapters focus on the 1810s and 1820s, when a new set of Calvinist reformers—many of them aligned with the Prison Discipline Society of Boston—prescribed more rigorous disciplines intended to break down and reshape inmates. They turned to the prophet Isaiah and spoke of the prison as a furnace of affliction in which God-ordained sufferings paved the way for receiving grace and reforming behavior. The prisons became increasingly harsh and violent in the late 1820s and into the 1830s. Chapters 4 and 5 follow a variety of reformers and ministers as they vigorously protested the violence in both the legislature and the public sphere. They insisted that retribution and degradation had no place in the furnace of affliction, that the fires should not be stoked too hot. They did not win the debate. Indeed, by the late 1840s and into 1850s, Protestant reformers and ministers viewed the prison as a hell on earth. Chapter 6 details their entreaties to other Christians, exhortations to follow Jesus's command to visit the incarcerated and bind up the wounds of those broken by prison regimes.

These visions of religion's place in the prisons—of wholesome gardens for the wayward, furnaces for transforming the guilty, and a hell where only mediating kindness could be offered—were contested by state officials, other reformers, and inmates with alternative visions of religion's public character. While Protestant reformers experienced episodes of partnership with state officials and other reformers, these moments rested on assumptions about religion that faltered when confronted with tough situations inside prison walls. Officials rejected reformers' nurturing garden when it failed to yield profit and maintain order. Although the furnace of affliction model seemed to offer wide agreement, it broke down over differences about the nature and extent of inmate suffering. While officials might have disagreed that prisons were hell, they certainly welcomed the Protestant reformers' and ministers' focus on ministries to the broken.

The source base for the book is textual. The texts are a testimony to the antebellum period's information revolution. More writers found publishers, and more citizens considered ideas they encountered in print. The prison debate was no exception. Partisans wrote legislative documents and official reports, diaries and letters, sermons and pamphlets, and articles for newspapers and magazines. Among the book's sources, the authors are usually Protestant reformers and clergymen or politicians and prison officials. Whenever documentation is available, of either inmates' actions or their words, I highlight the prisoners' experiences.[11]

Background

Understanding the debates concerning religion's role in the first prisons requires some background about sin and crime in colonial America. Whereas not all sins were crimes, all crimes were sins. Murder, theft, rape, and forgery garnered responses from both civil magistrates and colonial clerics. To be sure, religious commitment across the colonies varied dramatically. Protestant authorities hardly concurred on all theological issues, but most clerics preached a clear message about sin. All humans inherited it through their common ancestors, Adam and Eve. Everyone was responsible for it. Sin revealed the distance between God and humanity. Particular sinful acts spoke to the shocking degree of that distance in individual lives. The doctrines of original sin and predestination affirmed that human striving could not affect sinful status. Only Jesus's atoning sacrifice on the cross, made available and effective to human beings through God's grace, spanned this chasm. But even as these doctrines came under attack during the colonial era, the idea of sin persisted. Some colonial preachers discarded notions of common inheritance and human inability. At the same time, they reaffirmed that sin, because it was the most serious problem in human life, still demanded providential assistance. Consequently, religious life in the colonies amounted to prayerful acts and supplications for God's grace. Salvation usually followed a period of spiritual distress, if not agony.[12]

The problem of sin vexed spiritually minded colonists. Would God offer redeeming grace? If grace was available, would individuals continue to sin or live a life of moral perfection? How were communities to deal with sinful acts committed within their ranks? Developments in colonial religious life addressed these personal and communal questions. Purveyors of revival argued for religious renewal and moral living, even if they disagreed about some of the theological particulars. Communities also addressed the question of individual sinful behavior. Some advocated "strict moral standards" for admission to communion. Many religious bodies had disciplinary procedures, often borrowed from the Gospel of Matthew, that involved confronting sinners, offering modes of reconciliation, and requiring the withdrawal of the intransigent. If the offender was of high social significance or the offense particularly egregious, discipline sometimes took the form of church trials. In the colonial era, sin was considered a common condition that churches addressed either through older forms of discipline or through newer formats, such as sermons and songs aimed at individual awakening and moral reformation.[13]

Sin always offended the church. Sometimes it involved breaking the law. Colonists made concerted efforts to confront crime and deter lawbreakers. They generally relied on the British legal code to deal with offenders. Sheriffs, constables, and citizens on night watch administered jails, brought criminals to trial, and tried to keep the peace. Boston established a jail by 1635. The city later added both an almshouse for the poor and a workhouse for the unruly. New York established a court system by 1691. Criminals and the poor occupied the city's bridewell, or jail, until a separate almshouse was built in 1736. Colonial Philadelphia also boasted institutions for the poor and disorderly. But as historian David Rothman has observed, these institutions operated in an informal manner and did not have pretensions to affect social change. Keeping order was the primary goal, though it often went unrealized.[14]

Colonial justice was not only unorganized but also severe. Historians have suggested that colonists employed strict penal codes in an effort to bind together a culture that could easily spin out of control. Harsh public punishments made the lines of authority clear. Communities hanged first-time offenders who committed adultery or buggery. Repeat offenders of property crimes also went to the gallows. Punishments could be fiscal or physical, relatively mild or extraordinarily severe. In communities with strict religious codes, clergymen provided another layer of public support for these punishments that stigmatized crime.[15]

Colonial executions show the extent of the overlap between civil and religious authority in matters of sin and crime. As historian Michael Meranze has observed about colonial punishment, the criminal's body became "a symbol of the communal whole and the religious and political authority over it." This was especially true at executions. When New England townsfolk witnessed a murderer on the gallows, Puritan ministers guided them through the event. They reminded the crowd that civil government served as God's institution for keeping social order. They claimed that lawbreakers under judgment represented the entire community's sins. In short, one criminal's act signified that all had sinned before God. According to these ministers, capital punishment was a sign—one among many—that reminded Puritans to keep their part of the covenant with God. Even in parts of the colonies without New England's close connection between the civil and religious order, magistrates and ministers together used the gallows to support their quest for public order and God's favor.[16]

Whatever the difficulties and disagreements colonists experienced over questions of sin and crime, two principles marked their common considerations. First, sin was everyone's problem. No one could avoid it at a personal level, and no community could escape its negative effects. Second, while some religious communities designed disciplines to reconcile and redeem offenders to the community, civil punishments had no such aim. Fines and bodily punishments were believed to deter crime. Citizens affirmed that the pain of financial loss or bodily suffering paid the price due to the injured public. Magistrates did not intend these punishments to reform offenders. The transition to a system aimed at reformation, then, marked a significant departure from colonial-era legal practice.

Significance

For decades, historians heralded the early republic's prison experiments as a crucial step forward for humanity. Like Tocqueville and Beaumont, they affirmed that reformative incarceration essentially ended brutal corporal punishments and signaled a new concern for the pain and suffering of others. Prison historians no longer make such claims. Instead, they acknowledge that there was no sharp divide between harsh punishments practiced in the colonial period and gentler sanctions proffered in the early republic. They narrate the prison's uneven development and the ironies of its advent in an era of democratic revolution. As historian Rebecca McLennan has written, prisons have always been "unstable and highly contested." Their history abounds with "conflict and political crisis." Their advent certainly did not end corporal punishment. Instead, bodily sanctions resurfaced periodically throughout the nineteenth century. Historians account for this irregular development in a variety of ways. Some posit the weakness of emerging democracy, unable to extend political rights to all without incarcerating and disenfranchising felons. Others focus on labor relations and the effects of economic tumult on the earliest prisons and their regimes of forced labor. Still others point to the shadow cast by slavery, which prompted difficult questions about confining and punishing other people, as well as prospering from their unwilling work.[17]

The crises and questions occasioned by the early prisons show that antebellum Americans did not simply propose a system of reformative incarceration and support it without question. They remained unsettled about the prison. They responded to their perceptions of its successes and failures. Their opinions about the prison's purpose and its daily disciplines changed in response to the era's political, economic, and cultural transformations. Arguments about religion contributed to this instability in two ways. First, partisans in the prison debates used references to religion in order to advance specific disciplinary regimes. In their efforts to sway public opinion, proponents cited God, Jesus, the spirit of religion, and the brotherhood of man as inspiration. In particular, references to religion almost always played a key role in denying the prison's potential tyranny. Second, though partisans often rallied around religion and applauded its contributions to prison stability, they constantly disagreed about particular religious practices performed inside prison walls. They referenced God's justice and mercy. They noted Jesus's kindness. But they disagreed sharply about the practices necessary to cultivate a relationship with God and the extent of Jesus's mercy to wrongdoers. These differences led to further contention in places where many had assumed broad agreement.[18]

This book explores religion's role—as it destabilized debates about prison discipline and fostered disagreement rather than consensus—in an effort to contribute to our understanding of American prisons and American religion. For historians of nineteenth-century prisons specifically and early republic and antebellum American historians more broadly, it offers a careful account of the way Protestant reformers and chaplains articulated and implemented their disciplinary goals with varying degrees of success. It also serves as an exploration of how inmates reacted to the particularly religious elements of prison discipline through reports of inmate actions and through prisoner narratives.[19]

For historians of American religion, close study of the situation facing Protestant prison reformers—along with their negotiations over religion's role and content—reveals the challenges presented by simultaneous commitments to disestablishment and the nation's Christian character. Most prison historians have acknowledged the particular Protestant traditions that influenced prison reform programs. They note the widely held cultural assumptions about human sinfulness and redemptive possibility that informed the penitentiary movement. Some historians have offered more specific accounts, for example, connecting Quaker conceptions of the Inner Light to proposals for solitary confinement or some Calvinist support for continued use of the death penalty with the doctrine of original sin. Other historians have identified broad trends in American religious life, such as the decline in Calvinist orthodoxy or loss of clergy's privileged status in the early republic, to explain a move toward what was considered to be more humane punishment. Historians, then, have looked to the prison as representing the variety of and trends within antebellum Protestant Christianities.[20]

While historians have emphasized the prison reformers' and ministers' particularities, they have overlooked the way these activists cultivated common cause. Understanding religion's place in the antebellum prisons demands the exploration of the united front that reformers and ministers presented. To be sure, they disagreed over some specifics in rival disciplinary plans. More important, though, they agreed that incarceration had to have a reformative goal and that religion played a vital part in that goal's realization.[21]

Exploring the first prisons provides the opportunity to reconsider Protestant social reform for what it reveals about transformations in Protestant identity rather than its effects on American culture. This reconsideration is necessary, as much of the literature on American religion and reform has overlooked prison activism. Historians have focused instead on movements with broader participation and more measurable success. Though a few historians mention it, they offer minimal consideration in comparison to the attention directed at the movements to end slavery and curb alcohol consumption. Undoubtedly, the prison activists wanted to change things. They sought reformed criminals and reformed criminal punishment. They joined a massive interdenominational movement to evangelize the poor and friendless, fight slavery's expansion, and promote the virtues of temperance. They stood among thousands of American Protestants devoted to securing the nation's divine mission and articulating a vision of true religion that countered bad personal and political behavior.[22]

But as scholarship on American evangelicalism has shown, the impulse toward wider influence often involved the redefinition of Protestant piety. In order to secure their prison programs, Protestant reformers increasingly articulated a religiosity of citizenship focused on lawful living and obedience to secular authority. They advocated for "religion" even as Protestant particulars receded from public space. They stressed a Christian faith realized most significantly as moral living and obedience to governmental authority. These ministers and reformers were neither duped into this partnership nor calculating to achieve maximize political advantage. They recognized the need for negotiation. They tracked their gains and losses. Through the entire process, they struggled to hold together their notions of "saved soul" and "civil subject." Their prison experiences show, however, that they were ultimately unsuccessful. Or, as historian Mark E. Kann has remarked of prison reformers more generally, "[their] policies failed but their words succeeded."[23]

While the prisons received a lasting religious imprint, the most significant transformation happened within Protestant reforming circles. Indeed, this moment in the ongoing story of negotiating disestablishment provides another site for exploring what scholars have called secularization, or formations of the secular. The Protestant prison reformers and chaplains wanted to save souls and steer the nation toward godly behavior among individuals and government. This project became increasingly difficult, for, as historian Mark Noll has observed, "the reach of evangelicals has always exceeded their grasp." In a more traditional sense, then, this story tracks a secularizing trend. It follows Protestantism's declining public significance. More interesting, however, is the way their experience reveals how the project to Christianize the populace and its governmental institutions had a secularizing effect on the religion that the reformers recommended. In short, to secure a space in the prisons, the reformers excised the particulars of Quaker silence, Presbyterian prayer, and Methodist discipline. In their place, they articulated a vision of the redeemed life composed of common morality and hard work. As one theorist of secularization has put it, they preached a "true religion" that had significant "secular credentials and aspirations." Over time, this religiosity of citizenship overwhelmed the Protestant piety that the reformers tried to establish. Though they never wanted to abandon the "central role of grace" in virtuous living, a new era demanded narratives of "self-generated, personally chosen, public self-discipline." The ministers and reformers recognized the risks in their prison partnership. They never felt satisfied with the institutions they helped create. They sensed that the prison had changed them as much as or even more than it had transformed inmates. They concluded that America was not the sort of Christian country they once imagined. Their legacy remains with us. The Iowa case of 2006—one centered on the question of religion's role in inmate reformation and the place of religion in state institutions—shows that we have yet to settle the difficult dilemma that the prison presents.[24]

1

The Prison as Garden, 1796–1804

In the summer of 1800, fifteen convicts from Newgate Prison made a "daring escape" across the Hudson River to New Jersey. New York State legislators responded by establishing an armed guard on call in the surrounding neighborhood. The prison's agent, a Quaker and advocate of nonviolence, objected. He told state officials that overseeing the guard required duties that those "who are of the people called Quakers, cannot with propriety discharge." Legislators were unmoved. The armed guard remained, straining the prison's budget and vexing its Quaker administrators.[1]

During the prison's early years, the armed guard served on several occasions. Its ongoing presence clearly signaled that all was not well inside Newgate Prison. The controversy over the guard's necessity and morality proved to be the first of many conflicts between Friends administering the prison and state officials involved in governmental oversight. This situation seems almost absurd to the modern reader. Who put pacifist Quakers in charge of a criminal justice experiment? At the prison's founding, however, no one seemed particularly worried. If anything, many observers viewed the Friends as specially prepared and qualified for work with incarcerated criminals. Attention to the broadly held assumptions about religion's role in early republic society makes sense of this initial partnership. The Quakers running Newgate used a generalized religious terminology, calling for prisons to meet standards required by the "Christian religion," "humanity," "benevolence," and "morality." Legislators agreed and invited their participation.

The conflict over the armed guard, however, shows that agreement about religion faltered when particular Protestant practices failed to attain the state's desired results. The partnership weakened under pressure. The Quaker agent's protest served as the first in a long series of struggles pitting Protestant piety against state concerns about disciplinary order. Although the Friends took much inspiration and rhetoric from a transatlantic movement to reform criminal justice, once inside institutions they implemented practices drawn from Quaker tradition. They insisted on nonviolence. Daily routines and formats for prisoner counsel mirrored Quaker schools and methods of discipline. Conflicts with state officials arose when these particular practices failed to secure an orderly, profitable, and reformative environment. Because of the ubiquitous language about the prison's religious character, however, the parties seemed mystified by this breakdown.

Confronting Colonial Justice

In 1781 Thomas Eddy found himself in trouble. A young Quaker on a late night outing to visit his beloved, Eddy was set upon by New Jersey militiamen. The soldiers, keeping watch for potential enemies of the revolution, took aim at the young suitor. They shot at Eddy's boat, arrested him, and charged him with acting as a Loyalist spy. The twenty-three-year-old Eddy spent more than a week in a Monmouth County jail and later described his circumstances. He stayed with four or five prisoners in a room just "six or seven feet square," he wrote. They had only "dirty straw" to lie upon. "The stench," he wrote, made the place a "miserable dungeon."[2]

In this New Jersey jail, Eddy got his first glimpse of colonial-era punishments. Decrepit cells served as holding pens for those awaiting trial. Once convicted, offenders received punishments ranging from stiff fines to embarrassment in the stocks to death by hanging. Magistrates trusted that the prospect of flogging, fines, or banishment deterred potential lawbreakers. And if those did not work, the gallows always remained. New Jersey officials released Eddy when the spying charges proved unfounded. While he had avoided the worst possible punishments, Eddy remembered that stuffy and smelly jail cell for years. His reflections on the experience, according to historian Thomas Laqueur, functioned as a "conversion narrative" linking his own experience to the suffering of others.[3]

After the revolution, many American Quakers regained their social position in the nation's growing cities. By the 1790s, Eddy, a successful merchant and philanthropist in New York, had joined many members of the Society of Friends in the transatlantic debates over proper punishment. In agreement with those who were convinced that severe bodily punishments smacked of despotism, Eddy affirmed that "the peace, security, and happiness of society" depended on a new penal system "devised for the prevention of crimes."[4]

The early American push for criminal justice reform that inspired Eddy can be understood only in relation to its European backdrop. In the late medieval and early modern periods, new forms of criminal punishment emerged alongside, and sometimes overlapping with, strategies designed to deal with paupers, idlers, and other marginal people who had not necessarily broken the law. Criminals received punishments ranging from warnings and fines to whipping and agonizing death. States sometimes banished lawbreakers or marked them by mutilation and branding. Authorities placed them in institutions where they mingled with debtors, the insane, or the generally unruly. The early modern workhouse, where some criminals were forced to labor and other residents did so voluntarily, provides an example of the overlap between criminal justice and a wider effort to establish social order. Authorities targeted criminal misbehavior as well as the idlers and impoverished who had fallen through the cracks. Lawbreakers, however, received particularly tough sanctions. Punishments could be economically devastating and physically grueling. Though some countries experimented with imprisonment as a criminal penalty, incarceration was not widely practiced or considered necessarily reformative.[5]

While examples of punishment across Europe served as fodder for the New World, the colonists' systems of determining guilt and providing sanctions came directly from English common law. As on the continent, the English used a wide range of corporal punishments, public humiliations, and forms of confinement. But as historian Randall McGowen has noted, relatively few people were incarcerated for crime. Indeed, the majority of folks in England's jails and houses of correction were vagrants and debtors. Most lawbreakers received more immediate penalties, ranging from fines to periods in the stocks to capital punishment.[6]

Several factors in the seventeenth and eighteenth centuries brought dramatic changes to England's punishment practices. Crime rates rose. Imprisonment for debt increased. Authorities tried transporting criminals to the New World, but that solution became less tenable in the years leading up to the Revolutionary War. In the midst of these crises, English lawmakers expanded the list of capital crimes. For decades, the state had executed those convicted of serious offenses such as murder, rape, and treason. But in the eighteenth century, officials authorized the death penalty for a much wider range of crimes. Whereas the law included 50 capital crimes in 1688, it boasted 165 by 1765 and more than 200 by 1815. The expanded list of offenses punishable by death increasingly targeted petty crimes against property, such as stealing a sheep or pilfering fruit. Scholars have explained these developments as a response to the economic and social anxieties that gripped English culture. Whatever the reason, petty offenders risked their lives by committing even the smallest offense.[7]

Many historians link England's move toward harsher penalties for petty crime with the culture's increasing discomfort with the poor. Not only were more people incarcerated for debt, but ideas about poverty had changed also. For centuries, poverty was considered a humble, yet God-ordained station that gave people with resources a chance to share. As the ranks of the poor overwhelmed the social structures that had once accommodated them, citizens began to view penury as the result of idleness. More and more people became convinced that the poor, either unwilling or unable to work, would leach off society or, worse, commit crimes against it. New houses of correction hosted the poor, vagrants, and criminals, revealing the way in which ideas about poverty and criminality increasingly overlapped in English culture.[8]

Indeed, because criminal justice and poor relief reflect a society's norms and boundaries, Christian clergymen had ample reason to comment, if not participate, in this transformation. In England, ministers preached "condemned sermons" in prison chapels on the Sundays before executions. On the appointed day, clergymen offered prayers and the sacraments to offenders before processions to the hangman. Some ministers rode in carts to the gallows with the guilty party. Once at the site, they prayed penitential psalms. Particularly insistent ministers encouraged the condemned to recite the creeds as the noose was put in place.[9]

On the western side of the Atlantic, most colonial governments reproduced England's increasingly harsh criminal code to keep a disorderly situation under relative control. Punishments included the death penalty for the most serious crimes. Lesser crimes were met with fines and banishment, whipping and mutilation, the stocks and ducking stool, or letter wearing and branding. As in England, ministers supported modes of criminal justice, preaching execution sermons and evangelizing the condemned.

The colonists followed their English counterparts in understanding many crimes to be both civil and religious offenses.[10]

What is important to notice about both England and the colonies is that governments did not use imprisonment as a form of punishment. Historians have found a few instances of incarceration either combined with other public punishments or mixed up with other socially marginal populations. Colonial jails served primarily as holding pens for those awaiting trail and those confined for debt. For the most part, colonists did not see incarceration as the most fitting response to crime. It was most certainly not considered reformatory. Thomas Eddy sat in jail only as he waited for his alleged crime to be adjudicated.[11]

As punishments were becoming increasingly severe, a broad movement for criminal justice reform and reformatory incarceration was afoot. Historian Karen Halttunen has noted a new "sympathetic concern for the pain and suffering of other sentient beings" that prompted spirited activism on behalf of groups ranging from the insane to the enslaved to the criminal. Indeed, instances of cruelty took on a new shock value, prompting Anglo-American citizens to call them savage and uncivilized. Human rights scholar Lynn Hunt has argued that the period hosted transformations in notions of bodily integrity and feelings of empathy that "made possible new social and political concepts."[12]

Several European philosophers and legal thinkers sparked the move toward imprisonment's wider use by criticizing contemporary legal codes, decrying sanguine punishments, and outlining new principles to direct criminal justice. Even as England expanded its list of capital crimes, French philosopher Charles Louis de Secondat de Montesquieu wrote his 1748 *Spirit of the Laws*, questioning the propriety of monarchs' imposition of harsh punishments. He argued that moderate applications of better laws would lead to a more enlightened society. A generation later, Italian jurist Cesare Beccaria published his *Crimes and Punishments*. He called for judicial reform, a correspondence between offenses and their punishments, and laws that worked toward the prevention of crime. He claimed that the swiftness and certainty of punishment would lead to less crime. By the time Englishman Jeremy Bentham began his work on punishment as a deterrent to crime in the late eighteenth century, there was a transatlantic buzz about how best to deal with lawbreakers.[13]

Montesquieu and Beccaria questioned criminal codes in their broader considerations of good governance. But some thinkers and activists, particularly in England, moved from legal reflections into practical questions of how criminal justice should be administered. Bentham, for example, not only wrote widely in the philosophy of law but also created a famous prison design, the panopticon, that was copied around the world. Other Englishmen took a similarly practical approach to their criminal justice concerns. Reformer John Howard toured England's county jails after his election as a local sheriff. Drawing on his observations, he wrote a treatise exposing inmates' miseries. In 1773 he urged the House of Commons to clean up these filthy institutions. He recommended that inmates' daily routines be punctuated by stints at labor. These changes, he argued, would cure the moral and physical diseases that plagued criminals. Howard successfully petitioned for an overhaul of the British penal code, but the dramatic changes ordered by the new legislation were never put into place. Nevertheless, his work soon inspired change on the other side of the Atlantic.[14]

Americans joined this European conversation about criminal justice at a time particularly ripe for change. In the years after the revolution, citizens found themselves faced with the possibilities and problems of starting a new country. The prospect of new social, economic, and religious realities proved both thrilling and daunting. Americans joined a host of newly formed benevolent and reform societies aimed at improving the populous and creating a stable social order. While many focused on the slave trade or poverty, some Americans turned their attention to criminal justice. They claimed that removing sanguine punishments from criminal codes would distance America from "Bloody England" and the new nation's colonial past. The European reformers provided both the philosophy and the plans for new institutions. But even with this backdrop, as historian David Rothman has noted, most of the American experiments were decidedly "homegrown," primarily because the European nations had not implemented the reformers' ideas.[15]

American activists targeted state criminal codes and moved quickly toward reshaping institutions. According to historian Gordon Wood, their criminal justice experiments attracted more worldwide attention than any other reform movement. In 1785, Massachusetts moved to imprison convicted criminals—separate from debtors and idlers—in a Castle Island fortress. The experiment at Castle Island, however, lasted only a few years. Pennsylvania's reforms proved more lasting. In 1786 the state authorized public labor, rather than capital and corporal punishments, for crimes such as robbery, sodomy, and horse stealing. When the outdoor spectacle of criminals at work proved too troublesome, Philadelphians pushed for an alternative. A leading voice in the clamor was physician Benjamin Rush, who called for punishment to move off the streets and out of public view. Rush's plans adapted European reformers' ideas and combined with them a concern for inmate reformation through a terrifying solitude. Indeed, as legal historian Michael Meranze has observed, Rush "articulated a philosophy and psychology of private, penitential punishments." By 1790 Rush and his reforming colleagues secured a victory. Pennsylvania's criminals began terms of imprisonment in the old Walnut Street Jail. Inmates passed their days by laboring. The worst offenders occupied solitary cells in the jail's "Penitentiary House." According to Rush and the Pennsylvania reformers, the environment both reformed inmates' characters and deterred them from future criminal acts. The southern region of the new country also hosted criminal justice reform. Thomas Jefferson participated in the design for a new state penitentiary at Richmond. Rush's hopes for Walnut Street and Jefferson's experiments with individual cells in Virginia reveal the transformation in thinking about criminal justice. Instead of violence aimed at deterrence, many citizens advocated strict but humane environments designed for reform.[16]

Friendly Faith and Discipline

Many Quakers expressed particular interest in criminal justice reform. As with so much of their social activism, they brought their particular history and theology to bear on the matter. This spiritual grounding did not mean, however, that Friends eschewed philosophy and political theory about crime and punishment. They drew from the many treatises penned by members of the wider reform movement. Their history of religious persecution and ideas about spiritual experience and discipline, however, made them unique contributors to these discussions.[17]

Friends played a significant role in Pennsylvania's reforms. The Philadelphia Society for Alleviating the Miseries of the Public Prisons (PSAMPP) boasted a strong Quaker membership. Despite the participation of reformers from outside Friends' circles, the Pennsylvania prison experiment took on a decidedly Quaker cast. The PSAMPP proposed a prison discipline of inmate separation and silence, Bible reading, and simple labor. To be sure, the Friends' concern for prisoners grew out of their own history of suffering in England and the colonies. Many Society members had served time in jail. Others met a worse fate. But their participation in legal change, prison administration, and institutional reforms also reflected the foundational

Quaker idea of the Inner Light and the eighteenth-century development of elaborate systems of discipline within Friends' communities. Society members' proposals for the prison were grounded in their belief that proper environment allowed lawbreakers to experience God's presence within.[18]

The doctrine of the Inner Light originated with Quaker founder, George Fox, in 1640s England. It affirmed that every person had the "still, small voice" of God within. Friends traced this belief to scripture, namely John 1:9, which attested to a true light "which lighteth every man." Fox's claim had radical implications. Every person had the capacity to experience direct communication from God. Those who turned to the Inner Light could trust its leading. Consequently, they did not necessarily require direction from others. Fox's followers, especially Robert Barclay, preached the possibilities of the Inner Light in a culture that still assumed religious authority rested in the hands of a small, male elite. He claimed universal spiritual potential in a climate still dominated by Calvinist particularity.[19]

While Quaker apologists reveled in the Inner Light, they certainly did not dismiss all forms of outside authority. Indeed, historians identify both "externalist and internalist tendencies" in the Society's development. They point to a reliance on internal religious access and experience on the one hand, along with affirmations of human sinfulness, Christ's atoning sacrifice, and the authority of scripture on the other. While the Friends are well known for their quietism, namely their efforts to crucify "creaturely activity" and replace it with divine inspirations, other emphases are present in their history. In particular, some Quakers continued to affirm essentially Protestant doctrines of humanity's fall and the need for grace through God's loving work. This focus on personal holiness, combined with some Protestant doctrinal affinities and a later influence of evangelical perfectionism, provided the constellation of principles from which the prison reform movement emerged.[20]

Quakers in the colonies, including those involved in early penal reform, experienced this tension between the religious potential within all members and considerations of Christ's historical life of good deeds and death on a cross. In particular, Friends struggled over questions of behavior. Why did people sin if they had the Light within? Did the Light work in single, dramatic experiences or slowly over time? Was perfection possible? Historian Hugh Barbour has noted that a movement that "began as a spontaneous outpouring of religious fervor . . . survived because people found its institutions conducive to experiencing the Inward Light and developing Christian character." Earnest Friends felt that the community's potential for spiritual experience was compromised by the worldly temptations of wealth, fancy clothes, and ornamental speech. The holy life needed limits. In response, they proposed new strictures over social and political deportment. As with reforms in many religious communities, the Quakers named leaders to enforce these new strictures. Believers needed assistance to balance religious exuberance with earthly responsibility.[21]

As a result, the role of the overseer emerged in Society life in the mid-eighteenth century. Quakers understood the necessity of communal discipline from their founding. Those looking to lead good, Christian lives necessarily manifested certain fruits and avoided a long list of sins. But Friends were human and sometimes broke the rules. In response, they developed an elaborate process for dealing with transgressions. While any member could admonish another and communities met regularly for the purpose of discipline, the role of overseer took on particular import in these cases. Modeled on a form of confrontation in the Gospel of Matthew, overseers "treat[ed] with the offender." In this process, a "Christian-spirited" overseer approached stubborn sinners so that they would recognize their offenses and seek communal restoration.[22]

While Friends found themselves in the midst of an internal transformation toward stricter discipline, they also experienced changing relations with the political world. Concerned over issues of war and peace, most Pennsylvania Quakers abdicated political power by leaving the state legislature in 1754. Although they no longer held political positions and were wary of government interaction, Friends still desired to witness to the world. The question was how to wield influence in the social order while maintaining the community's purity. With their first social reform efforts, the Quakers mixed a commitment to personal spiritual truth and perceived responsibility to the world with concerns about the best methods for affecting change.

Quaker antislavery campaigns provide an apt example. By 1774, Friends in the colonies prohibited slave owning among their membership. They came to this decision after debating and then concluding that slavery threatened the apprehension of personal religious truth. Slavery's strict social ordering and capacity for violence prevented both the enslaved person and the slaveholder from following the Inner Light. Slavery confronted Quakers with an example of ordered relationships and strict discipline gone awry. Slavery allowed for slave owners' violence and enslaved people's debasement in ways that hid the Light. The Friends' questions about human bondage soon stretched beyond members of the Society. What started as an internal debate quickly went national. Quaker reformers soon sought to convince the world of slavery's evils. Indeed, John Woolman—the most vocal Friends spokesman against slavery—reflected the complicated legacy of the group's social activism. He combined a commitment to personal holiness inspired by the Inner Light with a sense of humanity's fall and redemption, made effective through Christ.[23]

As noted earlier, a similar concern about severe punishments prompted many Pennsylvania Quakers to form the PSAMPP. With their Protestant and more philosophically inclined colleagues, they affected significant legislative change. Caleb Lownes, a local Friend and PSAMPP member, administered experiments with solitary confinement at the Walnut Street Jail. While the institution initially housed men in common rooms, officials soon noted that mingling all kinds of offenders allowed older criminals to school younger, less experienced offenders. From that point, prison staff tried to separate, or classify, lawbreakers of different degrees. They also envisioned a new facility, the Arch Street Prison, where smaller cells allowed greater separation of inmates. The movement had begun.[24]

It would be an overstatement to argue that Quakers achieved significant criminal justice change alone. Pennsylvania developments relied on other reformers as well, namely Benjamin Rush. Nevertheless, Friends played a major role in the Philadelphia legal reforms and institutional experiments. Their affirmation of the Inner Light, along with their concern for disciplined living, provided a rich resource base for their disciplinary work.

Reforming New York

New York Quakers saw similar problems with their home state's criminal justice system and looked to Pennsylvania for inspiration. Thomas Eddy's brief sufferings in a New Jersey jail mirrored the awful conditions in New York criminal institutions. As a colony and during its early years as a state, New York followed the English common-law tradition. But several challenges made criminal justice especially difficult there. Ethnic and religious diversity undermined many citizens' sense of common order. Periods of population surge and economic fluctuation made residents uneasy. Historians have found that eighteenth-century New York had particularly high crime rates compared to other colonies, and instances of violent crime were especially high. The criminal code addressed these violations with severity. The jails were squalid. Onlookers described the jail located at New York's City Hall as cramped, dark, and disorderly. Just outside it stood the whipping post, pillory, and stocks. The gallows loomed not far away. New York punished sixteen crimes, ranging from murder and treason to highway robbery and forgery, with the death penalty. Other felonies, including grand larceny, embezzlement, and child rape, were punished by fines or corporal punishment for the first offense and death for the second. Recidivists of much more common crimes, including counterfeiting and horse stealing, also met their end at the gallows.[25]

Despite such harsh sanctions, New York's colonial-era system of criminal justice proved somewhat fragile. Casework was notoriously uneven, with more than two-fifths of cases brought to the courts never ending in resolution. More than 50 percent of criminals who received death sentences were eventually pardoned. As historian Douglas Greenberg has found, lawbreakers' experience of the criminal justice system varied widely depending on the county they lived in and the social categories they occupied. In sum, crime rates were high, and the systems in place to confront crime lacked organization and support. Nevertheless, punishments could be quite severe. According to Thomas Eddy, the system caused undue criminal suffering and demanded a complete overhaul.[26]

While Eddy took some of his inspiration from Pennsylvania Friends, he also read works by European reformers. He praised Montesquieu's call for a reformation of jurisprudence. He pointed to Beccaria's many contributions, particularly the principle that punishments be proportional to crimes. Eddy reserved his highest praise for English reformer John Howard, whom he called a "friend of man" for his work to expose prisoners' miseries. Each of these writers, according to Eddy, "awakened the feelings of humanity and justice." Their programs prescribed good governance and good religion. Quoting Montesquieu, Eddy wrote that the best civil laws stood second only to religion as a culture's greatest good. "The Christian Religion," he claimed, "which ordains that men should love each other," was a nation's greatest blessing.[27]

The postrevolutionary impulse to emphasize distance from England also shaped Eddy. He boasted of America's economic and cultural progress. This work was marred, however, by a striking weakness. The new nation "thought not of unhappy beings who suffered under the numerous oppressions of tyrannical laws." The state and most of its citizens prospered, Eddy complained, while its criminal offenders met ignominious ends. In response, he started a one-man campaign to change the situation. He persuaded New York leaders that colonial-era punishments were both undemocratic and un-Christian. Riding a wave of criminal justice reforms in Europe and America, Eddy sought nothing less than a disciplinary revolution.[28]

Convinced of the need to reform New York's criminal justice system, Eddy turned to Pennsylvania's penal experiments as a basis for his proposals. He visited Philadelphia institutions with General Philip Schuyler, a New York legislator. They met Caleb Lownes and toured the Walnut Street Jail. Like so many eighteenth-century penal thinkers, Eddy believed that a society could be evaluated by its treatment of criminals and that current use of harsh bodily practices belied the goodness of American life. But with the Pennsylvania reformers, he concurred that criminal reform depended on the correct calibration of right circumstances and oversight within prison walls. From his reading of John Howard and corresponding and visiting with Pennsylvania Quakers, Eddy fashioned a plan for New York offenders that reflected the broad spectrum of reform impulses. His humanitarianism prompted his efforts to transform the sanguinary legal code. His more radical tendencies pushed him to view criminal justice as an index of a nation's holiness. But another impulse demanded that his work not end with legal revision. Indeed, his inclination toward moralism drove him to create a prison environment designed for inmate reformation. He envisioned not only the end of afflictions delivered on the gallows and pillory but also the sufferings imposed by poverty and bad life choices. Eddy and Schuyler returned to New York with the intention of lobbying the legislature for a reformatory prison modeled on the Walnut Street Jail.[29]

Eddy tested his reform ideas through valuable friendships with members of New York's upper echelons. He circulated a report on Pennsylvania's revised criminal code to two legislators and encouraged Senator Schuyler to propose legislation removing bodily punishments from New York's criminal code. The bill, abolishing the death penalty for everything but murder and treason, passed in March 1796. Corporal punishments, such as whipping and branding, were abolished. Criminals now faced imprisonment, which could be accompanied by "hard labour or solitary confinement, or both." All sentences longer than one year were to be served in state prison.[30]

New York, however, did not have a prison yet. Eddy and a handful of Quakers made up the majority members of a committee charged with the prison's construction and management. Eddy turned to Caleb Lownes for assistance. In a 1796 letter, the Philadelphia Quaker answered several of Eddy's questions, offered advice, and included drawings for the new prison's plan. Lownes assured Eddy that a combination of good architecture, careful regulations, and respectable staff eliminated potential security concerns. After his experience in Philadelphia's Walnut Street Jail, Lownes believed that good prison order guaranteed success. Eddy took Lownes's recommendations to heart, inviting the Philadelphia Quaker to New York to oversee the prison's construction.[31]

Eddy shared Lownes's optimism but knew that selling his ideas to the public would be difficult. He reckoned that "the work of reformation is slow, and must encounter many and strong prejudices, and the force of long-established opinions." Passing legislation and building the prison were only the beginning of the journey. Eddy needed to prove that a milder penal code would work—that it would protect the public and lower the crime rate. He had to show that prisoners would improve themselves if given the opportunity. Eddy recognized the public's reticence. He counseled the impatient to "turn their eyes inward upon their own hearts" and consider the need for dramatic social change before deciding between "mild and sanguinary" laws.[32]

While Eddy acknowledged the public's reticence, he never wavered in his support for a slow-going, milder-tempered plan to replace the inordinate suffering produced by colonial-era criminal sanctions. He wrote that the prison's success depended on "long and persevering attention." He defended his position by pointing to the "nature of man" and the "history of society," both proof that patience would be necessary. Eddy assumed the value of this long-term endeavor and believed that those working to reform criminals were "fulfilling the highest duty of humanity." If the system he proposed was the "only just and beneficent system yet devised for the punishment and correction of criminals," it certainly required just and beneficent men to administer it. According to Eddy, the prison could be the best reflection of a government's wisdom and a population's Christian faith. It offered the only opportunity for reforming lawbreakers.[33]

At least in one respect, Eddy's concern for inordinate criminal suffering both at the gallows and in the prison itself differed with some of the Philadelphia reformers not associated with the Society of Friends. While Eddy almost single-handedly envisioned and orchestrated the New York transformation, the Pennsylvania Friends dealt with reformers from other denominations and those with a more philosophical bent. Such reformers believed that incarceration avoided the sanguine and monarchical overtones of the gallows, even as it preserved punishment's purpose to deter. Yet, in their view, prison deterred potential lawbreakers only insofar as the prospect of incarceration terrified them. The reforming ideas of Benjamin

Rush exemplified this position. Rush sought the reformation of prisoners and believed it would be achieved through the prison's horror. He hoped the new institution would work its power on both the convicts within and the public blocked from view. Both groups would feel the "terror" imposed within this "abode of discipline and misery."[34]

Indeed, Eddy's plan for New York's first state prison looked quite similar to the experiments in Philadelphia. But unlike some of the Pennsylvania reformers, especially those outside the Friends circle, Eddy saw his new prison as a completely positive experience. He believed that prison would put an end not only to state sanctioned afflictions at the stocks and whipping post but also to sufferings created by social factors such as poverty, alcoholism, and urban decay. The prison provided an escape from both the gallows and the slum. It was designed not to terrify but to edify.[35]

Creating His Garden

Caleb Lownes advised Eddy that a prison garden would do much for "engaging the minds of those under your care." He testified from six years of experience at the Walnut Street Jail that extensive grounds and regular employment would not only bolster security but also "raise the prisoners both in their own and others' estimation." Lownes assured Eddy that a careful night watch and days full of wholesome activity protected from outside influences and rehabilitated inmates' character.[36]

Eddy certainly needed Lownes's advice. After successfully campaigning to rid New York State of its long list of corporal punishments, as well as trimming the state's capital offenses from thirteen to two, he now had a prison to build. Indeed, Eddy borrowed many ideas from Pennsylvania Friends, including plans for workshops and worship space. But he initially avoided Philadelphia's growing emphasis on solitary confinement. Philadelphia Friends saw their focus on solitude as consistent with Quaker principles. But Eddy's prison, which emphasized communal living and work, was no less Quaker. He looked less toward the Friends' legacy of solitude and reflection and more to recent innovations to address children's education, disciplined living, and the welfare of the nation's most vulnerable inhabitants.[37]

His choice to follow Lownes's advice about a garden is telling. In Eddy's time, Quakers reared their children in a structured home life and educational environment that historians have called an "enclosed garden." For many Friends, this enclosure shut off worldly evils such as gambling and theater, politics and violence, and, perhaps most important, marrying non-Quakers. As a child grew, the local meeting also played a role in social formation. Friends' meetings developed patterns of discipline for those who broke the guidelines impressed on them since childhood.

Eddy's prison ideal combined these internal traditions of childrearing and group discipline with the Quaker external concern for other people. Namely, he worried about the dangers of bad social environments in general and particular social practices that targeted marginal groups, such as African Americans and Native Americans. Like antislavery Friend Anthony Benezet, Eddy believed these populations' problems were caused not by their base characters or lesser humanity but rather by their dreadful social situations. Indeed, the degradations of poverty and slavery stifled the capacity to flourish and blocked the expression of the Inner Light. Eddy followed many Quakers' affirmation that both the inner and outer world mattered for the children they raised and for people mistreated by the wider world. The divine presence in each person demanded a proper environment. His prison brought together the removal from worldly distraction and a positive claim about the potential of a good environment for all those who carried the Light within.[38]

As literary critic Gail Finney has written, garden images generally embodied an "idealized alternative to social reality." In her study of nineteenth-century fiction, she noted the way in which gardens served as reminders of a simpler, country life in a rapidly urbanizing world. In particular, Finney has shown the way gardens often worked as symbols of ethical character, representing a cultivated example of "self-restraint and control" in the "midst of a tangled landscape." Indeed, Finney's examples from literature reflect Eddy's efforts inside Newgate Prison. In the tangle of New York City's criminal elements, he hoped to cultivate an ordered and prospering, if not fruitful, harvest of reformed behavior.[39]

While Eddy made much of enclosure, order, and discipline, he said little about suffering. Indeed, he mentioned mental and spiritual affliction—never physical—in regard to only the "more hardened and daring offenders." While inmates certainly disagreed, Eddy did not regard a state prison term as unduly painful or a loss in any way. In fact, his public accounts of the prison always heralded the institution as a bastion against worldly distraction and a setting for wholesome living. The prison was everything a chaotic city was not, and offenders ought to welcome it. In this way, Eddy imagined inmates to be somewhat like the average Quaker meeting member. He expected them to follow the rules and avoid things that prevented godly living. Prison, then, prevented not only the harsh sanctions of the stocks and gallows but also the social situations that led many into sin.[40]

Although some historians locate the beginning of reformative incarceration in the 1820s, Thomas Eddy designed his prison toward one principle end: the rehabilitation of criminals. He asserted that Newgate Prison reclaimed offenders, prevented further crime, and served as a site of reparation to the offended community. Eddy believed his prison countered the negative effects of fines, corporal punishments, and executions. The threat of those punishments, Eddy claimed, lacked hope and usually contributed to the offender's alienation. The prison, on the other hand, served as "the only means of reclaiming an offender from evil." The city received the added benefit of reduced crime, along with the satisfaction that the community supported a humane rather than a despotic and bloodthirsty institution.[41]

Eddy began with the prison's structure, built to keep out bad influences. Newgate's buildings spread across four acres bordered by Greenwich Street at the front and the Hudson River at the rear. Four wings of rooms extended from a central apartment for the prison's staff. With 8 men to a room, Newgate could hold about 336 inmates. These cells contained beds and the inmates' night buckets for their toilet needs. At the end of each wing was a stone building with seven cells for solitary confinement. Workshops ran along the stone wall by the river's edge. Newgate's north wing contained a large gallery for Sunday worship, although it was not complete upon the prison's opening. Along with various sheds for materials and fuel, the prison grounds hosted a garden in which inmates grew vegetables for themselves and their keepers. A twenty-three-foot wall enclosed the grounds and its inhabitants.[42]

This wall and the structured world inside it mirrored Quaker efforts to rear good and faithful children. With their days seeking outside converts long past, Friends relied on their offspring to transmit the tradition and keep it alive in the world. Beginning in the mid-eighteenth century, Quakers treated their children's education with utmost urgency. It began, of course, in the home. Here, parents protected their children from the vice and greed that permeated the outside world. In contrast, they offered up the value of a simple and disciplined life. Home life transitioned into Quaker school, where students received a formal education among teachers and children who shared their commitment to a Friends' lifestyle. This upbringing, it was hoped, culminated for each child in adult life as a responsible member of a local Friends meeting. And beyond the simple following of Quaker regulations, Friends hoped that this heritage would be

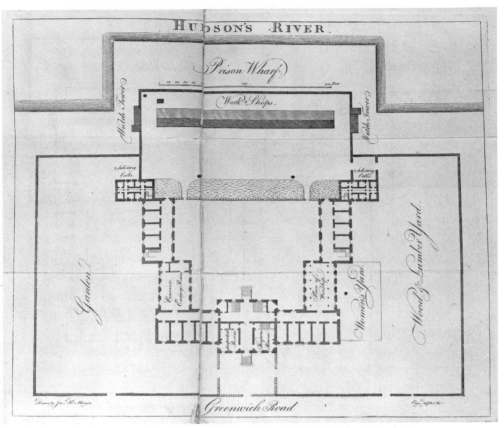

Front elevation and ground plan of Newgate, 1797, from an engraving by Gilbert Fox from the original by Joseph F. Mangin, architect. Note the garden in Newgate's architectural plan. From Thomas Eddy, *An Account of the State Prison or Penitentiary House, in the City of New York*. (Collection of The New-York Historical Society. Negative #61487)

confirmed by the adult's experience of the Inner Light and following of the true path throughout his or her life.[43]

Once sequestered in the prison, convicts encountered a similar regime for rebuilding their characters. The list of rules read to new inmates presented its behavioral demands. Newgate forbade "swearing, idle stories, gaming, quarrelling, disrespect to the keepers, idleness . . . or want of cleanliness." The habits, mores, and pastimes of the outside world were not welcome.[44]

Eddy not only sought to replace bad behaviors with good but, more important, instituted regular labor for those he assumed were accustomed to idleness. To be sure, some inmates had struggled on the outside because decent work was not always available. But others, Eddy concluded, simply lacked the resolve to labor when given the opportunity. He took inspiration from John Howard's prison reform campaigns in England. Work amended criminals by keeping idleness at bay and retraining offenders in honest trades. Under Eddy's direction, Newgate included several workshops for shoe making, nail making, spinning, weaving, sawing marble, and grinding paint. This work did more than stave off sloth. Eddy also hoped it that would train convicts for future jobs and produce enough goods to make Newgate a self-supporting institution.[45]

Eddy also insisted on replacing filth with cleanliness. He concluded that most criminals came from lives of chaos and squalor. Having seen the city's jail, it was clear that prisoners experienced gritty conditions while confined in other disciplinary institutions. Eddy maintained that a clean and ordered environment was integral to running a decent institution and had salutary effects on prisoners' hearts and minds. In his first report to the state legislature in 1797, Eddy and his fellow prison inspectors claimed that the first batch of prisoners they transported from the jail to Newgate needed clean clothes and tidier rooms. He demanded that prison holding rooms circulate fresh air and that workshops be supplied with clean water for washing. Floors of the prison were washed weekly and swept daily. Inmates received a clean shirt weekly and shaved twice in that period. With these innovations, Eddy offered a hygienic routine for those who appeared to lack it in their outside lives.[46]

Eddy also instituted a healthy, though plain, diet to combat the ravages of malnutrition and alcoholism. His directions for Newgate's kitchen allowed for a breakfast of rye coffee and bread, a dinner of soup, potatoes, and bread, and a supper of hasty pudding and molasses. In summer months, he added clams and codfish to the menu, along with produce from the prison's garden. In many of his written pieces on prison life, Eddy reiterated the importance of pumps with clean water in Newgate's kitchens and workshops. These innovations, taken along with the prohibition of alcohol, would build up an inmate's constitution.[47]

Eddy also hoped to restore prisoners' health. He provided a hospital for those who took sick. A doctor paid by the state visited twice a week to see patients. A live-in apothecary attended to the prison hospital, which had its own kitchen, "a means for cold and warm bathing," and an exercise "machine" for those who could not venture outdoors. Eddy insisted on these measures because so many inmates arrived at Newgate "greatly impaired by excessive drinking, debauchery, and vicious habits." The hospital, along with the prison's order, allowed sick inmates to "become healthy and vigorous," according to Eddy.[48]

Finally, Eddy sought to replace bad habits with more wholesome activities. He proposed education and religious meetings as a cure to the drinking, dog baiting, and dueling that pervaded city life. "Diffusion of knowledge" was necessary, Eddy explained, because "it is generally from ignorance and corrupt manners that crimes proceed." Within a few months of Newgate's opening, prison inspectors placed Bibles and schoolbooks in prison rooms and began a series of evening reading classes. In 1801 they completed a room capable of holding six hundred people in public worship. While Eddy encouraged local clergymen and other Christians to visit Newgate on Sundays, the inmates themselves played a leading role in Sabbath services. As Eddy reported of the prisoners' Sunday gatherings, "one of their number reads a sermon and prayers." During the week, Eddy and the inspectors took it upon themselves to provide spiritual counsel. Every part of Eddy's regime reflected the robust anthropology he inherited from the Friends. Confident that the Light was present in all and satisfied that Quaker living was the best way to let it shine, Eddy hoped to close off the old and create something new.[49]

Indeed, Eddy believed that most offenders would eventually welcome this dramatic change. He sensed that inmates desired relief from the growing stresses of the city. Historian Christine Stansell has described these challenges well: a swelling population competing for work, yellow fever epidemics, and widespread poverty among even able-bodied men. Never in his public comment and writing did Eddy consider that Newgate's discipline might cause distress, pain, or harm. In contrast, he believed that prison provided the means to end past sufferings. But to realize these plans fully another step was necessary. Inmates also needed guidance, praise for good actions, and censure for bad. Eddy believed that the staff's attention to educational and spiritual matters was vital. Because staff played an important role in guiding inmates, Eddy carefully controlled the selection and training of those who worked inside Newgate.[50]

Tending the Garden

Eddy's concern for inmate guidance reflected the reforms sweeping the meetinghouses of eighteenth-century Quaker America. Friends worried about their children's behavior. They longed to see them become lifelong members of the community. They were loath to see them marry outside its bounds. The development of the institution of overseer reflects this concern. Meetings for discipline intensified, and Friends who pushed the boundaries found themselves being "treated" by an overseer hoping to restore them to good conduct.

Eddy mirrored the overseer's work in structuring Newgate's Board of Prison Inspectors. Members met regularly for discussion of prison affairs. Two were assigned to visit the prison weekly. Eddy believed that the inspectors held duties beyond their state-mandated charge to "inspect the general state of the prison." They also investigated for cleanliness and order, ensured fair and just treatment of inmates, admonished and advised prisoners, encouraged reformation, and supported efforts at moral improvement. Eddy held that the position should be unpaid to ensure that inspectors were motivated by "principles of benevolence, and love of justice and humanity." The inspectors' goodness was vital as Newgate was hidden from public view. With their privileged access, the inspectors served as the only defense against possible deviation from the prison's proper character, Eddy argued. Convinced of the precarious nature of this new institution, he wrote that "the efficacy and success of this new experiment in the penal law" would "depend on the board of Inspectors."[51]

Even though he created an institution in which inmates wore the same clothes, ate the same food, worked the same hours, and lived in communal rooms, Eddy hoped to tailor prisoners' experiences to their individual needs. He believed that knowledgeable inspectors and staff could use conversation, labor assignments, and classification systems to give each prisoner the right environment for turning around a disordered life. Eddy wrote that judges did not have the power to personalize a sentence. In contrast, "it is in a penitentiary house, that an opportunity is afforded of distinguishing the shades of guilt in different offenders, and of correcting error and injustice." According to Eddy, such a task demanded benevolent men.[52]

It should come as no surprise that Eddy ensured that Friends dominated the board's early membership. Including Eddy, four of the six original prison inspectors held membership in the New York Yearly Meeting. Robert H. Bowne was reared in the city's monthly meeting and remained a member in good standing until his move to Oswego in 1802. Thomas Franklin participated in the Philadelphia Yearly Meeting in his young life before settling in New York. The final Society member, John Murray Jr., shared many reforming sensibilities with Eddy. The two went to school together in Philadelphia before starting successful mercantile careers in New York. Murray's interests, like Eddy's, ranged from education and anti-poverty societies to work with the antislavery and Native American fair treatment movements. With these fellow Quakers, Eddy shared a commitment to religious experience, discipline within their community, and a sense of responsibility to the world.[53]

The prison's staff was equally important. Newgate's agent handled prison operations, including delegating labor assignments, buying supplies, establishing security, and hiring personnel. A staff of keepers served guard duty, watching over inmates at both work and rest. Eddy served as Newgate's first agent and laid out several rules for staff hiring, especially the keepers who maintained order in daily operations. As with the inspectors, a keeper's character mattered. An 1802 legislative report includes a long reflection on keepers' necessary concern for religion. Hiring required a recommendation from "respectable characters of some religious denomination." In addition, applicants had to provide proof of their "attachment to religion" and evidence of "their disposition to promote the reformation and real good of their fellow-men." To this end, Eddy and the inspectors insisted that keepers should not use bad language. Confident that "kind-hearted visitors would soften the hearts of prisoners," Eddy ruled that only principled and committed men should take supervisory and directorial roles at Newgate.[54]

For Eddy, the staff and inspectors' ability to guide demanded extreme patience and a commitment to the institution's rules against corporal punishment. Eddy demanded that no prison officer was "permitted to strike a prisoner" because the "indulgence of anger" would diminish the prison's good effects. Eddy quoted John Howard on the matter, who wrote that "prisoners are made desperate by the profaneness, violent hasty tempers, inhumanity, and ill usage of their keepers." The public, Eddy determined, could not expect prisoners to act any better then their keepers. He insisted that they serve as spiritual guides with the hope of reclaiming the lost. With the new patterns of labor, attention to wholesome living, and the inspectors' counsel, even the most resistant inmate could be transformed by a stint in Newgate. As with overseers in a Friends meeting, character mattered with prison staff because demeanor and actions had an invaluable effect on the person receiving "treatment." The prison as a garden hosted good life and good people.[55]

Life in the Garden

By November 1797 Newgate was ready to accept inmates. Sixty-eight convicts arrived the first evening. More trickled in over the coming weeks as prison inspectors gathered them from county jails around the state. Statistics from the end of 1798 offer a snapshot of these inmates. Newgate's prisoners were overwhelmingly white and male. Only one out of thirteen inmates was African American and one in five female. Foreigners constituted more than a third of the inmates; the majority came from Ireland, followed by the West Indies and England. Most were convicted in New York City of property crimes ranging from grand larceny and forgery to arson and petit larceny. Only one in ten inmates had been convicted of a violent crime, usually assault. Only a few inmates, less than 1 percent, were guilty of greater physical harm, namely manslaughter. From these early statistics kept by Thomas Eddy and Newgate's inspectors, it is clear that the prison held an inordinate number of foreigners and other recent transplants to the city. In short, the prison contained the city's poorest and least connected residents. Most stole goods or passed counterfeit money as a way to get by in a fast-paced, rapidly changing urban environment.[56]

From their entrance into the prison, these offenders confronted Newgate's alternate world. A newly arrived convict was brought to a special room in which he was "stripped of all his clothes" and "obliged to wash and clean himself." Prison staff then consulted with inmates about their occupational skills. The next day prisoners began labor in one of Newgate's workshops. Waking, working, eating, and sleeping commenced at the sound of a bell. Meals were taken in silence and the workshops and night rooms watched by circling keepers. Prison inspectors visited new convicts to take personal histories and "collect all the information" in order to determine the "treatment of the prisoner during his confinement." Newgate was a new world, ordered, scrutinized, and laborious.[57]

Slowly, and not without difficulty, Eddy established daily routines. Labor in workshops began. Night rooms filled up. Prison days passed one upon the next. Eddy sensed that his garden was growing. But even with all these pieces in place, he knew from his correspondence with colleagues in Philadelphia that not every offender would be easily reached. While many inmates complied with the inspectors and keepers, some resisted. These inmates, whom Eddy called "the most obdurate," warranted a treatment beyond Newgate's usual routines of labor, order, and counsel. As in Philadelphia's Walnut Street Jail, prisoners who broke the rules were placed in solitary confinement cells. Newgate had twenty-eight such compartments. Eight feet long, six feet wide, and fourteen feet high, the cells had high windows to let in light and air but prevented inmates from seeing outside. Cells contained no beds or chairs. While confined in solitary, prisoners received only bread and water, none of the coffee, soup, or meat contained in the prison's regular rations. Eddy believed that in this situation, the inmate could "ruminate at his leisure," hopefully feeling the "pangs of remorse." In this space, the stubborn prisoner might acquire a disposition to "future amendment" through a spiritual awakening:

> In the silence and darkness of night, the voice of religious instruction is heard; and, if any circumstances can be imagined, calculated to impress the warnings, the encouragements, the threats, or the hopes of religion upon the mind, it must surely be those of the convict in his cell. . . . These instructions frequently discover to the guilty tenant of the cell, what seems often not to have occurred to him, the simple fact, that he has a spiritual nature. . . . This is a discovery which alone may, and does effect, a great change in a man's whole character.

The solitary cell stood as the final option for confronting inmates' resistance to a reordered and, Eddy hoped, redeemed life. It embodied the Quaker affirmation that shutting out distractions opened up the way for communion with God. It crucified "creaturely activity" insofar as the human will sometimes resisted the work of God.[58]

It is important to note that Eddy recommended solitude and its potential discomfort only for the most obstinate rule breakers. He estimated that 10 percent of Newgate's inmates resisted Newgate's routines. Only this subset of offenders warranted this test, with its possible afflictions, designed to reveal their spiritual nature and emphasize their responsibilities to God and society. Other inmates, like so many Quaker children, could benefit from simple changes of environment, routine, and influence provided by Newgate's enclosed garden.

Though Eddy emphasized the way his prison saved many offenders from swinging at the gallows, his disciplinary imagination stretched much further. His mission included the minor offenders who had formerly moved beyond the clergymen's gaze. Pastors preached at executions but not as often at the stocks. Ministers had not paid attention to those who had formerly been fined for their misdeeds. Eddy's mission involved disciplining every sort of offender, including those who had never before been subject to sermons and routines of redirected behavior.

With his prison built, discipline established, and the first batches of inmates arrived, Eddy was hopeful. To the legislature, he proclaimed that the "number of crimes, in all probability will be lessened." There was "good reason to hope," he continued, that the habits instilled in the prison would create not only law-abiding citizens but also self-supporting and honest individuals. The state benefited as inmate labor supported the institution, requiring no outside funds for its maintenance. Most important to Eddy, other states and governments in Europe would be inspired to reform their bloody penal codes and establish a humane system of punishment on New York's model.[59]

Despite Eddy's efforts, things did not go smoothly at Newgate. To begin with, his garden was not exactly enclosed. When Newgate opened in 1797, the outer wall remained incomplete. The worship space and some workshops were also unfinished. With the prison in this state, Eddy could not implement his plan for complete segregation from the world, full inmate employment, and regular Sabbath worship. If structure was crucial, having an incomplete set of buildings hindered Eddy from the start.

But even after the walls were completed in early 1799, Eddy realized that Newgate remained permeable. Indeed, changes in the outside world affected daily operations. The city's residents, and therefore the mix of people sent to prison, seemed to surprise Eddy. In an 1801 report, he mentioned "the great influx of foreigners" in the city and in Newgate. He added that their presence "contributes very much to the increase in crimes," although he did not specify how. These immigrants usually arrived at Newgate with poor job skills and serious health problems. The increased foreign population was not the only urban change that distressed Eddy. The next year he named increased "population, commerce, wealth, and luxury" as factors contributing to rising crime. He also mentioned the increasing number of inmates convicted of petty larceny. Second offenders and foreigners, especially, were caught up in cycles of poverty and waywardness that led to common thievery. Newgate was not saving hordes of hardened murderers from the gallows. Instead, it housed small-time criminals new to the city. Reaching these inmates became paramount, although Eddy seemed continually surprised by the makeup of the crowd to which he ministered.[60]

Indeed, the baggage these common offenders brought to Newgate jeopardized Eddy's entire program. Some inmates were simply too weak to work. Years of malnutrition, illness, and, in some cases, alcohol abuse simply incapacitated some prisoners. For others, undiagnosed mental illness made long days of monotonous labor impossible. Lack of job skills also contributed to difficulties in the workshops. Inspectors interviewed incoming prisoners and often found that they had neither skills nor regular work histories. In light of these circumstances, Eddy had the option of offering extensive and costly training for these inmates or making only the simplest items. Inmates brought the difficulties of the outside world into Newgate, hindering the prison's smooth operation.

Eddy's effort to reach first-time and petty offenders was also threatened by their contact with Newgate's more experienced and intransigent criminals. The outside world invaded in the very bodies, words, and actions of these men. This danger encroached most dramatically in Newgate's common night rooms. In them, prisoners of all ages and criminal backgrounds spent the dark hours between the end of supper and the dawn. Convicts were crowded together in late-day conversation and shared beds for the remainder of the long nights. In these spaces, beyond the gaze of keepers, inmates directed the subject and tone of conversations. Eddy quickly concluded that the night rooms allowed hardened offenders to lead more impressionable inmates into further iniquity. More than anything, the night rooms undermined Eddy's idea of the enclosed garden. In the whispered words of the most depraved convicts, the worst aspects of the outside world found a space inside Newgate. Here, Eddy concluded, inmates had the "chance of corrupting each other."[61]

The contamination of nighttime conversation appeared to spread. Indeed, outright inmate resistance constituted the key labor difficulty at Newgate. While some inmates worked willingly, if not taking a lead in the workshops, others simply refused. Able-bodied and even skilled convicts sometimes shrugged off their work. Of the experienced shoemakers Eddy had in his workshops, he reported that "only two [were] good, and five indifferent." This indifference could easily spread as resistant inmates directed common-room chatter.[62]

With tough city life producing more criminals and raucous night rooms causing labor troubles, Eddy considered alterations to his prison program. Most important to these efforts, Eddy strived to enclose inmates further, cutting off opportunities for contamination. He began with a limited program of inmate classification. In their 1801 report, the inspectors noted that they found it "necessary" to separate out the "worst, and most hardened men." Eddy placed these "notoriously bad characters" in their own wing of the prison where keepers watched diligently over the inmates' constant employment. Eddy hoped this regime of strict supervision and labor would benefit these tough cases. More important, he believed this separation made the rest of the inmates "less exposed to corruption." Considering this early experiment of classification a success, Eddy soon called for further "assorting and discriminating."[63]

Eddy expanded his ideas for classification with requests for inmate separation at other correctional institutions around the city and state. He argued that New York had an obligation to lessen the possibilities for criminal contamination at every level. He began with the county jails, where upstate offenders sometimes stayed for months before their trial, sentencing, and removal to Newgate. In these jails, inmates of all ages, sexes, and levels of crime mingled. Loose supervision allowed for the free access of visitors bearing liquor. Realizing that a stint in the county jail led to further corruption of the men and women bound for Newgate, Eddy requested stricter regulations starting as early as January 1799.[64]

He also turned his attention to the city's jail, known at that time as the bridewell. This institution, too, allowed for inmate mingling and regular access to outsiders and their alcoholic wares. It was also filthy and had no structures for occupying inmates' long days within. Indeed, Eddy argued in 1801, the bridewell's "contagion of example" made its residents "an hundred-fold more vicious and intractable." Rather than a clean and decent holding cell for offenders before entering Newgate for a reformative term, it was instead a "nursery for criminals." Once again, Eddy called for inmate separation to stave off contagion and, possibly, initiate redemptive contemplation. He recommended that the bridewell's petty offenders receive thirty to ninety days in a solitary cell on a "low diet," which would convince most of them to amend their ways before they were sent to Newgate. These changes, he reported, were "more likely to reform the offender" and prevent crimes worthy of a state prison sentence.[65]

His campaign to prevent contamination also encompassed city life. He advocated shutting down sites for illicit pursuits and expanding opportunities for more wholesome ones. As early as 1799, Eddy and the inspectors advised the city to limit the number of permits for "petty taverns and grog shops." After interviewing hundreds of inmates, Eddy determined that these places, along with "horse races, cock fighting, and houses of ill fame" encouraged vice. Vice led to small crime, which later led to major offenses. According to Eddy, the city boasted more than twelve hundred taverns. He asked why the city did not support an equally expansive network to employ the working poor instead of intoxicating them.[66]

Despite his concerns about the contaminating effects of New York's social environment, Eddy continued to hope. In his first report to the legislature, Eddy wrote that "an amendment in minds and manners of several [inmates], is very apparent." In 1801 he still affirmed "the rectitude of the system" and his ability for "carrying it into effect." Even in 1803, as difficulties mounted at Newgate, Eddy reported that many inmates "expressed their thankfulness to Providence, for being stopped in their career and criminality, and placed in a situation where they have been led to reflect on their past conduct, and to see the advantages of sobriety, industry and religion." Nothing, Eddy and the inspectors insisted, could "shake their faith in the rectitude of the establishment." It must be a "humane and christian institution."[67]

Eddy emphasized the good outcomes at Newgate in order to bolster the state's fledgling commitment to reformative incarceration. Indeed, Eddy faced great resistance. Crime in New York was rising rather than falling. Some leaders and citizens questioned Eddy's system. To the doubters who considered reverting to colonial-era corporal punishments, Eddy insisted that all citizens were redeemable under the right circumstances and that the prison prevented crime. He held up New York as a beacon of humanity in contrast to tyrannous governments that exacted "unequal and cruel" sufferings on lawbreakers. He praised the system that avoided the financial disasters that befell families after a member's criminal offense brought the sentence of an exorbitant fine. An enlightened nation, Eddy argued, regarded the humanity of each person. It sought not to destroy its unruly citizens but instead to assist in their flourishing.[68]

Eddy cringed at the thought of undue suffering. He resisted a return to the gallows. Just as fervently, he rallied against the dangers of the slums. Despite his aversion to suffering, however, Eddy was unable to recognize that his own institution caused so much of it. From late-night conversations about the prison's gloom to elaborate escape plots, prisoners expressed their dissatisfaction with their lot. As noted earlier, offenders complained and refused to work. Others went farther. Three inmates absconded in 1798, before the outer wall was finished. As noted at the beginning of the chapter, fifteen convicts attempted escape in the summer of 1800, prompting legislators to summon an armed guard. Even with their guns, they could not quell inmate efforts to flee. In April 1803 a "considerable disturbance" occurred as twenty inmates attempted to escape. Guard members arrived and unsuccessfully commanded the convicts to desist. They fired into the crowd, killing four prisoners, including one who was not party to the escape plot. Prisoners not involved in the escape set fire to a room. Others threw brickbats and hammers at guard members called on to suppress the riot. Despite the chaos and the death of an inmate uninvolved with the plot, Eddy looked on the bright side. He reported that the rest of the convicts, despite dramatic inducement, "refused to be concerned in the enterprise."[69]

The regular occurrence of riots and escapes reveals that a significant portion of inmates refused to accept the Protestant patterns of piety imposed on them at Newgate. Planning the garden and making it into a reality proved to be very different things.

Prison Politics

Legislators and city officials had ranked among Eddy's early collaborators. He relied on their ongoing support for his prison program. From the earliest record, it seems that state and city officials appreciated their partnership with Eddy. His work reflected the Quaker traditions of care for the marginal and concern for disciplined living. He brought just the sort of religion that officials needed. Or so it seemed. Newgate's disorder, along with developments in New York political life, allowed for conflicts over religion to come to the fore. Under mounting pressure, officials resisted the spiritual particulars of Eddy's disciplinary regime.

The turn of the nineteenth century brought significant turmoil to New York state politics. Previously, Federalists in the tradition of Alexander Hamilton and Democratic-Republicans inspired by Thomas Jefferson had competed actively. But in 1800 emerging Republicans won national and statewide elections and secured victory over the Federalists. Once in power in New York, they created the Council of Appointments, which controlled thousands of political appointments. While the Republicans dominated state politics for several years, factions within it clashed endlessly. Control over the legislature, and hence appointments, bounced back and forth between these blocs. As a result, political assignments lasted only as long as any faction's tenure in power. As the political historian Alvin Kass has written, these blocs pushed out good civil servants, a system of political spoils developed, and principle rarely ruled over electoral victory in party faction decision making. While political parties had been forming in New York since the revolution, after 1800 the winner truly did take all.[70]

Changes in the political landscape affected partnerships with Protestant reformers. In previous years, magistrates and humanitarians came from the same social class and considered themselves partners in governance. But after the turn of the century, politics took a new turn. Members of the opposing parties parried over new ways to make political appointments. The developing structure of spoils dominated political life. Benevolent reformers sometimes found themselves in the new position of having no voice in the state legislature. In Eddy's case, this process meant he had less of a say over appointments to Newgate's inspectors' board.[71]

According to Eddy, the politicization of state jobs jeopardized the prison's proper oversight. He believed that the prison required proper staffing and the influence of Quaker disciplinary practices. Men appointed by Republican factions simply did not fit the bill. They possessed neither the right plan for reformation nor adequate character to see it through. The tide, however, had turned against him. One of the Quakers on the inspectors' board moved away, making him ineligible to serve. In 1803 the appointments council removed two Friends from the board, leaving only Eddy. He, too, lost his inspector's position in 1804. Soon after, Eddy resigned his post as agent and left Newgate utterly confounded. The legislature replaced him with a sailmaker with no experience—and little interest—in prison affairs.[72]

As Quakers and other Protestants brought particular aspects of their faith to the penal debate, leaders of the new nation were in the peculiar position of not knowing what to do with their input. Religious leaders and thinkers had long contributed to debates in many colonial American communities. But the creation of a new nation brought this pattern of influence into question. With the disestablishment of religion and the separation of church and state, many leaders were unsure about religion's role in the public sphere. As historians Richard Pointer and Jonathan Sassi have noted, the new republic experienced a decline in public-private partnerships, including former collaborations between magistrates and ministers to direct the culture. Working in New York City in the 1790s, Eddy and his Quaker colleagues faced these changing conditions. Eddy and other religious reformers worked within an emerging political system in which loyalty and spoils ruled. Within this political landscape, religious leaders had no prescribed role in containing the social stresses of the new republic.[73]

Losing Newgate

Eddy argued that the spirit of religion demanded a mild yet firm approach to offenders. He believed that most inmates—eventually—would acknowledge the benefits of Newgate's enclosed garden. It promoted labor over idleness, clean living over filth and decay, good food over malnutrition, benevolent companions over partners in poverty and crime, and a pattern of reformed living over the sufferings caused by bad environment and choices. But Eddy clearly underestimated the difference between Quaker childrearing and criminal justice. Newgate's inhabitants were not Quaker children. These criminals were not reared in Friends communities and decent schools. They were adults who had experienced traumatic migrations, urban poverty, and a world that offered few possibilities for their material success. They were the city's newly arrived immigrants and country folk, the poorest of its residents. Eddy believed that Newgate could reshape them. His enterprise met its match in the inmates' difficult lives and their refusal to concede their liberty. Eddy responded with calls for separation, removing opportunities for "contamination" to spread. He believed that classification and isolation blocked out the insidious whisperings of hardened convicts. He began to call for individual cells to protect inmates from bad influences. Once separated, they could begin the reformative process of labor and good living, reflection and education. Quaker religion, in this case the call for clear boundaries and separation from wickedness, offered a new set of structures for the revised needs of reformative incarceration. Eddy referred to his prison as a garden, a trope that reflected a widespread attraction to a pastoral ideal. But, as historian Leo Marx has shown, some citizens of the early republic also embraced the idea of the machine or mechanism. They saw technology's potential for dramatically improving the new nation. Eddy affirmed a new technology—the prison—and its capacity to accomplish his age-old vision of a righteous community.[74]

But just as Eddy anticipated changes he hoped would address Newgate's problems, he lost his singular authority over New York prison affairs. While he convinced many New Yorkers of the need for more solitary cells, he lost his public platform for directing their meaning and use. As a young man, Eddy had spent a few days in prison. By 1804 he could not get inside no matter how he tried. He had hoped to make Newgate a garden. Clearly, at least some inmates resisted. Now, a new spate of administrators took his institution in a new direction.

By 1804 the historical moment in which Protestant reformers had the greatest impact on the New York prisons was over. Eddy's naiveté was partly to blame. The Quaker prison agent never administered a reformatory institution that maintained basic order and operated without a deficit. Both inmates and politicians refused his Quaker garden, resisting his effort to implement redeemed living among criminals and nonviolent criminal justice in the nation.

Other factors also contributed to the broken relationship between Eddy and state officials. Assumptions about a common commitment to religion's role in the prison obscured real differences. Protestant reformers and state politicians thought that they agreed about religion's vital role in New York's prison experiment. Eddy spoke with legislators about their common goal to create a "humane and christian institution." He authored documents with utmost confidence that the public shared his assumptions about inmates' "spiritual nature" and God's communication of "religious instruction" through solitary cells. He proposed a series of rules about hiring prison keepers based on proof of their religiosity. No one in the legislature objected. In fact, they actively supported these aspects of his reformative program. With the exception of the prison guard debacle, there seemed to be no problem. At least, not at first.[75]

Developments after 1800, especially the Quakers' removal from the inspectors' board, reveal the fragility of religious discourse in the early republic. The situation with the armed guard shows that interested parties did not agree about what constituted a "humane and christian institution." Friends adhering to strict pacifism were not the right partners for state officials concerned with prison order and profit. The development of political spoils, with its emphasis on giving appointments to up-and-coming politicians, put an end to Friends' ability to direct prison affairs. Dissatisfied state officials removed the Quakers, hoping that their own appointees would bring Newgate order, profit, and reformation.

The concern about religion's place in the prison did not go away with the Quakers' exit. State officials simply looked to a different sort of Protestant to share their common cause. They found a willing partner in a Baptist minister of English birth. Soon, Newgate officials hired the nation's first prison chaplain in an effort to secure the right sort of religion within prison walls.

2

The Furnace of Affliction, 1805–1823

In 1822 an evangelical press published *Sword of Justice, Wielded by Mercy*, an anonymous dialogue between Newgate prison inspectors and an inmate about to be released. Reflecting on the sentence he served and punishments he endured, the prisoner quotes from the book of Proverbs: "I experienced the truth of the declaration that 'judgments are prepared for scorners, and stripes for the backs of fools.'" In response to the inmate's reference to the whip, the inspectors explain that they found it "painful" to administer such severe sanctions. The convict assures them, however, that he understands their position, that stripes were "inflicted in mercy" and "designed for my good." Acknowledging the inmate's contrition, the inspectors offer "forgiveness of [his] trespasses." Before venturing out into the city, the ex-convict replies: "I accept pardon as a gift from heaven."[1]

This anonymous pamphlet reflects more than the missionary spirit of antebellum tract literature. It offers a particular point of view on New York's controversial reintroduction of corporal punishment. It is one example of how partisans invoked religion to bolster their arguments about evolving prison discipline. The pamphlet writer speaks through a convict's voice to assure the public that God redeemed inmates through incarceration featuring the whip. The piece was surely intended to persuade New Yorkers concerned about a variety of prison issues. Crime increased after the War of 1812. Newgate's workshops remained unprofitable as staff struggled to force inmates to work. Overcrowding prompted calls for a new prison design featuring more solitary confinement. As the pamphlet attests, the reintroduction of whipping also provoked considerable controversy.

At this key moment of communal questioning, parties on all sides presented plans for effective prison discipline. They considered new possibilities for labor, space, and discipline to address the failures of Newgate's early years. They debated labor's purpose and how prison agents might create successful prison labor regimes in a tough economic climate. They reflected on spatial organization, especially as Newgate became increasingly overcrowded and inmates found themselves crammed together in common rooms. They pondered new disciplinary options, as current practices did not quell everyday acts of resistance and periodic riots and revolts.

Even as citizens disagreed about labor, space, and discipline, they concurred that prisons must continue to have a redemptive purpose. Increasingly, New Yorkers used language about religion in order to win practical arguments about prison organization and score rhetorical points about the institution's reformative potential. As Newgate's discipline became more severe—especially when corporal punishment was reinstated—partisans appealed to religion to underwrite their approaches to inmates and institutional life. Whereas observers once invoked religion to abolish corporal punishment, they soon used it to defend its reinstatement. Newgate's new chaplain played a particularly important role in this process by articulating a prison religion of suffering and redemption that could be interpreted as supporting inmate whipping. The chaplain replaced Thomas Eddy's garden with a new and enduring model: the prison as furnace of affliction.

Prison Troubles, City Troubles

Life in Newgate remained chaotic after Thomas Eddy's departure. When prisoners set fire to a workshop, communal labor came to a stop. Milder forms of inmate intransigence took place everyday, mainly in the form of work stoppage and workshop sabotage. The new slate of civil servants assigned to administer Newgate encountered an expanding criminal population that overwhelmed the prison's physical space. Prison keepers found it nearly impossible to maintain silence in common rooms. Inmates, it seems, found myriad ways to resist the inspectors' effort to establish strict discipline.[2]

Newgate's problems reflected pressures felt by the entire city. After 1805, New York's faltering economy left multitudes out of work. A yellow fever epidemic killed many and devastated families left behind. The emerging slum called Five Points, just north of City Hall, proved a public embarrassment. The War of 1812 put further pressures on the community. After the conflict, the war's unemployed veterans increased the number of residents seeking jobs and public aid. Impoverished immigrants entered the city at increasing rates. They competed against the free black population for the lowest-paying jobs. The expanding city government and a growing army of charity and mission workers tried to keep order in this difficult mix.[3]

The prison's growing population reflected a city in which residents weighed the consequences of property crime against their situation in poverty-stricken, jobless families. Inmate numbers surged. By 1806 Newgate held a third more inmates than the 336 for which it was designed. With each passing year, legislative reports noted increasing numbers. By 1816 Newgate held 600 prisoners, almost twice its intended capacity. The public, including some state and city officials, worried that crime was out of control. As the prison became increasingly overcrowded with property offenders, many began to wonder if the corporal punishments of former years ought to be reinstated.[4]

Newgate's residents experienced the stresses of the overcrowded institution. The workshops could not accommodate the growing numbers, and the same was true of common rooms used at night. Administrators struggled to keep workshops supplied with sufficient materials. When supplies ran low, even prisoners willing to work loitered about the grounds. Tensions from the outside also influenced Newgate's daily routines. Inmates brought with them the antipathies of New York street life. Tensions between rival gang members, black and white, Catholic and Protestant, native-born and immigrant were only amplified in Newgate's close quarters.

Despite considerations of returning to the system of criminal justice that preceded the turn to prison sentences, New Yorkers took no such action. Instead, officials struggled to bring order to the institution they inherited. Thomas Eddy's departure from his roles as prison agent and inspector left Newgate's discipline and administration wide open. With the exception of laws against corporal punishment, Newgate officials had great freedom to direct inmate experience. They used this authority to wrestle the prison toward a single goal: maintaining an ordered and profitable institution. Along the way, they argued for corporal punishment to be reestablished and promoted a theology of divine justice and mercy in which inmate reformation sometimes demanded the lash.

An 1812 amendment to state law revealed the new inspectors' focus on a prison order marked by profitable labor and strict discipline. Of course, the new inspectors had the same list of responsibilities as their predecessors. They were to maintain a regular rotation of prison visits. Their reports on these visits, however, focused narrowly on the institution's business side. The state required inspectors to provide a "complete and comprehensive view of the transactions during the previous year." These transactions included number of convicts, reports on the various workshops, and net profits. The revised law made no mention of reports on inmate reformation or education as a part of the inspectors' annual report.[5]

Initially, state officials argued that they could achieve both order and profit without resorting to physical penalties to make inmates work or perform other aspects of their daily routine. In 1805 the new inspectors reported that they remained committed to the "present system of mild punishment." They insisted that the prison, no matter how flawed and expensive, reflected the values of the new republic. They also hoped that inmate labor soon would generate profits for state coffers. But experience prompted a change in approach. Confronted with overcrowding and unruly inmates, officials soon argued that a revised criminal code and changed daily prison discipline would alleviate their problems. Increasingly, they believed the prison's disorder threatened not only the prospect of inmate reformation but also the potential for Newgate's—and therefore the state's—financial security.[6]

As inmates jammed into every available space, they strapped Newgate's financial and material resources. From 1805 to 1817, the prison regularly ran a deficit. Except for the years 1812 and 1813, inspectors noted "the indispensable necessity of further supplies of cash" and endless "pecuniary embarrassments." Board members worried that the state would give up on the penitentiary experiment on account of its costs. They frequently assured the assembly that they strived to make Newgate "as little burthensome to the state as possible." At the same time, former inspectors, including Eddy, sought reimbursement for the personal funds they had used to run the prison.[7]

Under financial pressure, prison officials felt they hardly enjoyed the leisure to dwell on programs to support reformation. Instead, they responded to the cash and crowding crisis with policy reforms and a reorganization of prison life toward order and profit. The new agent and board of inspectors began by revising sentencing rules. They asked for longer sentences in order to maximize inmates' time doing profitable labor. They also argued that petty criminals from the farther reaches of the state ought to remain upstate rather than travel to Newgate. This change served two purposes. Petty criminals would not mingle with the prison's population of hardened criminals. More important, the state would not bear the cost of transporting criminals to and from the city. As the new agent reported in 1805, the "considerable expense" of transport made these inmates a financial "dead weight to the institution."[8]

Inspectors also asked for changes to the pardon process, hoping to ameliorate the prison's financial situation and alleviate inmate overcrowding. Typically, the governor offered these reprieves to large numbers of inmates to make room for the incoming criminal population. Mass pardons of forty to fifty inmates led to the simultaneous release of convicts who then formed gangs and soon found themselves back at Newgate. While city security proved to be an immediate problem, the inspectors also complained about pardons' financial implications. Namely, shortened sentences decreased inmates' time to provide productive labor for the state. Officials argued that profits depended on newly trained prisoners serving out the full length of their sentences. Once again, the reordering served primarily a financial purpose. Or, as another agent put it in 1814, more discretion over pardons would make "the [prison] factories less interrupted."[9]

Despite every effort to create profitable workshops and stabilize the inmate population, Newgate struggled to stay afloat. The prison held more inmates than its workshops could employ. As a result, many remained idle, neither learning helpful trades nor making profits for the state. With inmates milling about doing nothing, the common rooms served as schools of criminality. Crowded together in rooms with other offenders, greenhorn lawbreakers learned the tricks of the trade from the more experienced. Debtors, murderers, juveniles, rapists, and thieves wiled away the hours together. Inspectors rightly concluded that Newgate had the opposite effect of the disciplinary environment they desired. They decided that overcrowding, while impossible to eliminate, might be managed through a system of inmate classification.

Before 1805, Thomas Eddy and his fellow prison inspectors experimented with inmate classification. The board members that replaced them, however, had not continued the practice. By 1810, though, the inspectors changed their minds, complaining to the legislature that mingling criminals of all kinds was "injurious," particularly to the "inexperienced and early offender." In 1812 they claimed that "promiscuous association" had "nearly defeated" any opportunity of inmate reform. In 1814 they requested that the "best behaved" be separated from the rest and given the first chance at pardons. And in 1815 the inspectors asked to "separate boys from men and black women from white women." But, they acknowledged, such inmate classification required more space. More rooms cost money. Worried about the expense, the inspectors ended their 1815 report with an admission that the expense made classification basically impossible. Indeed, the cost kept them from ever attempting it.[10]

While classification seemed out of reach, the inspectors introduced other changes. In 1804, even before Eddy quit his post as agent, the new inspectors altered the discipline. The new head of the inspector's board posted a revised set of prison rules. Almost all of them dealt with silence and order in prison workshops and rooms. The first decreed, "Assistant-Keepers shall have power to command silence, and enforce decent behavior." The rules offered no details about enforcement provisions. The fourth rule emphasized the role of labor in organizing prison life. "Whilst the prisoners are at labour there shall be no talking allowed . . . as an indulgence in this respect would not only impede the work, but have the tendency to create disorder." The new inspectors imposed a silence that had nothing to do with Eddy's dual sense that quiet maintained the peace of the prison and provided the best environment for the Inner Light to shine. Rather, silence and work were the only weapons for containing prisoner laziness and potential insurrection. They made an environment for orderly labor and production.[11]

The new rules produced little effect. Inspectors continued to complain of Newgate's chaos. They soon began a series of public musings on religion, in case anyone doubted their commitment to inmate reformation. For five years following Eddy's departure, Sabbath services and educational programs were sporadic at best. Hoping to improve the situation, the inspectors turned to New York's clergymen. By 1810 the inspectors asked local ministers to reinstate regular Sunday services. In 1812 the state revised its visitation rules to allow ministers that "reside in the city of New-York, and have charge of a church or congregation therein" to visit Newgate regularly. That same year, the inspectors urged state officials to hire a part-time chaplain.[12]

The effort to reinstate religious services at Newgate shows that the new inspectors and agents had not entirely forgotten about the reformative goal. In his reflections on the prison's financial troubles, Eddy's successor as agent remarked that it would be "a matter of real joy" if Newgate could realize the community's wish of inmate reformation. In 1816 Newgate inspectors argued that the legislature should do all it could to make the prison "both a place for punishment of crime, and a school of reclamation." But they concluded that achieving these goals demanded "another prison" and punishments "a little more severe." While these officials remarked on reformation's importance, they also seemed unsure about how to combine their hope for an orderly institution with the environment necessary to rehabilitate. They viewed inmate reformation as something achieved outside the daily routines of forced labor. Indeed, it required a spiritual specialist.[13]

The need for a chaplain dedicated to a reformative project was so acute because the new inspectors did not identify themselves—as Eddy and his colleagues had done—as inmate guides. Inspectors after 1804 did not understand themselves as instructors and probably did not possess the expertise to do so if they had tried. Drawn from the ranks of the emerging corps of civil servants, Newgate's new inspectors focused on their roles as administrators and financial managers. The prison's internal chaos and New York's erratic politics hampered even the most basic administrative tasks. Political developments in Albany resulted in rapid turnover in the inspectors' board. These frequent changes contrasted with inspectors' continuity during Eddy's tenure. With little experience and no chance to acquire it, new board members struggled to accomplish great things with little guidance.[14]

Along with the short terms they served, political appointees to the inspectors' board had little experience in benevolent work. After 1804, New York's Council of Appointments organized the inspectors' board out of entry-level party operatives. Few had experience in reform movements or benevolent service. Most were local merchants. Newly introduced to the idea of prison work, greenhorn inspectors admitted in reports to the legislature that "short experience" and "short tenure" affected their ability to evaluate the prison properly. As with the inspectors, the role of prison agent also became a post for new and inexperienced civil servants. In 1805 the inspectors appointed Peter Wendover as agent. According to the city directory, Wendover had worked most recently as a sailmaker. His departure in 1810 coincided with a complete turnover of the inspectors' board that year. His successor had worked as a merchant, but after his short service at Newgate, he moved up to the position of city alderman.[15]

The new inspectors confronted the prison's problems and attempted to secure an order marked by strict discipline and profitable labor. They noted that new spatial organization might assist in reaching their goals but balked at the cost of hundreds of new solitary confinement cells. Unable to adjust the space, they made changes to the disciplinary regime. They instituted a strict physical routine with the hope of avoiding deficits. They demanded silence to stem potential inmate riots. They wanted fewer inmates in New-gate for many reasons but primarily so that "profit would be increased." To that end, practices that encouraged reform but increased costs were rarely put in place. Inspectors complained that mingling tractable and hardened offenders could hardly produce good results. Nevertheless, they confessed that "expense alone" had "deterred them from undertaking" classification of any kind. State officials now hoped that Protestant ministers, working inside the prison as chaplains, would serve the prisoners' spiritual needs, which had largely been neglected during their tenure. Concerned that lan-guage about reformation be entirely lost from the conversation, inspec-tors suggested offering an annual salary of $250 to a minister willing to contribute to their effort to establish an orderly prison that could reform inmates.[16]

The Furnace of Affliction: Creating a Prison Religion

The Reverend John Stanford kept a copy of the first sermon he preached at Newgate. He took his text from Isaiah 48:10: "Behold, I have refined thee, but not with silver; I have chosen thee in the furnace of affliction." In the sermon, Stanford noted that the prison hosted the fullness of di-vine action, including the suffering necessary for redemption. He believed that criminals necessarily experienced state-imposed physical and psycho-logical pain. While humiliating and awful, such torments were necessary. By prompting redemption, they helped achieve the institution's primary goal. Reformative incarceration, Stanford affirmed, was especially suited to American life. Democratic governments, when overseen by Christian leaders, had a special capacity for administering the best sort of punish-ment—one that chastised and reformed.[17]

A prominent worker in the city mission movement, Stanford brought to Newgate his effort to uplift and evangelize the urban underclass. His other ministries took him to the city orphanage, jail, almshouse, and hospital. His role as one of the nation's first prison chaplains—at a time when the course of prison discipline was so fiercely debated—makes his Newgate tenure of particular interest. Unlike many of his Protestant colleagues with a reforming persuasion, Stanford tried to stay above the political fray. He offered few comments on labor, space, and discipline. He stayed away from particular positions on matters of prison organization. At the same time, he offered copious comments on inmate reformation. For Stanford, the reason for the prison's existence was inmate reformation, which demanded an orderly institution. Although he remained aloof from the particular inner workings of the prison, he constantly commented on the prison's larger purpose and the religious realities behind its power. The prison was to be a furnace of affliction, a well-running, orderly machine designed to put great pressures on inmates, who would then emerge transformed by the experience.[18]

Though Stanford evoked a house of woe and furnace of affliction, his ideal prison was no frenzied experience of pain and suffering. In fact, he valued quiet, order, and submission. While prisoners might experience terrible moments of physical and psychological stress, the ideal was to face the challenge calmly. An impassioned response to prison stimulus could cause God's work to be undermined. In fact, order was necessary for God's redemptive acts. Stanford urged inmates to follow rules, avoid trouble, and accept their punishments as the price God exacted for sin. His allusion to the furnace of affliction implied more than just the fire the prophet Isaiah referred to but also the mechanism of the antebellum furnace in which myriad parts worked together to create heat and produce a measurable end product.[19]

Stanford had acquired this theology of sin and redemption in his years journeying from Anglicanism to Baptist life, from Britain to America. Stanford hailed from England, where he was reared in an Anglican family. His memoir details a youthful conversion that resulted in a ministry to the poor. In time, Stanford found his Episcopal prayer book inadequate for these ministries and began extemporaneous prayer. Soon after, he became a Baptist. While some Baptists had already moved toward newer religious ideas, Stanford was drawn to the Particular Baptists and their affinity with Calvinist theology. Ordained in 1781, Stanford was baptized and received into fellowship by a London church. In the 1780s he printed tracts in London. His memoir elusively notes that in 1786, he became "dissatisf[ied] with his situation" and sailed for America. Arriving in New York City, Stanford again instigated cooperative ministries to the poor. He opened a church on Fair Street in 1795 and began work on some religious writings. Despite all this activity, he sought more ministerial work. After the turn of the century, Stanford found a new role in institutions for society's outcasts, including orphans, lawbreakers, and the mentally ill.[20]

Stanford's first visits to Newgate in 1807 coincided with the order emerging under a new set of inspectors. He watched as prison officers tried to enforce silence and struggled to contain the chaos of overcrowding. Stanford responded to the circumstances with a theological interpretation of the prisoner's experience of Newgate. First and foremost, he believed that inmates could be reformed. But his vision of how that transformation occurred differed substantially from Eddy's. Stanford emphasized the state's prerogative to punish offenders and the chaplain's role to deliver the message of potential salvation. Stanford's discipline reflected a Baptist faith in redemption steeped in Calvinist understandings of God's sovereignty. In a prison tract he penned years later, Stanford summarized his approach with a quotation from Job 36: "If they be bound in fetters, and be holden in cords of affliction; then [God] sheweth them their work, and their transgressions that they have exceeded. He openeth also their ear to discipline, and commandeth that they return from iniquity. If they obey and serve him, they shall spend their days in prosperity, and their years in pleasures. But if they obey not, they shall perish by the sword, and they shall die without knowledge." The minister believed that God ordained sufferings as a part of sinners' redemption.[21]

The Baptists from which Stanford came shared with Eddy and the Quakers a lineage of dissent from the English state church in the seventeenth and eighteenth centuries, but beyond their genesis in dissent, they had little in common. These Baptists in America adhered to the Philadelphia Confession, a statement of belief with only slight differences from the Calvinist orthodoxy represented in the Westminster Confession. Particular Baptists affirmed the utter depravity of humankind and the need for Christ as mediator. God had created humans without sin, but the fall from grace led to imputed sin for all. According to Particular Baptists, God demanded a reckoning for this sin. Humans needed Jesus to relieve their condition as "children of wrath, servants of sin, the subjects of death, and all other miseries, spiritual, temporal, and eternal." So Jesus "underwent the punishment due" and "satisfied the justice of God, procuring reconciliation" for the elected faithful. For those gifted persons, God offered grace that could be accepted as faith in Jesus's sacrifice.[22]

Along with personal faith, the law and civil authorities played a role in this formula for the sinner's redemption. God's moral law—as known in the Ten Commandments—served as a rule for believers' lives, binding them to God's will. The law convinced believers of their ever-present sin and need for Christ. At the same time, Particular Baptists affirmed that the law worked on nonbelievers. It restrained their corruption, revealed the depths of their sin, and detailed the penalties they deserved. As with Calvinists in England and on the Continent, American Particular Baptists affirmed that civil authorities enforced many of these moral laws. God authorized the state to use force "for the punishment of evil doers." To be sure, Baptists had received their share of persecution at the hands of English authorities. But believers understood those instances to be the result of the wrong people occupying positions of power. They affirmed that good magistrates would be wiser, upholding God's laws and chastening the hearts of wayward lawbreakers.[23]

While strict in their belief in predestination and the role of government, American Particular Baptists also had an evangelistic side. They did not wait for the afterlife to find out who was among the elect. They shared in the legacy of Jonathan Edwards and more recent Puritan divines, convinced that the truths of Calvinist Christianity allowed for spirited ministry to human beings. God had predetermined the elect, saved them through the blood of Christ, and offered the free gift of justifying grace. But Stanford and his colleagues believed that God used their preaching, prayer, and counsel as tools of effectual calling to these people with salvation potential. Ministers of the Word were needed because one never knew if God might use a sermon, a visit, or a tract to propel the sinner into the regenerative experience of God's grace. Stanford respected the law and governmental authority. But he also firmly believed that God's grace was available to all and that it could be known through evangelistic efforts such as tract writing, preaching, and benevolent work.[24]

Baptists such as Stanford did not believe that state authorities held sole responsibility for disciplining sinners. In this period, they had practices of internal church discipline as well. They shared with the Quakers a commitment to following the "rule of Christ." Laid out in the Gospel of Matthew, this rule provided procedures for dealing with offenses in the church. The Philadelphia Confession affirmed that every church had the power and authority for "order in worship and discipline." This Baptist confession compelled every church member to "perform duty required" by the rule of Christ and "wait upon Christ" as the church worked through particularly difficult offenses. Baptist church covenants from this period attest to the way congregations enacted the rule of Christ to mediate disputes. Members promised to "submit to the discipline of the gospel" and "to exercise, practice, and submit to the government of Christ in this His church."[25]

Despite having an internal system for dealing with offenders, Baptists proved wary to push these pastoral practices into the wider public as Quakers such as Thomas Eddy had done. Their commitment to liberty of conscience demanded that state authorities refrain from interference with the church's internal workings. Baptists were concerned that civil government should remain within God's proper order. Neither church nor state should overstep its proper boundaries. Though the church could patiently "wait upon Christ" as disputes were settled, the state could not. The state had to do its God-given duty to protect the good and punish the bad.

Stanford's Particular Baptist theology and experience colored his approach to New York's offenders. Indeed, his chaplaincy introduced a theology of redemptive suffering into the state's prisons. Crucially, his ministerial program emphasized the prison's gloom. Newgate was a furnace of affliction. But Stanford tempered this affirmation with caveats to the mildness of American prisons and the work of God inside these institutions. From Stanford's pulpit, inmates received the negative message that they deserved a certain amount of suffering at the government's hands. They had broken the law, making them subject to the state's punitive measures. At the same time, convicts also heard that they could receive the gift of the gospel. A thief could experience God's mercy just as any upstanding minister could. Despite his difference with Eddy, then, Stanford shared in the Quaker's emphasis on the reformatory aims of incarceration. In his visits to Newgate, Stanford articulated this theological understanding of the prison through a variety of texts and tasks.

Stanford used the pulpit as his primary platform for communicating the prison's dread. Some sermons put it mildly. For instance, Stanford reflected on the command to visit prisoners found in Matthew's gospel. He encouraged the listening audience, which was mostly made up of inmates but included some local visitors, to enter Newgate's "gloomy shades of confinement." Other sermons contained more dramatic images. Reflecting on Psalm 79, Stanford addressed convicts as "suffering fellow creatures" who experienced "exquisite pain."[26]

If inmates proved unaffected by his sermons, Stanford hoped that special reading materials might reach them. As early as 1808, Stanford began writing tracts and trying to have them distributed. In a piece for prisoners that he published through the American Tract Society, Stanford evoked the "horrid prison," where chains pulled at inmates' legs, barred windows and gates separated them from family, uniforms scratched the skin, and a thin layer of straw served as a meager bed. Indeed, Stanford wrote, the prison produced "overwhelming grief" and "a flood of tears."[27]

Frontispiece from John Stanford, *The Prisoner's Companion*. (Texas Baptist Historical Collection, Baptist General Convention of Texas, Dallas, Texas)

Despite his focus on the prison's gloom, Stanford constantly referenced the mild conditions of American institutions in comparison to European penal practices. "Perhaps you need not be told," Stanford wrote in a prisoner tract, "that for many ages, the laws of European nations have been strongly marked with blood; and that, for trivial offenses, the life of the offender is sacrificed." Pointing to criminal justice reforms in the new nation, Stanford boasted that "wisdom and humanity" propelled the revisions. Indeed, he went further, "the beams of the Gospel of Jesus have so benignly illuminated our legislators." Although the prison constituted a painful and sorrowful experience, its pressures were not inordinate. According to Stanford, Jesus authorized them.[28]

Stanford's endorsement of reformative incarceration depended on this point. God not only approved of the prison but also worked through it. Stanford spent the bulk of his ministry articulating just how prisoners should understand this crucial point. According to the minister, prisoners underwent chastisement and humiliation that revealed the depths of their sin and need for God's grace. Within Newgate, he advocated a prison discipline that combined the powers of state officials and Christian ministers to convince criminals of their wrongs and bring them, if God willed it, into the realm of grace and faith. In this process, the sufferings of prison life were redeemed.[29]

Indeed, Stanford pointed to the Bible and its multiple affirmations of God's presence in moments of dread and humiliation. In his scripture directory for prisoners, Stanford quoted Psalm 107: "Such as sit in darkness and in the shadow of death, being bound in affliction and iron. . . . He brought down their heart with labour. . . . Then they cried unto the Lord in their trouble, and he saved them out of their distresses." God had not abandoned the criminal to the state's severity. Rather, God used the state's occasion to incarcerate offenders as a way to reach them. The Bibles placed in convicts' cells carried the message. The minister made this point over and over again. In a tract for young offenders, he wrote that the Bible "contains the promises of God for [prisoners'] direction, support, and comfort, when everything else fails." Or as he argued fervently in another sermon: "Take the contents of the Bible for your own; view the variety of providences, however afflictive, as designed to promote your best advantage."[30]

Along with tracts, Stanford offered Sunday services, weekday prayers, and occasional visits to persuade inmates to accept God's salvific offer. He preached that "sensible sinners" would see God's hand in their imprisonment and accept the offer of Christ as a ransom for their sins. On his Wednesday visits to the hospital and female ward, he offered prayers but also answered "religious questions." His goal, as attested in his catechism for young offenders, involved scripture and teaching that resulted in inmates' thankfulness for salvation, penitence for their sins, and resolution to live honorable lives.[31]

The choice between grace and damnation became strikingly clear in Stanford's sermons and pamphlets on sick and dying inmates. Stanford both preached and published on the salvation of George Vanderpool, a repentant arsonist. He used the prophet Zechariah's words to describe the dying convict as a "brand plucked out of the fire." Stanford's sermon at Vanderpool's funeral told the story of the offender and his accomplice, who were both sentenced to death. Vanderpool, who was white, received a commutation to life imprisonment. His partner in crime, who happened to be African American, did not. He was hung just a few blocks from Newgate in 1816. Vanderpool lived for a few more years, succumbing to illness in the prison's hospital, though, according to Stanford, not before he had made the choice to accept salvation. God's pardon of Vanderpool mirrored the pardon offered by the state.[32]

Not everyone made Vanderpool's choice. Stanford used the stories of those who did not convert in time as a warning. In 1815 he preached about the death of an "unfortunate youth" at Newgate. He hoped that God would "use this early death to our advantage" and make all prisoners aware of their sins against God, parents, and community.[33]

Often, Stanford reasoned, a helpful guide proved to be the difference between a good outcome such as Vanderpool's and the sad end of the impenitent youth. Like Eddy before him, Stanford was convinced that inmates needed guides who were driven by spiritual concerns. But he saw this as a minister's, rather than an inspector's, responsibility. "Perhaps more than others," Stanford wrote, "the confined needed instruction." While the prison served as the teacher of deep humiliation, Stanford understood himself as a fitting companion and guide to interpret God's justice and graciousness. In his journal, he affirmed that salvation belonged to God alone. "But," he continued, "God can appoint guides that can work with the help of the Spirit." Inmates needed guides to help them, but Stanford always acknowledged that both parties stood in similar positions before God. "Take away grace," he wrote, "and we would all be going to the gallows."[34]

Guides took on great importance as a counterweight to the majority of the prison's population. In his sermons and writings, the chaplain referred to the bad characters at work against God's designs for the prison. Stories about contrary inmates pervade Stanford's work. Of young inmates, Stanford asked their opinion on "those persons under confinement with you, who would imbibe in your mind pernicious principles and prompt you to more evil practices?" When addressing the general inmate population, Stanford warned of convicts "hardened in iniquity" who reveled in "prison mirth" and evidenced "little regret." These characters, the chaplain argued, ought to be avoided because they "subvert the designs of punishment."[35]

Sensible inmates, Stanford said, recognized the truth in his words. Prison delivered terrible sorrow and affliction. But things were worse in other parts of the world. And God offered dramatic opportunity within the walls of America's prisons. Wise convicts, then, reformed their habits. Stanford offered clues for what the redeemed life looked like. He pointed to biblical models for inmates' correct habits and disposition. He used the Genesis story of Joseph's stint in an Egyptian prison as an extended reflection on prisoners' appropriate behavior and the public's right to expect submission. Though imprisoned wrongly, Joseph offered "correct conduct" through "submission and virtue." Stanford concluded that Joseph's actions pleased God and his keepers, resulting in his eventual release. Submission to the prison order showed inmates' progress in mercy and grace. In obeying rules of silence and bodily order, prisoners showed their respect for civil authority and, further, their respect for God. Indeed, Stanford preached that the required physical submission originated beyond the earthly realm by the "command from Heaven: Be still and know that I am God."[36]

With the Bible to inspire and a clergyman to guide, inmates could travel their path of labor and gloom toward a glimpse of God's glory. In this environment, criminals who previously had recognized neither their sinfulness nor the authority of law soon came to new knowledge. Convinced of the prison's potential for good, Stanford showed off the facility. He hosted touring dignitaries. In 1816 he invited President James Monroe to visit. The inspectors ensured the president that Stanford did much to "promote [the prisoners'] eternal welfare." In 1818 Stanford hosted New York's governor, DeWitt Clinton, on a similar tour. During these visits, he affirmed his message that the prison had much to offer both inmates and the world.[37]

Stanford said little about labor, space, and discipline. He thought inmates ought to work, that they deserved decent surroundings, and that consistent, firm discipline worked for reform. He could not imagine a redeemed life without conversion and moral living. He focused, though, on the prison's theological potential. Though lacking the passionate stirrings of frontier revival tents, Newgate—at least for Stanford—amounted to a place where equally dramatic divine wonders could take place.

Debating the Furnace

While Stanford's theology permitted, if not advocated, inmate suffering, he never offered specifics. Throughout the second decade of the century, other interested parties earnestly debated the severity of prison punishments. They measured their proposals against the standards of religion, which made Stanford's position as chaplain one of public importance.

Reports to state government spoke to these concerns. Reporting to the legislature in October 1816, Newgate's head inspector admitted that crime had increased, the prison was nearly bursting with 722 inmates, and current prison discipline had a better chance to "demoralise than to reclaim criminals." In December of the same year, Newgate's agent worried that "a strong prejudice [had] gone abroad about this institution" and that punishments that served as an "insult to the divine Majesty of Heaven" loomed on the horizon. While both men worried that inmate reformation and a system pleasing to God were in jeopardy, their proposed solutions reveal a philosophy in which order and profit amounted to the inmate's good and

God's approval. The inspector asked for punishments beyond the solitary confinement practice they had at their disposal. The agent begged for legislators to assist him in "perfect[ing] this liberal system of ours" by expanding workshops and getting the best prices on raw materials and the lowest possible rates for prison provisions. Even as they admitted problems and referenced the reformation ideal, they articulated plans to achieve these ends by using profitable labor and strict discipline to achieve order.[38]

This enthusiasm for stricter discipline only increased. Newgate's inspectors clamored for the legalization of corporal punishments. They had particular concerns to sanction prison rioters and arsonists. In 1816 the inspectors reported "some other kind of punishment ought to be inflicted . . . and that the Legislature should enact a law for that purpose, a little more severe; for it is a fact, that the convicts have become hardened to [cell]blocks and chains." By 1819 the inspectors secured the sanction they sought: the right to whip disobedient convicts. With this change, inspectors could direct keepers "to inflict corporal punishment" with up to thirty-nine lashes at a time. Placing inmates in irons and stocks also became a legal option. While solitary confinement was still a choice, it was now one of several options at the inspectors' "discretion, proportionate to the offense."[39]

Under pressure, prison staff and officials adjusted their notions about religion to align with the disciplinary options they sought. In 1816 Newgate's agent had defended a milder approach. "Our present system," he declared, "is far, very far from answering the ends anticipated by the really christian like spirit that first proposed and finally adopted it." By 1818, however, the same agent told legislators that "sympathy" for criminals was a virtue "often carried to extremes." After whipping was reauthorized in 1819, inspectors explained that a system of "punitive justice" was appropriate. They would establish forms of lashing that had a "severity [that] will harmonize with the spirit of christianity." The furnace of affliction, according to them, included the limited use of corporal punishment. In fact, it demanded it. The inspectors continued, "lenity, when ill directed and excessive, is in fact cruelty."[40]

Some disagreed—Thomas Eddy, in particular. He had expressed his concern already in the months after his ouster from Newgate. In letters to fellow reformers, he lamented the prison's disorder. He found the staff ineffectual. He noted a fire that inmates recently set. He wrote to Scottish reformer Patrick Colquhoun that Newgate's discipline was "more severe than necessary" and new administrators were "not so suitable characters."[41]

While many observers lobbied for stricter sanctions, Eddy recommended spatial reorganization instead. If Quakers or other appropriate guides could not oversee inmate reformation, Eddy decided to reach offenders—and other social outcasts—in a different way. He called for new prison architecture and routines to make administrators less influential. He proposed changes to Newgate that limited the negative effects of the staff he deemed unsuitable. If enclosure had only secured the negative elements within its walls, then Eddy would have to devise even more dramatic possibilities for separation. He sought isolation to arrest the spread of contamination. And if the prison was not the garden he imagined, he would work to make the city a more agreeable place.

At an 1810 Humane Society event in New York City, a committee called for legislation to reshape the broader social environment. Eddy and other committee members asked city officials to limit liquor licenses and outlaw forms of gambling and animal baiting. He had long hoped to limit the social vices that led to criminal acts. His 1801 treatise on Newgate included his concerns about liquor. But stopping the flow of liquor and the crimes it subsequently produced became all the more important to Eddy after he left Newgate. Earlier, he had believed that Newgate might reform drinkers who broke the law. But with state officials running the place, Eddy no longer held such hope. He believed Newgate to be disorderly and crowded, led by officials with no concern for reformation. The jail, he reported, was no better. He had asked the city to build solitary cells there in 1801. The state legislature had supported his request, but nothing came of it. The Humane Society's 1810 report observed that the setting was "extremely dirty" and inmates "lay promiscuously on the floor." Even worse, guards refused to stop drinking and violence in the jail. Eddy reported that his visit exposed him to every "sort of corruption" that "wickedness and poverty can produce."[42]

Beyond decrying the liquor problems plaguing the city and its jail, Eddy used the 1810 Humane Society meeting to call for changes to Newgate's prison discipline. Just as he had proposed for the bridewell, Eddy wanted more solitary confinement at Newgate. Inmate mingling had long troubled him. He admitted that Newgate's common rooms were designed with a "most striking error." Such mingling, he had argued in an earlier letter, "entirely destroys the designs of a penitentiary establishment." But inmate interaction was not the only problem solitary confinement solved. It also reduced prisoner interaction with staff.[43]

Once again, Eddy recommended that petty offenders serve a sixty-day stint in solitary with no labor and no contact with other prisoners or prison

officials. Time alone for the first-time criminal became even more important as Newgate's rooms overflowed, labor was becoming increasingly difficult, and administrators bore no benevolent interest. These cells could be
built in county prisons, too, keeping new offenders in their home county
rather than shipping them to Newgate. Eddy wrote to British Friend and
prison reformer William Allen of his "favorite object" to get county prisons
with solitary confinement for sixty days for first-time offenders. Whether
in the city or in the rural counties, short-term solitary confinement made
the proper environment, keeping petty offenders away from the worst influences. It gave them space for reflection. Eddy also wanted solitary for
Newgate's more experienced offenders.[44]

The 1810 Humane Society meeting proved only the beginning of his
campaign. He later advised prison inspectors at Massachusetts's new state
prison to try solitary at night and labor by day. He counseled New York's
governor to follow a similar plan at a prospective prison upstate. Eddy realized that Newgate might be a lost cause. He knew the state would have to
deal with overcrowding. In some respects, he shifted his focus to delibera-
tions about new penal institutions.[45]

Eddy's new focus on solitary confinement reflected his misgivings not
only about inmate mingling but also about the state's capacity to provide
proper discipline. He continued to voice concern about inmate oversight.
He successfully lobbied to get three commissioners to investigate the New
York prison and to consider "what amendments, if any, are necessary." He
asked that they "point out the defects" of the present administration and
suggest alterations. His letters continually lamented the prison's bad administration, assuring correspondents that "when Friends had the management, it was entirely different."[46]

Stanford, though he promoted a theology of redemptive suffering, also
worried about developments inside Newgate. Overcrowding and harsher
punishments poisoned inmates' daily experiences. Stanford witnessed
the effects, especially on the youngest offenders. In 1812 he petitioned the
city to allow "Christian teachers and private benevolent persons" to organize an "asylum for vagrant youth." Stanford hoped that the institution
would reclaim offenders who had been "cast out as youth." If volunteers
reached these unfortunates through a course of education and job training,
they might prevent a fair number of them from serving a prison sentence
someday. An asylum provided a better chance for reformation, a goal that
seemed increasingly elusive at Newgate.[47]

Stanford's 1819 pamphlet on the execution of an African American

woman also attests to his unease with the developing system. Rose Butler was accused and convicted of setting her mistress's kitchen on fire in
the middle of the night. The state sentenced her to hang. New York law
had recently added arson to the list of capital crimes. Urban construction
practices meant that a fire in one house almost inevitably spread to others.
Stanford understood the necessity of dealing strictly with such a significant crime. Butler spent nearly a year in jail in which Stanford and other
local ministers offered multiple reasons for confessing her crime, asking
for forgiveness, and accepting God's pardon, even if the state's would never
come.[48]

Nevertheless, Stanford had misgivings about hanging Butler, despite her
conviction for setting a fire that could have killed her employer and many
others. The pamphlet reveals that Stanford remained unsure if Butler was
the arsonist. He included two conflicting confessions allegedly made by
the condemned. In the first, made to Stanford himself, Butler relayed a
story in which two white men who had a problem with her employer tried
repeatedly to convince her to set the house on fire. Time and again, Butler
refused. In this statement, Butler maintained that the two men not only
set the house on fire but also arranged a series of obstacles on a stairway
so that the employer and her family could not escape. The bizarre account
does not end there. Butler's first accuser is not a witness but a fortuneteller
whom the employer sought out to learn how the fire was set. And after
Butler was imprisoned, a "short fat white woman" named Mrs. Scott passed
a secret note about the fire's origin to her in a loaf of bread. The account,
from Stanford's perspective, includes a black servant, possibly wrongly accused by a fortuneteller and paying the ultimate price for a trio of white
villains still on the run.[49]

After this account, Stanford's pamphlet features another, more traditional telling of a criminal's repentance on death's doorstep. In this narrative, given to a white woman named Eliza, Butler confessed to lighting the
fire and blocking the exit on account of her poor relationship with her employer. "My mistress was always finding fault with my work, and scolding
me," the maid reported, "I never did like her." While Butler mentioned the
male accomplices who prompted her, she took sole responsibility for the
criminal act. Even worse, she showed no regret for her crime. Her answers
to Eliza's questions are described as "cool" and "deliberate."[50]

Stanford's inclusion of two differing accounts of Butler's situation—
however confusing—ends with the criminal's punishment. Throughout
the entire scene, Stanford presented the condemned as unaware of her fate

and strangely uninterested. How does Stanford explain Butler's torpor? A few lines at the end of the second confession narrative provide a clue. In it, Eliza, the white prison visitor, reminded Butler that she had never shown a "hardened and wicked disposition" while working for her employer. Indeed, Eliza wonders, what made her so "altered"? Stanford's text provides an intriguing answer. In it, Butler states, "I have been kept in prison so long that it hath hardened me—I shall never be otherwise."[51]

For Stanford, something went wrong for Rose Butler. The problem seemed not to be rooted in her human depravity or resistance to the gospel. The issue was her punishment at the hands of the state. According to Stanford, Butler's crime—if it happened at all—did not receive a pardon. She spent her days languishing in city jail where there was no labor to occupy her days. The trade of alcohol made up a brisk business and inmates faced extortion from their keepers. The state had done her wrong. And Butler was "launched into eternity . . . almost without a struggle." To Stanford, this was a terrible thing. The state was responsible for making punishment a place for holy and redemptive struggle, rather than an experience that squelched its possibility.[52]

Stanford found New York's jail far worse than Newgate Prison, but his complaints about bad environment and staff reflected his concern that poor institutional conditions made reformation impossible. Stanford weighed his concerns for criminals against his many other ministerial charges. His work took him into realms of suffering across the city. Disease, immigration, economic fluctuation, and war made life difficult for multitudes. Many city residents relied on food aid to feed their starving families. And every day, Stanford preached to the sick, the insane, the fallen women, and the abandoned children of New York. If so many innocent people suffered, how much more could be expected for those who broke the law?

With his commitment to the right use—in fact, the positive spiritual potential—of suffering and an urban context in which so many people led difficult lives, it is easy to understand Stanford's reticence to confront the legal structure, even if he had questions. Stanford searched his understanding of God's providence to make sense of the prisoner's experience. When some of Newgate's conditions troubled him, the Philadelphia Confession reminded him:

> The most wise, righteous, and gracious God doth oftentimes leave for a season His own children to manifold temptations and the corruptions of their own heart, to chastise them for their former sins, or to

discover unto them the hidden strength of corruption and deceitful-
ness of their hearts; that they may be humbled; and to raise them to a
more close and constant dependence for their support upon Himself
. . . so that whatsoever befalls any of His elect is by His appointment,
for His glory and their good."[53]

Stanford's theology—his notion that the prison served as God's furnace
of affliction—had its nuances. He certainly did not intend it to support
inmate torture. He sometimes questioned whether the prison's discipline
supported inmate reformation. Nevertheless, his call for redemptive suffering opened a door for a new understanding of how religion contributed
to prison discipline. His theology offered a way not only to interpret the
workings of new practices at Newgate but also to plan for new institutions
upstate.

Life in the Furnace

Even as Stanford hoped inmates' spiritual transformation would contribute to prison order, Newgate's inspectors made headway in their goal to
achieve peace through stricter sanctions. Inmates certainly protested these
changes. As historian Rebecca McLennan has noted, Newgate experienced
"serious insurrections" in 1818, 1819, 1821, and 1822, the years surrounding
the whipping debates and the lash's reauthorization. Those found guilty of
harming prison guards or setting fires in prison could be hanged under
new state laws.[54]

Beyond these acts of resistance, prisoners began to add their voices to
the public debate about prison discipline. They contributed their own per-
spectives on developments at Newgate. In 1823, ex-prisoner William Coffey
published a book on the prison's ills. In more than two hundred pages, he
offered a critique of the widely held view that the nation's prisons fostered
reformation. He argued from his experience that Newgate did no such
thing. Indeed, it had the opposite effect. Bad conditions, cruel guards, and
rooms brimming with felons created desperate men unable to choose the
good. Coffey's narrative joined a chorus of voices claiming that Newgate
had become a "seminary of vice." Within its walls, he wrote, "no contrition
can be expected."[55]

Coffey noted that some inmates had long records of bad behavior that
defied logical explanation. He pointed to fellow convict Jacob Coolman,
who committed his first crime—the theft of an oxen team—for no appar-

ent reason. Unable to give an account of the missing animals, Coolman was sentenced to ten years at Newgate. Upon release, he perpetrated more crimes. Caught counterfeiting, Coolman served a second sentence in Newgate. According to Coffey, Coolman offered even more counterfeit cash to whoever could get him a pardon. His case involved a lifelong criminal whose acts defied explanation.[56]

Coolman's criminal behavior, though, stood out among the convicts Coffey profiled. Newgate's felons were bad men, Coffey admitted, but they had not started out that way. Indeed, many of them ended up in prison after a series of harrowing circumstances, including poverty, parental abandonment, and intemperance. Down on their luck, these men made bad choices resulting in criminal convictions and stints in Newgate. Once there, Coffey contended, any good within them was forever lost. Criminal companions in night rooms regaled the life of crime. Cruel guards excited thoughts of revenge. The stigma of being an ex-convict both demoralized inmates and resulted in alienation from family and friends. In prison, Coffey wrote, men teetering on the precipice between good and bad behavior were lured to the worst.

Coffey supported his argument with sorrowful tales of convicts' difficult circumstances. He wrote of David Smith, who, after losing his father, suffered continually in his efforts to survive. Lacking both direction and means, Smith wandered New York's slums and got caught up in a band of mischievous boys. Another story that Coffey relayed had to do with William Schropson, a Dutch immigrant. Schropson's father abandoned the family, and his mother later took up residence in a brothel. The child was sent off to a tailor to help support his impoverished family. Coffey also profiled James White, an Irishman who had a good father but lost him when his parents left for America out of economic necessity. Left on his own, White emigrated as well; falling in with "low company," he never found employment and eventually enlisted. In all these cases, Coffey highlighted family and economic circumstances leading to vulnerable situations. Without social support or financial means, such young men—or even children, as the case of Schropson indicates—turned to crime.[57]

In recounting these sad cases, and others, Coffey insisted that the young men's sharp moral decline occurred *after* they entered prison. Smith, who served a sentence of two months for insulting an elderly woman, spent his days with "several convicted and desperate felons." "Here," Coffey insisted, "commenced his career of infamy." The Schropson case looked similar. Sentenced to years of hard labor with older felons, the child found "his feelings very soon were in unison with theirs, and their depravity was soon familiar to him." Coffey's most dramatic case involved Ezekiel Wadler, a Vermont youth who claimed he was falsely accused of rape. According to Coffey, Wadler was guilty of no crime at all and entered prison only after a witness's perjury. Once there, though, environment had its way. "Vice had lost its odious aspect to his mind," Coffey argued. "The stream of virtue, had become somewhat turbid in his soul."[58]

Coffey's narrative confirmed what reformers such as Thomas Eddy already believed. Poverty, family breakup, and limited opportunities prompted some young men to turn to crime. The prison, intended to reform them, instead made them infinitely worse. Overcrowding and internal chaos made life miserable. The worst offenders mingled indiscriminately with youthful offenders, schooling them in further iniquity. Worst of all, harsh guards lacked all sympathy for inmates. According to Coffey, they acted on inmates with a "brutal and unfeeling hand." The keepers were "inflated with their mighty consequence, and eager to show their power," he argued. "They practice upon the convicts, without scruple or reserve, every thing abominable, disgusting, and inhuman." Despite the efforts of those interested in prison reform, the inmates themselves attested that incarceration did not humanize them. It made them into beasts.[59]

Spreading Prison Religion

In the period after Thomas Eddy's removal, New Yorkers interested in Newgate Prison continued to call for inmate reformation, although their priority remained securing order and profit. As they debated modes of labor, spatial organization, and daily discipline, deep disagreements emerged. Newgate officials worked within the prison's existing architecture, using corporal punishments on inmates unwilling to labor in pursuit of prison profit. Reformers such as Thomas Eddy insisted on the importance of labor but opposed the lash. Concerned that the new slate of prison inspectors could not be trusted to handle discipline, he focused on space. He called for the separation of inmates through evening confinement in solitary cells. Silent labor by day and solitary confinement at night, he argued, protected inmates from the contaminating influences of other inmates and incompetent staff. At a moment when Newgate's future was wide open for disciplinary experimentation, state officials and Protestant reformers took decidedly different positions.

Chaplain Stanford presented an agreeable demeanor and desire to stay above politics. But his career at Newgate—especially the theology he articulated—offered officials a new way to bolster their arguments for strict inmate sanctions. His connection between the early national prisons and Isaiah's furnace of affliction affirmed the need for an orderly institution and God's desire for reformation without engaging the particular debates over labor, space, and discipline. Stanford had little to say about the question of prison profits versus deficits. He never commented on the potential for broad application of solitary confinement. And even though his career coincided with the whip's reintroduction into New York criminal justice, his notebooks, sermons, and reports include no reflections on this development. To be sure, he supported an effort to reach juvenile offenders. He played a key role in the creation of New York's House of Refuge for underage criminals. His pamphlet on the Rose Butler case shows that Stanford harbored worries that the prison sometimes worked against inmate redemption and reformation. The bulk of his work, however, showed no signs of these concerns. By supporting Stanford's ministry, state officials could claim that they worked toward reformation even as they focused on workshop profit and applied new and stricter forms of bodily discipline.

Other interested Protestants spoke where Stanford remained silent. The evangelical publishers of *Sword of Justice* put their stamp of approval on Newgate's use of corporal punishments. In a dialogue between inspectors and an inmate, the author associates whipping with God's redemptive work. The convict reports that Newgate's officers explained to him that every punishment given was "intended to reform." Having committed himself to being an "honest man and a good citizen," the convict informs the inspectors that he deemed his confinement, and all its difficulties, as "an act of mercy."[60]

Other Protestant reformers also moved in this direction, especially as they turned their eyes upstate to a new institution built in Auburn. Armed with a prison religion based on suffering and redemption, they advocated a new prison partnership. They argued for the chaplain's essential role in establishing and maintaining prison discipline. As New Yorkers experimented with new disciplines upstate, the reformers were ready to make their furnace of affliction a disciplinary reality.

3

The Furnace at Auburn, 1816–1827

In October 1826 a young minister sat in on a conversation between Auburn Prison's resident chaplain, the Reverend Jared Curtis, and an African American inmate, Jack Hodges. Hodges was serving a ten-year sentence for his role in a murder plot. According to the visitor's account, Hodges considered himself a sinner and an unbeliever upon his arrival at Auburn. After many visits from Chaplain Curtis and a long period of spiritual suffering, however, Hodges experienced conversion. The visitor listened to Hodges recount his movement from repentance toward belief and moral living. "In the providence of God, you have a long sentence," Chaplain Curtis observed. "Can you say, Thy will be done?" Hodges answered, "That is my prayer." Moved by this exchange, the visiting minister asked Hodges again to reflect on his prison experience. "Yes sir," Hodges began, "I feel grateful that I was brought here."[1]

The visitor's account of Hodges's testimony became a favorite among Protestant reformers. It affirmed that the prison allowed God's will to be done and that at least some inmates embraced the institution's reformative discipline. In the 1840s the American Sunday-School Union printed a book on Hodges's conversion, *Black Jacob: A Monument of Grace*. The publication testified to the popularity of the new discipline established at Auburn Prison. It also spoke to widespread acceptance of the furnace of affliction theology advocated by a new set of Protestant prison reformers. The Reverend Louis Dwight, a Congregationalist minister and reformer from Massachusetts, worked with Auburn officials to create a partnership between administrators and prison chaplains. For years, chaplains sponsored by Dwight's organization walked Auburn's halls, counseled inmates, preached the word, and kept notebooks full of statistics on prisoners' backgrounds and habits. His chaplains worked in tandem with the institution's keepers and their lashes. According to Dwight, the Auburn system of prison discipline maintained order, stayed under budget, and prompted inmate reformation. In this way, it promised to fulfill America's destiny to create regimented, solvent, and Christian prisons. Auburn became the perfect furnace of affliction.[2]

As it emerged in the 1820s, the Auburn system of prison discipline featured a new level of cooperation between prison officials and Protestant reformers. Under the administration of Auburn's agent, Gershom Powers, prison staff and Protestant activists saw particular benefits to this arrangement. For reformers, the advantages seemed clear. More than any time since Thomas Eddy's early years at Newgate, Protestant prison activists had a voice in New York's disciplinary regime. They watched over—and therefore sanctified—daily prison routines. Prison officials appreciated their presence. They recognized the institutional and public value of resident chaplains, religious services, and a broad reformative program. Specifically, they approved of the reformers' message about suffering and redemption that produced the obedient inmates they desired. The Protestant reformers' presence inside the institutions, along with the rhetoric about inmate reformation, also protected Auburn from public disapproval when scandals threatened the prison's viability. Even though the public registered some dissatisfaction with new prison practices, these religious specialists helped the institution secure widespread approval.

Despite the partnership that was welcomed on both sides, some tensions appeared even in Auburn's earliest years. One particular prison official scoffed at ministers' reformative goal and argued for stricter corporal punishments. Even one of the chaplains displayed moments of incredulity at the prospect of widespread inmate reformation. Despite these countervailing voices, the new partnership between prison officials and Louis Dwight prevailed. Religion bolstered prison discipline, and prison discipline bolstered religion. The furnace of affliction garnered wide acceptance and praise.[3]

Finding Auburn

The Auburn—or congregate—prison discipline developed over several years as New York officials responded to both failures at Newgate and new issues upstate. Eventually, it organized prison life around silent, communal labor by day and solitary confinement by night. This was not the original plan. Starting in 1816, officials planned for a replica of Newgate Prison, primarily to relieve the city institution's overcrowding. In Auburn's early years, prisoners slept in large common rooms and labored in collective workshops. A host of problems—the same ones faced at Newgate—quickly emerged. Raucous common rooms seemed to do more harm than good. Keepers struggled to enforce inmate labor. In the early 1820s, Auburn administrators tried different versions of solitary confinement until a combination of daytime communal labor and nighttime solitary confinement provided a pattern that worked. The new discipline provided order, seemed budget-friendly, and appeared to promote inmate reformation.

A collection of Protestant reformers advocated for the new discipline's development, argued for religion's role in its administration, and promoted its spread to other American prisons. They claimed that the Auburn system struck the perfect balance. It required inmates to labor strenuously but not excessively. The solitary cells prevented mutual corruption and enforced a space in which self-reflection would likely occur. In this difficult regime, they hoped, prisoners would see the error of their ways and repent. With such redemptive possibilities, the Auburn system avoided the unduly harsh treatment convicts received in other prisons. Ready to support the Auburn discipline's spread across the nation, these clergymen served as the institution's primary boosters. At Auburn, they argued, God inflicted the chastisements necessary before redemption.

Auburn's original design and its particular setting upstate reveal a great deal about New York's efforts to reform criminal punishment. By 1816 the state was almost twenty years into its experiment with reformative incarceration. Many of the early backers were frustrated. Legislators believed that Newgate suffered not from bad planning but simply from overcrowding. The overflow included scores of criminals transported into the city from upstate. Officials resolved to keep them upstate in a new institution based on the older model. Inmates would labor in workshops and retire to common rooms. Prisoners who broke the rules faced stints in solitary confinement.

Indeed, more reflection went into where the new prison would be built than to how it would be organized. The intricacies of the state's developing party politics played an important role. The debate over the new prison's location reveals the way such decisions reflected strategic deal making, with public institutions such as prisons offering status and economic support to small towns. The village of Auburn, in central New York, aspired to host the state's new prison as a symbol of its emerging success on the frontier. Incorporated in 1815, Auburn's citizens believed that a prison in their midst would "confer importance and prosperity" on their growing town. They soon got their wish. The newly elected majority in the state house owed a favor to the Auburnites who had supported them so vigorously. As a token of thanks, the legislature authorized local assemblyman John H. Beach to take charge of the prison's construction. It was just one of many institutions signaling Auburn's growing importance. The village chartered its first bank in 1817, hosted several new religious societies, and laid a cornerstone for a Presbyterian seminary in 1819.[4]

The state engaged former military officers to plan and build Auburn Prison. The main contractor, a master builder named Captain William Britten, constructed large inmate common rooms, workshops, and more than one hundred solitary confinement cells. After the south wing was finished, the first inmates arrived and mingled indiscriminately within its compartments. Britten served as the prison's agent, supervised a staff of keepers, and interacted with a board of inspectors drawn from the local community. With part of the building complete, Britten set to building the north wing to house the upstate offenders who had formerly been sent to the city.

The decision to keep rural offenders upstate reflected concerns about New York City and its criminal population. Newgate's inmates exhibited alarming trends in urban life. A growing class of impoverished people—often set apart by race and religion—had an increasingly difficult time managing life in the metropolis. The city was bursting. The population grew by 27 percent between 1810 and 1820. Immigrants fueled this growth. The percentage of foreign-born residents rose from just under 10 percent in 1819 to more than 20 by 1825. They arrived from Ireland, the majority of them male and single. Their ranks boosted the city's Catholic population and transformed older, ecumenical trends. Earlier Catholic immigrants tended to be upper class and made connections to their Protestant neighbors. But the difficult social circumstances faced by the new arrivals, including earnest evangelization campaigns by Protestants, provoked a more defensive stance. As historians Burrows and Wallace have written, the 1820s witnessed New York's Catholics becoming "more working class, more militant, more Irish . . . [and] less respectable." Some of these young Irish men entered Newgate, confronting its grim interior and its devout Protestant chaplain.[5]

The growing ranks of free African Americans added to the urban mix. Although this population had experienced some advances, including a statewide movement to abolish slavery and the celebration of Emancipation Day in July 1827, New York's black residents struggled economically and experienced many barriers. African Americans were barred from most social, cultural, and educational arenas and from many modes of transportation. They found themselves increasingly pushed into poor, racially diverse neighborhoods, including the notorious Five Points. Mixed with the newly arrived Irish, Africans Americans and other residents of Five Points lived in overcrowded rooms, often with insufficient light, furniture, and privies. Outside the boardinghouses and apartments, scores of pigs roamed the streets. Residents needing supplemental food kept the animals and participated in "hog riots" when mayors tried to remove them. In sum, the city's poorest residents, including both newly arrived Irish and free blacks, often lived in rough conditions and faced a less than sanguine economic outlook.[6]

City residents sought release from life's stresses in various ways. Alcohol had long been associated with daily life in the city, but the scale of drinking changed in the 1820s. Advances in grain farming, whiskey distillation, and transportation made the city "awash in cheap liquor." The number of taverns skyrocketed, along with the establishment of brothels. Historians have pointed to a boom in the sex trade in 1820s New York. As thousands of unattached immigrants arrived and the city's population swelled, more and more citizens sought illegal sexual contact. Others turned to gaming. Bear and bull fighting had been prohibited by 1820, but dog and rat contests took place all over the city. Whiskey, sex, and animal baiting provided release for many urban residents, but it also prompted a trip to jail and eventually Newgate for those who got caught.[7]

Newgate's interior became increasingly volatile. The pressures experienced in the city were amplified in the prison. More inmates crowded into increasingly disorganized workshops and common rooms. Tensions grew between different inmate populations, including blacks and whites or Protestants and Catholics. Prisoners resisted forced labor in a city where jobs with decent salaries could be so hard to find.

Hoping to avoid the volatile urban situation, particularly inside its prison, Auburn officials set to work. Before the structure's completion, however, problems ensued. Captain Britten enlisted 140 inmates from neighboring county jails to build the prison between 1816 and 1818. The prisoners worked alongside local Auburn artisans. Trouble soon developed as inmates and laborers became friends. When a local blacksmith whipped three disobedient prisoners, a crew of inmates and laborers tarred and feathered him. This solidarity between prisoners and local workers, however, did not last long. Observers noted that prisoners soon "learned to be rebellious, transgressed the rules of the shop at every opportunity, set fire to buildings and destroyed their work whenever they dared." Villagers soon felt "oppressed by fear" of an "eruption of criminals into the town." The city formed an armed guard to watch prison walls and bought a fire engine specifically for the purpose of dousing prison conflagrations. Suddenly, the prison became a political gift of questionable value.[8]

Officials failed to realize that Auburn's inmate population did not differ dramatically from Newgate's. Demographic data collected in the prison's first decade reveal the population's character. As with its sister institution in the city, Auburn's inmates were inordinately white and male. The array of criminal offenses also reflected Newgate's statistics. Crimes against property ranging from grand and petit larceny to forgery and counterfeiting made up 79 percent of offenses. Violent crime, including rape, arson, and murder, accounted for just under 10 percent of Auburn's incarcerations. The population did not include a kind of homespun, country offender in contrast with the city's more dangerous criminal classes. Instead, it reflected the growing number of immigrants moving beyond the boundaries of New York City into other parts of the state. By 1824 Auburn had inmates born in Ireland, England, and Germany. To be sure, the percentages were lower than at Newgate. But Auburn's inmates reflected the changes—changes feared by many more-established residents—afoot in upstate New York.[9]

Indeed, upstate villages such as Auburn experienced many social disruptions in this period. As historians Mary Ryan and Paul Johnson have shown in studies of Utica and Rochester, the 1820s hosted the transition from frontier flexibility to more urban establishment. Residents experienced upheavals in family and work life, along with periodic outbursts of corporate religious enthusiasm. Upstate communities changed from colonial households where fathers directed the family's common subsistence labor to a more dispersed economic system that often undermined old lines of authority. As a result, upstate residents expressed concern about societal change, especially as it affected their children. According to John-son, religious enthusiasm in its evangelical form provided an important format for reining in a culture and its children that could potentially spin out of control.[10]

Questions asked of inmates—and answers received—by prison officials reflected these societal shifts. Administrators pointed to myriad examples of breakdown and flux in religious and family life. In 1828 more than 43 percent of discharged inmates were between the ages of twenty and thirty. These young people—almost entirely men—testified to failures in frontier culture. Among them, 36 percent claimed to have had "very poor" educa-tion or none at all, and 37 percent to have been deprived of their parents through either death or abandonment. The statistics about alcohol use come then as no surprise. In light of life's stresses, more than 49 percent claimed to have been intemperate before their commitment to Auburn.[11]

Prison officials wanted to prevent Auburn's demise into a Newgate-like chaos, but they had all the ingredients for such a result. They ruled over a stressed population that was not eager to labor in workshops and enjoyed consorting with each other in common rooms at night. To their advantage, the officials did not have to deal with overcrowding and managed to main-tain a generally orderly routine. But the night rooms were always a struggle. Captain Britten responded first with corporal punishments, which recently had been reauthorized. Rule breakers also spent periods in solitary confine-ment. While these punishments had some effect, Auburn was still chaotic. Prisoners rioted and set fires before the walls could be completed. Desper-ate administrators sought a way to control the situation.

Thomas Eddy had been focused on Auburn from the moment the legis-lature authorized its construction. He began a letter-writing campaign to state officials who could influence Auburn's development. In 1817 he sent John H. Beach, the state assemblyman from Auburn, several prison dis-cipline pamphlets. He highlighted Englishman John Howard's proposals for daytime labor and nighttime solitary confinement. He counseled New York's Governor DeWitt Clinton to do the same. Eddy reminded Clinton that prison officials in London and Philadelphia also experimented with versions of solitary confinement. Referring to the state's refusal to use in-mate classification or separation at Newgate, Eddy argued to Clinton, "It is in vain to look for Reformation [there]—it has not been produced." He hoped officials would use some of his disciplinary ideas at Auburn.[12]

Eddy also campaigned for a state board of commissioners dedicated to better prison oversight. The commissioners, he hoped, would control the changing cast of local politicians appointed to the prison inspectors' boards. Since he left Newgate in 1804, turnover on the board had been rapid and inextricably linked to political battles in Albany. For several years, Eddy lobbied to get three commissioners to investigate the New York prisons and suggested that they "consider what amendments, if any, are necessary," "point out the defects" of the present administration, and suggest alterations. When the state finally appointed three men, Samuel Hopkins, George Tibbetts, and Stephen Allen, in 1819, Eddy hoped that the commissioners, along with the state officials he lobbied and reported to, would heed his call for a reorganized prison discipline both at Newgate and at the new institution in Auburn.[13]

Creating the Auburn System

It is unclear what prompted the Auburn experiment—it might have been John Howard's pamphlets, experiments in Philadelphia, or Thomas Eddy's prompting—but Captain Britten planned for more individual cells in the prison's north wing. The agent soon looked to these compartments as a possible answer to his disciplinary problems. On Christmas Day in 1821, Britten put eighty-five of the "most dangerous and impenitent" offenders into solitary cells. In these spaces measuring seven feet long, seven feet high, and three and a half feet wide, inmates spent twenty-four hours a day alone and in silence. It was widely reported that guards did not allow prisoners to sit or lie down during the daytime. Short conversations with prison staff or a visiting doctor or minister provided the only exceptions to the solitude.[14]

According to later accounts, Britten's initial experiment soon proved disastrous as five inmates died, one "became an idiot," and another committed suicide. After ten months of continuous solitary confinement, the remaining prisoners "begged pitifully to be taken back to the shops and set to work." Concerned that total solitary was untenable, administrators considered a variation. In 1822 Captain Elam Lynds, Britten's replacement, put inmates to work together by day and enclosed them in solitary cells at night. At all times, prisoners were to be silent. Breaking prison rules brought swift and sure corporal punishment. With Lynds's experiment, the Auburn system of prison discipline was born. It would be copied in almost every prison built across the country.[15]

Lynds enacted this system at the same time Thomas Eddy published a lengthy report on the state of American prison discipline. With his col-

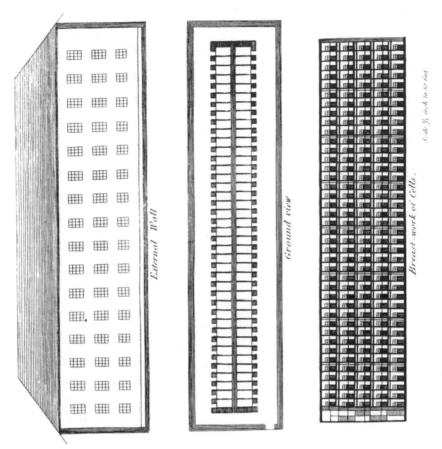

Architectural plan for Auburn State Prison. (*Reports of the Prison Discipline Society of Boston*, 1855)

leagues from the Society for the Prevention of Pauperism (SPP), Eddy recommended that New York's prisons should be built to accommodate solitary punishments in one of two ways. First, they should have some cells for short-term, round-the-clock solitary confinement. These cells were reserved for first-time petty offenders, with the hope that a time of reflection would turn them to right living. A second option included new prison architecture that supported inmate classification by day and solitary confinement by night. By separating inmates according to severity and longevity of the their criminal careers, the system halted inmate corruption. Right prison design included more than the building. The committee called for more religious and moral instruction as these programs had dwindled, if not disappeared altogether, from Newgate. They maintained that cleanliness, a wholesome diet, and basic healthcare would assist the process of reform. While they suggested improvements to the current system, the SPP carefully avoided the appearance of coddling prisoners. It strongly recommended that there be "no inviting comforts in the penitentiary." Good design involved a delicate balance between austerity and provision.[16]

The report concluded that state officials often forfeited reformative discipline out of concern for costs. The legislature insisted that the prison be financially self-sufficient, which led to several negative consequences. First, the quest for productive labor forced the prison agent to abandon inmate classification. Eddy had long feared that obdurate criminals corrupted those who might yet reform, making classification necessary. A proper penitentiary, the SPP argued, placed inmate classification above immediate financial concerns. Second, proper classification actually prevented crime and therefore lowered costs to the state. While the SPP argued the pragmatic effects of classification, it also referenced a higher end. The SPP warned that the state's "narrow fiscal views" would "defeat [the prison's] great moral purpose," inmate reformation. At Newgate this had clearly been the case, but Auburn had the potential for achieving reform.[17]

Just as Eddy argued that inmate separation was necessary no matter the cost, Auburn's Agent Lynds affirmed that his regime of nighttime solitary confinement could make money if the daytime labor was an efficient operation. Lynds became legendary for the order he established at Auburn Prison. His system had elements that seemed so elusive at Newgate. First, it was strict and organized. There were no raucous night rooms or insolent inmates. Inmates moved about in an orderly fashion in a routine repeated day after day. Second, it had elements aimed at inmate reform. The agent was open to the presence of ministers and allowed for educational efforts. Finally, it was affordable. Indeed, some years it made money.

Lynds, a former military man, instituted strict order and discipline at Auburn. He expected prisoners to move quickly and quietly between their cells and the workshops. He introduced the lockstep, in which prisoners walked in perfect, military order with their arms held tight to their chests or with one hand down and the other resting on the arm or shoulder of the prisoner ahead of him. Prisoners moved in this formation at the sound of a keeper's whistle. In lockstep lines and at workshop benches, inmates were held to strict silence. Lynds looked for ways to remove the temptation to communicate with other prisoners. He moved convict meals from a com-

Auburn prisoners in lockstep. (Image courtesy of Cayuga Museum of History and Art; from John Warner Barber and Henry Howe, *Historical Collections of the State of New York . . .* [New York, 1841])

mon dining room to individual cells. Prisoners who talked in any common area were subject to whipping. Though outsiders remained uncertain about the extent of whipping at Auburn, Lynds used the lash liberally to achieve the prisoners' "perfect submission."[18]

Lynds's tenure initially received approval because it allowed for elements believed to bring inmate reform. The pattern of labor and solitude he established hearkened back to English reformer John Howard. Onlookers sensed that the work contributed to reformed habits. They believed the solitude provoked self-reflection and rehabilitation. Beyond the pattern of work and rest, Auburn also boasted the presence of a new chaplain who provided counsel to inmates and directed religious and educational services. With inmates hard at work and removed from the contaminating influence of a common room full of jabbering criminals, it seemed that reformation was a much more likely prospect than at Newgate.[19]

Finally, Lynds developed a system that seemed likely to prove financially beneficial to New York State. The small individual cells cost less than ones built to accommodate the unmitigated solitary confinement practiced in

Philadelphia's prisons. Lynds argued that the Pennsylvania model, which limited inmates' capacity to labor profitably, could never sustain the institution. Indeed, the agent believed that the combination of daytime congregate labor and nighttime separation offered the best of all possible worlds.[20]

During the first years of Auburn's new discipline, both Thomas Eddy and John Stanford supported the regime. It seemed the best chance for inmate reformation that either had seen for years. They approved of the system's orderly environment, believed in the instructive capacity of physical labor, affirmed the salutary effects of solitary confinement, and emphasized the role ministers could play to guide prisoners' wayward souls. Compared to the chaos of Newgate and other New York institutions of confinement— the Magdalen house, the jail, and the hospital—Auburn was the picture of order. Its setting offered the possibility of inmate reformation. Eddy proved especially keen, writing in an April 1825 letter that Auburn was "the best constructed [prison] of any in this country" and "I think the penitentiary will succeed."[21]

Warning Signs

As the Auburn system began to take hold, outsiders had no way of knowing what happened inside the walls. Interested observers such as Eddy and Stanford had no access to episodes of physical violence that bolstered Auburn's daily routines. But others began to protest. Auburn citizens complained of Lynds's unfair advantage in the production of prison goods. Local craftsmen argued that free prison labor violated the rules of the market. Other citizens responded to rumors of Lynds's cruelty toward prisoners. The inspectors' board defended Lynds, reporting to legislators that "mistaken motives of humanity" led several Auburn residents to testify about harsh prison discipline before grand juries. Detractors alleged that Lynds instituted degrading practices, such as removing forks, knives, and plates so that inmates had to eat out of slop buckets with their fingers. In December 1825 tensions boiled over when a female convict died, allegedly from the effects of a whipping. Within a month, state officials relieved Lynds of his duties and named an investigative committee to look into Auburn's disciplinary practices.[22]

That same month, Eddy wrote to a friend, "As a disciplinarian, it would be difficult to find [Lynds's] equal." But, he continued, "I am exceedingly mortified to find my friend Captain Lindes [sic], keeper of Auburn prison, advocates and practices inflicting corporal punishment." Eddy apparently tried but failed to convince Lynds to use other means. "I have in vain urged to him, that whipping is totally inconsistent with the principles of the mild system we wish to establish. I cannot persuade him." Eddy asked Lynds to forgo bodily punishments. Overlooking some of the outbursts during his own tenure at Newgate, he wrote to the agent that "perfect order was completely preserved" at Newgate without resorting to the lash. While Eddy worried that Lynds threatened "principles of the mild system," he wrote that he firmly hoped that the agent would "in time, alter his opinions."[23]

Soon after Eddy wrote his letter, state officials relieved Lynds of his duties. The controversy that provoked his removal provided a learning opportunity for interested observers. It revealed what could happen with few eyes inside the prison. A system intended to provide an orderly setting and encouragement toward reformation could easily turn into something else. Lynds, who had enforced the Auburn system and whipped inmates with the legislature's approval, was soon replaced by Gershom Powers, the prison's head keeper. Powers saw his role as no less than saving the penitentiary system from the disrepute it acquired under Lynds.[24]

Saving Auburn

Gershom Powers, a local lawyer and common pleas court judge, struggled to implement a viable prison discipline. Across the country, prison experiments evidenced serious weaknesses. Communal confinement at Newgate made for a riotous situation and allowed criminality to spread as "pestilential vapors" and carry a "moral plague through the land." Pennsylvania's total solitary confinement in prison had clear defects. Many believed it caused insanity. Most agreed it cost far too much money. And while the public appreciated Auburn's new routines, it certainly resisted Lynds's methods for achieving order. Powers, too, appreciated the Auburn system of prison discipline, but he was repulsed by Lynds's extensive use of the lash. He needed to modify the system in order to save it. "If the present mode of punishment, by classification, labour and solitude, fails," he argued, "then the whole system must be given up in despair; the hopes of the philanthropist must perish; and scourges, the gallows, or guillotine must administer to the demands of sanguinary laws." Powers's 1826 pamphlet on Auburn's discipline focused on this crisis. He needed to maintain control of the inmates but not through so much violence as to raise public ire. Or, as one judge ruling in a prisoner abuse case warned, the whip's role in maintaining the current system had the potential to "render the Penitentiary discipline so completely odious and revolting to the best feelings of the community."[25]

Hoping to use the Auburn system without resorting as often to the lash, Powers sought a way to convince inmates of the institution's integrity and their duty to submit to its discipline. He looked to Protestant ministers for help. Indeed, his program focused on religion's role in a way not seen since Thomas Eddy's early years at Newgate. After Eddy's departure in 1804, Newgate's administrators allowed religious programming but hardly paid attention to the work of chaplains and reformers. They were either too overwhelmed by prison problems or uninterested in the whole endeavor to make religion a vital part of their prison discipline. For years, Eddy and Stanford worked for inmate reformation without much support from state officials. But Powers hoped to harness the energies of Protestant prison workers. He determined that Christians had a vital role to play in his disciplinary order. But he needed a new figure to support his regime.[26]

Powers began his changes by smoothing out some of the harsher edges of Lynds's regime. He strove to be strict, but not harsh. He allowed more educational programs, resumed the original practice of inmates eating in a common room, and used the whip less frequently. The discipline, however, was by no means easy. By day, prisoners still labored in silent workshops. At night, they slept in tiny individual cells. Guards on evening watch assured that inmates could not tap messages to each other through pipes or walls. Powers used the lash less frequently than Lynds, but the whip by no means disappeared. The new agent continued to use the lockstep, which inmates found degrading. In his 1826 pamphlet on the prison, Powers noted that the lockstep kept order and gave "to the spectator somewhat similar feelings as those excited by a military funeral; and to the convicts, impressions not entirely dissimilar to those of culprits when marching to the gallows." While Powers fancied himself less harsh than Lynds, he still enforced a prison discipline based on absolute submission and the threat of corporal punishment. "The whole duty of a convict in this Prison," he wrote, "is to obey orders, labor diligently in silence, and whenever it is necessary for him to speak to a Keeper, to do it with a humble sense of his degraded situation." While they were not beaten continually or treated as animals, prisoners had become the walking dead—bodies in disciplined motion, without the will to resist.[27]

Powers expanded on Lynds's sense of the reforming potential of the labor and cells, emphasizing the place of Christian ministers to guide inmates on their journey. He made chaplains a crucial part of his emerging prison discipline. He wanted ministers not only to teach basic reading and writing to inmates in Sunday school but also to instruct inmates in the humility and degradation proper to their position. In his 1826 publication, he wrote, "actuated by motives of public policy and Christian benevolence," chaplains positioned themselves with prisoners to find out their particular needs and prepare them for "salutary impressions."[28]

According to Powers, the chaplains' benevolent concerns did not keep them from communicating the dramatic fact of prisoners' guilt and need for repentance. In his pamphlet, he wrote that the minister should "dwell emphatically upon [the prisoners'] deep depravity and guilt, in violating the laws of God and their country—convince them of the justice of the sentences . . . and make them feel, pungently, the horrors of their situation." Chaplains worked on prisoners to bring them low and then offered a lesson in the inmate's proper response. Powers wrote that the chaplain "awaken[ed] remorse in their consciences—press[ed] home upon them their solemn obligations . . . and, by all other means, [made] them realize the necessity and duty of repentance, of amendment, and of humble, and strict obedience, to all the regulations of the Prison." For Powers, the path toward Christian repentance also led to prisoner obedience.[29]

Powers believed that chaplains encouraged the psychological suffering necessary to turn chaotic, intemperate criminals into subdued and ordered citizens. He assumed that ministers would, "force [inmates] into reflection, and let self-tormenting guilt harrow up the tortures of accusing conscience, keener than scorpion stings; until the intensity of their suffering subdues their stubborn spirits, and humbles them to a realizing sense of the enormity of their crimes and their obligation to reform." While the language is somewhat reminiscent of Stanford's, the earlier reformer's sense of sufferings' purpose was markedly different. Newgate's chaplain affirmed that affliction sent by God would surely be followed by divine deliverance. But for Powers, suffering taught inmates to obey prison rules.[30]

In short, Powers wanted chaplains' work with prisoners to "make them better convicts; and whenever restored to their liberty, better citizens." He needed chaplains to use the language of heaven to reinforce the disciplines of earth. Powers's story of a "grossly ignorant young Indian" in the prison Sabbath school provides an apt example. The inmate realized his wickedness and wanted to change his ways. But rather than go to the chaplain or pray on his own, the young prisoner "wanted to go before the Agent, confess and promise he would never disobey God any more." In his pamphlet, Powers idealized a prisoner's confession made to a state authority, not to the clergyman present in the prison or in a conversation directly with God.[31]

Powers needed willing partners to rehabilitate the Auburn system. While New York had a history of part-time chaplains such as Stanford, the agent needed Christian organizations willing to support him in a public campaign to direct the course of America's prison discipline. He found that support in the Reverend Louis Dwight and his Prison Discipline Society of Boston (PDSB).

Preaching the Furnace of Affliction

Louis Dwight committed his life to prison reform after a January 1825 visit to the District of Columbia's jail. In a letter to his family, he described the plight of four children held there. "The little girl was sick, and lying in faintness on the floor. . . . For that sick child there was no bed in the narrow and dark cell." Dwight described the girl's three brothers standing over her and the "misery in this room." Clearly shaken by the encounter, Dwight asked, "Could nothing be done for them in prison? I hope so; but it is hope against hope."[32]

Dwight wrote to his wife that he "could do nothing," but the next day he penned another letter to the Reverend S. S. Woodhull of the American Bible Society. In it, he mentioned his visits to jails and prisons throughout the Mid-Atlantic. He complained that Philadelphia's prison lacked a chaplain, that Delaware's had "great abuses," and Baltimore's suffered under "disgraceful management." Unlike most northern prisons, none south of Pennsylvania had inspectors to ensure even a modicum of decency. "Consequently," Dwight wrote to the minister and reformer, "there is great filthiness, disorder, wickedness, and misery."[33]

The shocking scenes in the Washington jail were repeated many times over during Dwight's 1825 journey. He had embarked on the trip to distribute Bibles but found that access to scriptural guidance was the least of prisoners' problems. Inmates suffered under incompetent administrators, lived in wretched conditions, and often lacked due process. Dwight handed out literature and preached when he was able. But increasingly he understood himself as a witness to the church on behalf of prisoners. As literary critic Thomas Laqueur has noted, Dwight's southern journey functioned as a conversion moment might, bringing him into reform campaigns to alleviate others' suffering. As Dwight wrote to his wife from Washington, "When I shall bring before the Church of CHRIST a statement of what my eyes have seen, there will be a united and powerful effort in the United States to alleviate the miseries of prisons."[34]

When he arrived home in Boston, Dwight gathered important New Englanders to his cause. By the time the Prison Discipline Society of Boston issued its first annual report in 1826, fourteen ministers, four lawyers, and four judges served as officers of the society. These included the presidents of Williams, Amherst, and Brown Universities. Andover Theological Seminary professors, local ministers, and officers from the American Board of Commissioners for Foreign Missions served as well. Donors included Horace Hills, a member of Auburn's Board of Prison Inspectors since 1821. With this stately list of names, Dwight commenced on a campaign to educate Christians about the plight of prisoners and crusade for the cause of the Auburn system as the most hopeful possibility of prison discipline and inmate evangelization.[35]

Dwight brought the changing face of New England Protestantism to his prison work. His early years confirmed him on the path to the Congregational ministry. Born in 1777 in Stockbridge, Massachusetts, to a family of "old Puritan stock," Dwight grew up in the church. His memoir details a classic Puritan religious experience in which great psychological suffering preceded the experience of conversion. His plans to enter the ministry were interrupted, however, by a chemistry accident in school that left his lungs permanently scarred and weakened. Despite his inability to sustain a career in public speaking, Dwight attended the recently founded Andover Theological Seminary. Once there, he experienced the changing world of New England Calvinism. Andover students found themselves stretched between the ascendant liberalism of Boston's Unitarians and the campaign to defend the faith by New England's stricter Calvinists. They occupied a Calvinist middle ground walked by Jonathan Edwards before them.[36]

Dwight entered Andover—and attended the Park Street Church in Boston—as the Calvinist New Divinity movement came into its own. These moderates had shed some of Calvinism's strictest tenets. While they still affirmed the need for conversion and grace, they modified several Reformed concepts. First, as historian David W. Kling has argued, "they reversed the emphases . . . on the sufficiency, design, and effectiveness of the atonement. The New Divinity stressed the unlimited sufficiency of atonement." Believing that salvation was available to almost everyone willing to accept it, Andover students and others imagined the social implications of their theology. As a practical matter, almost all people could receive the gospel if they heard about it, repented, and accepted it. New efforts, therefore, were necessary in order to spread the Christian message, which according to one New Divinity preacher, was "suited to govern mankind of every nation and climate." Andover students combined a Puritan emphasis on God's sovereignty with a tireless energy to proclaim grace to the world.[37]

As historian William Sutton has put it, the New Divinity men wanted to "reconcile Calvinism with personal moral accountability." People could not deny their responsibility for sin because of predestination and election. Believers faced the reality that their sinful acts disrupted God's good order and were the sad but necessary step before experiencing saving grace. The New Divinity thinkers, then, had a theology in step with some emerging republican ideals, at least as they pertained to moral behavior. Virtuous living was the goal and sinful acts signaled rebellion against God and the common welfare. As historian Christopher Adamson has observed, Dwight's prison work reflected a Calvinist theology shaped by evangelical public-spiritedness and widely held concerns about the direction of antebellum society.[38]

Andover Seminary students, and other young New Englanders steeped in the New Divinity, sought ways to profess their convictions to the world. Their best-known effort, the American Board of Commissioners for Foreign Missions, sent out missionaries for decades. Other students joined a growing network of benevolent societies. Through these outlets, young preachers and benevolent workers asked people in America and around the world to read the Bible, pray, attend revivals, and give up sinful habits. Their Calvinism kept them from claiming that such practices were effective in receiving grace. If anything, the gospel's claims reminded them that all were lost and in need of God's grace. The ideal mission asked people to pray for God's mercy, realize their fallenness, repent of their sins, and allow God to work upon them.[39]

After graduation, Dwight considered the ministry. Because he lacked the commanding voice needed for the pulpit, he looked for work with the growing host of Protestant benevolent societies. Dwight served short terms with the American Tract Society and the American Education Society between 1819 and 1824. Both agencies sought to turn the culture toward God, the first through tract distribution and the second by educating new ministers. In both cases, Dwight and his colleagues hoped that with a little prodding, humans might open themselves to the grace and redemption that could come only from God. Dwight's lung ailment often interrupted his work, however, demanding long breaks from labor. During a period of convalescence, he determined that the sedentary life did more harm than good and decided to take a trip on horseback to the South. Almost as an afterthought, he decided to carry Bibles to prisoners along the way. In the associational spirit of the time, Dwight sought the "sanction and cooperation of the American Bible Society." He went to the society's board of managers meeting in New York City in November 1824. Thomas Eddy was among the ministers and reformers gathered there. The society listened to Dwight's presentation and approved his mission.[40]

As with his tract society and educational work, Dwight brought the changing face of Puritanism to his emerging ministry to prisoners. He believed in sin and the necessity of conversion by God's grace. Like many Puritan ministers before him, he affirmed the civil authority's duty to restrain offenders and protect the innocent. But Dwight was a child of nineteenth-century America, not the seventeenth. The language of covenant that had bound earlier church communities was no longer useful in a more mobile and diverse society. Punishing offenders no longer involved public whippings and hangings but incarceration behind walls and bars. Earlier, Puritan ministers spoke to crowds at public punishments. They reminded the people that a criminal's guilt reflected their own sin. Dwight faced a situation in which there were far fewer public gatherings around punishments. There was no longer a tight-knit community bound by covenant to God.[41]

Hidden from view, the prison represented the opportunity to evangelize those who formerly would have been executed or whipped soundly and sent on their way. The prison became another mission field. While Dwight affirmed that the prison's first purpose was criminal punishment he believed that the state had a duty to make prisons orderly enough to promote evangelism and reform. Christians reminded the state of its duty and brought the full force of Bible and mission societies to convert prisoners. Criminals no longer stood for humanity's collective depravity but represented Christians' opportunity to convert all sinful people.[42]

For Dwight, then, the condition of American prisons was not only the legislator's problem but also the Christian's. Ideally, the government worked to maintain strict, orderly prisons. Christians then visited and evangelized inmates, helping to turn a situation of moderate suffering toward a redemptive end. Dwight's experience in the Washington jail made him question how the message of a just and merciful God could penetrate such gloom and filth. If it could not, he felt compelled to make the prison a place more amenable to God's work. Through the PDSB, Dwight affirmed the state's duty to punish criminals and argued for systems of punishment that fostered inmate reformation through Christian conversion and a disciplined life. He became an ardent proponent of the Auburn system, which included its special role for chaplains under the direction of Gershom Powers. He mentored and financially supported Congregational and Presbyterian prison chaplains. When the Auburn system came under serious public scrutiny, he served as its staunch defender. He argued that Auburn's was the best way, if not the only way, to organize prison life with an eye toward good order and inmate reformation.

The goals Dwight articulated for the PDSB upon his return reflected these commitments. First, PDSB members were "not to screen [prisoners] from merited punishment; but to protect society from their depredations." Second, members were "to save [prisoners], if possible, from further contamination." To do this, they lobbied for decent prison conditions. Their list of improvements included clean environments, inmate classification, and good prison order. As his memoirist noted, Dwight believed that "the terrible neglect" and "many abuses" of inmates had to change before "the light of holy truth could penetrate into [prisoners'] minds and hearts." Only then, could the society's third goal be met. Members were "to preach to [inmates], 'CHRIST AND HIM CRUCIFIED.'" The prison signaled the Christian's duty to evangelize all those outside Christ. In this way, Dwight's work in the prison reflected his heritage that affirmed the state's rightful role to punish and the changing face of Calvinism that made the world its mission field. Dwight was convinced that redemption could be achieved through afflictions rightly directed.[43]

With these goals, the society's work was broad in scope and dramatic in its effects. Members inspected institutions across the country, including new prisons built in Maine, Pennsylvania, Connecticut, and Washington, D.C. They published reports on their findings, including their assessment of each institution's religious programming. They lobbied state legislatures and federal officials in Washington. They carried on a vast correspondence with prison officials throughout the United States and Europe. Their reports gathered copious statistics on everything from prison deaths and diet, escapes and illness, punishments and reforms. They called for better order, nutrition, cleanliness, and administration.

In his PDSB reports and particularly in letters to public officials, Dwight focused on the terrible conditions he witnessed in his initial southern journey. In March 1826 he wrote to the Speaker of the U.S. House of Representatives and called for prison reform legislation. He cataloged the horrors of Washington's jail, describing urine that "descends through the ceiling"; the overwhelming dampness, filth, and vermin; and the holding of prisoners without charge for months on end. Again, Dwight recounted the story of the sick little girl and her brothers. He reminded the Speaker of his responsibility to stand "against the continuance of a system, under the immediate eye of Government, exhibiting a compound of mismanagement, oppression, and wretchedness."[44]

But Dwight wanted influence beyond the state and federal legislatures. He pushed into the prisons themselves. Indeed, he worried about the lack of religious education at most of the nation's prisons. His first annual PDSB report noted deficiencies at institutions in New Hampshire, Vermont, Massachusetts, Connecticut, New York City, New Jersey, Pennsylvania, Maryland, and Virginia. One institution, however, met with his approval. In 1825, Dwight managed to send his own minister to Auburn Prison.[45]

Dwight looked to Auburn Prison as a near-perfect model for the state's goal to punish offenders at no cost and for the Christian missionary's hope to evangelize a captive audience. Neither society nor God could be served by the terrible conditions and lack of order in southern prisons. But Auburn's self-sustaining labor, inmate classification, and strict order served the public well and gave missionaries their best chance to reeducate and reform offenders. Auburn kept inmates working, allowed for religious services, and barred all spirits and tobacco from its grounds. Its administrators claimed a recidivism rate of one in twenty compared to Newgate's one in four. Dwight noted that Auburn had a "few cases of unjustifiable severity in punishment" and could not entirely support itself financially. But these concerns were overwhelmed by the list of fifty reformed convicts published in the PDSB's 1827 annual report. Having followed up with local sheriffs, Dwight testified that discharged convicts J.P. of Batavia was "altogether reformed," T.H. of Tyrone had his "bad habits cured," and E.B.D. of Sacketts Harbor was "penitent and humble."[46]

Auburn's discipline also suited Dwight's vision for inmate education and evangelism. Both Agent Powers and the Reverend Dwight understood the work of chaplains to include gaining conversions and improving inmate behavior. Dwight's support of Powers and the Auburn system was significant because most American prisons had no chaplain at all. On his 1824 trip, Dwight met only one chaplain, Stanford at Newgate. Philadelphia's Walnut Street Jail, which had many other good qualities, boasted no leader for religious and educational services. Further south, the lack of religious instruction was just one of myriad problems. The prison society's first report noted the "inadequate supply of moral and religious instruction to prisoners." Even when state officials hired chaplains, the ministers were overworked. Dwight noted that Stanford's part-time salary could not begin to support his workload. How could one man minister to somewhere between 2,100 and 3,500 inmates held in New York's prison, penitentiary, jail, debtor's jail, hospital, and almshouse? The solution was clear to Dwight: dispatch chaplains immediately.[47]

One might ask why Dwight enthusiastically promoted a system that could be so easily misdirected, as had so recently occurred under Elam Lynds at Auburn. For Dwight, this was simple. Compared to the horrors of southern prisons, conditions at Auburn were a reformer's dream. Even with its corporal punishments, the prison seemed a picture of order after the chaos he witnessed on his southern journey. Dwight befriended Auburn's agent Gershom Powers. He accepted Powers's invitation to partner with the state in the prison discipline enterprise. While all three men—Eddy, Stanford, and Dwight—approved of the Auburn system for at least a brief time, it was only Dwight who did so with such unabashed and continued enthusiasm. He lacked experience in other New York institutions, and his Puritan background provided confidence in the state's ability to play a leading role in God's discipline of sinners. He was a perfect match with Auburn's prison administrators. Dwight accepted their call to supply chaplains. And he used the PDSB to advocate for the Auburn system across the country and around the world.[48]

Dwight's advocacy depended on his partnership with Agent Powers and the unprecedented opportunity it provided to integrate Protestant ideas about suffering into state-run prison discipline. The minister appreciated the prison's environment, praising its "unremitted industry" and the prisoners' "entire subordination." He trusted prison agents more than inspectors. The habits of labor, solitary confinement, and the lockstep built order. Dwight even accepted the lash, considering it to be "less severe" than solitary confinement. In short, he believed that chaplains could fully support the state's project at Auburn. Even the lockstep, which prisoners resisted, and the lash, which inmates and some of the public abhorred, could be used for the good of society and God's kingdom.[49]

Both Powers and Dwight emphasized order, economy, and reformation, but they differed on questions of emphasis and purpose. Agent Powers saw inmates as citizens gone wrong. They needed redirection, and religion could play a part in that process. Dwight viewed inmates primarily as sinners. Good citizenship was certainly important, but secondary to and usually a result of becoming a redeemed believer in Jesus Christ. The externals of their programs looked alike--labor, cells, and a limited use of the lash. But ideas about motivations and outcomes diverged.

Powers envisioned a new role for the chaplaincy at the same time that the Reverend Louis Dwight of Boston established a coalition of Protestant reformers concerned with prison affairs. In Dwight and his host of chaplains, Powers found willing partners in building up the Auburn system of prison discipline. Dwight advocated the expansion of Protestantism's public role even as Powers narrowed its reach in his concentration on inmate obedience. They both embraced the furnace-of-affliction model, even as they conceived of its power in decidedly different ways.

Tensions at Auburn

The historical record includes one inmate's voice from Auburn's first decade. Horace Lane served a three-year term in Auburn after a tumultuous life as a sailor. In 1835 he published a book focused on the inhumane treatment he received while serving a second sentence at another New York institution, Sing Sing Prison. His reflections on his first term at Auburn, then, served as a foil to brutal physical treatment elsewhere. Indeed, the piece is a dialogue between prisoners recently released from the two institutions. Lane's character articulates some of Powers and Dwight's ideals, although in this case to establish a contrast with more strenuous prison regimes.[50]

Like Powers and Dwight, Lane extolled the Auburn discipline, especially the staff that enforced it. In his preface, Lane referred to "worthy keepers at Auburn." He noted the mild application of Auburn's discipline: "For my part I never had cause, nor inclination, to find fault with any keeper. . . . The rules were strict, yet there was not much flogging. . . . Once I got a light touch of it, but it was my own fault, for I deserved it, because I was so foolish as to get into a fair conversation with a fellow." Lane assured readers that Auburn's was a humane regime, even if it sometimes utilized the whip. "The keeper seemed very loath to do it," he wrote. "I did not blame him."[51]

According to Lane's narrative, the firm but humane discipline resulted from Agent Powers's approach. The Auburn inmate in the dialogue extolled the judge, calling him "one of the most benevolent and tender-hearted men that I ever saw." The prisoner further described Powers's farewell to the inmates to take up a seat in Congress. He noted the agent's faltering voice and "heart so full he could scarcely speak." Anyone who worried that humane prison staff sacrificed order, the inmate insisted, was far off. Agent Powers and "the good order of Auburn Prison" attested to the transformative power of the Auburn system mildly administered.[52]

While Lane's publication offers a window into one inmate's experience of the Auburn discipline during the system's early years, it has much more to say about the way convicts experienced the religious messages they received during their incarceration. The pamphlet's first fifteen pages contain multiple references to reading prison-cell Bibles and the possibility of finding redemption. Lane's later work, a memoir, also reflects on his Auburn sentence. Lane claimed that he read his Bible attentively, all the way through, seven times. He listened to instruction from teachers and chaplains. With a few exceptions, he followed prison rules. Though prison life was not physically grueling, he found it spiritually painful. I was "in the valley of humiliation," full of regret, and cognizant of the "obligations [I] owed to God."[53]

Nevertheless, the prison did not work on this inmate as Powers and Dwight had planned. Even Lane seemed confused about why he never experienced conversion at Auburn. Despite availing himself of all the religious resources, "there was something lacking," he wrote. "I did not believe I was a Christian." Dwight's hopes that the furnace of affliction led prisoners through suffering to redemption did not work on Lane. Agent Powers's goal of making a law-abiding citizen also failed. Upon release, Lane took up drinking. He committed more crimes and was arrested. He was sentenced to prison again in 1830. His writing, then, is no simple tale of a reformative prison regime. As scholar of antebellum narratives Anne Fabian has observed, convicts like Lane did not write to provide a "moral lesson" but instead had "multiple, competing purposes," from long explanations for criminal behavior to passing judgment on American criminal justice. Even his positive comments about Auburn served the rhetorical purpose of criticizing other New York institutions.[54]

Like Horace Lane, even some of Auburn's PDSB-sponsored chaplains remained ambiguous about the institution's reformative potential. The prison's first resident chaplain, the Reverend Jared Curtis, arrived in November 1825. He took up his ministry just before the scandal that precipitated Elam Lynds's resignation and Gershom Powers's ascension. A Congregational preacher from Stockbridge, Massachusetts, Curtis preached a revivalist Calvinism like that of Louis Dwight and other New Divinity preachers. Upon arriving, Curtis found the prison both impressive and daunting. In letters to his son, he commented on the "neatness, the order and regularity, and the perfect system which prevails" in the prison.[55]

Curtis received instruction about his duties from Agent Powers, who had specific ideas about a chaplain's contribution to prison discipline. According to the agent, the chaplain would befriend inmates and support the institution's policies. To this end, a chaplain would "become acquainted with [the prisoners'] views and feelings," getting to know inmates personally. At the same time, personal contact did not mean adjusting the regime. Powers insisted that chaplains "strictly conform to the rules and regulations of the institutions." Within this disciplinary framework, Curtis organized an inmate Sabbath school, taught mostly by students from the Presbyterian seminary down the street. He preached on Sunday mornings. He tried to learn more about the inmates by reading collections of letters that recorded interviews of inmates soon to depart. In an effort to prove that the system worked, Curtis wrote to officials in the towns to which discharged convicts returned. He collected data about how the ex-convicts performed upon release.[56]

Under Powers's direction, Curtis told inmates that they had sinned and deserved God's judgment. Then he offered words of encouragement and support. Powers demanded that chaplains "dwell emphatically on [the prisoners'] deep depravity and guilt." They were to "convince them of the justice of their sentence . . . and make them feel pungently the horrors of their situation." Curtis shared with Agent Powers a belief that mortifications were proper to punishment and the first step to reformation. He referred to the prisoners as "unhappy outcasts," whose stories involved sorrow and frequent "tears."[57]

Chaplain Curtis—and his employer Louis Dwight—extolled Powers's approach. They applauded Powers's 1826 pamphlet on prison discipline. Dwight quoted large sections of the text in his next PDSB report and Curtis sent copies to his son for dissemination at Williams College. Curtis quickly concluded that many criminals were made better by their time in Auburn. He reported to Dwight that only one in twenty men was recommitted and that many men were very "much improved," "remarkably industrious," or "penitent and humble."[58]

Curtis's reports to Dwight maintained a positive perspective on the Auburn discipline. His letters to family, however, reveal a more ambiguous posture toward the institution and its inmates. The chaplain regularly noted the way in which the prison's darker realities—its gloom, its despair—overwhelmed the impetus toward a redeemed and hopeful future. His earliest letters attest to Auburn's gloom. He wrote to his son that the prison was like "the old castles of Romance, full of passages, intricacies, dismal places and dungeons." Curtis earnestly prayed that revival would break out in his hometown of Stockbridge or where his son studied in Williamstown. He seemed less certain that God's fiery revival would spread to Auburn Prison. Such an unlikely miracle was necessary, he wrote, to change "this gloomy establishment."[59]

Curtis's ambivalence extended to the inmates. In contrast to his prison work, Curtis wrote emotion-laden letters to his son with pleas for his conversion and regeneration. His reflections on inmates were much less fervent. In June 1826 he wrote, "I think I feel for [the prisoners] and I try to pray for them." It is no wonder, then, that Curtis counted few total conversions during his time there. "Now and then," he wrote, an inmate would be "anxious about salvation." Auburn boasted only a "few friends of the Lord Jesus Christ." The prison shared, after all, in a sad similarity with the rest of the world. Only a few would manifest true faith in Christ. And the only thing that saved them, as in every other place, was the reviving power of God. According to his letters, Curtis never experienced that overwhelming power while working at Auburn State Prison. Or, at the very least, he appeared to doubt that God would send adequate revival energies in such a dark place with such irreligious inhabitants.[60]

One veteran reformer was less ambiguous than Curtis. By the mid-1820s, Thomas Eddy despaired. To be sure, his displeasure stemmed primarily from the continuing chaos at Newgate. When state prison commissioners asked for his comments in 1825, Eddy offered caustic remarks. His answers to the commissioners' questions reflected his anger and sadness over the course of the prison's development. He declared, "The New-York State Prison [Newgate] is not a real system of punishment calculated to prevent crimes." Rather, it was a system of confinement that schooled criminals in deeper iniquity and squandered public funds. After cataloging the system's deficiencies, Eddy reminded the commissioners of the public's purpose in administering the penitentiary. He criticized those who decried "the attempt to reform convicts by exercising kind and conciliatory means." These critics forgot that "to advise and admonish the most profligate and abandoned, is the usual practice of life, and is solemnly enjoined by the precepts of the Founder of our holy religion." To that end, Eddy maintained that criminals could be redeemed and that the work of reformation served the greatest demands of both God and society. Unfortunately, state officials had subverted that end. As a result, Eddy remarked that he could "only recollect two cases of complete [inmate] reformation," and one of them had taken place in New Jersey.[61]

In many respects, Newgate was an easy target. But Eddy's concerns about prison discipline extended beyond the bad planning and politics he identified as the cause of Newgate's problems. Even good plans could be nullified by the wrong spirit and the wrong people. Eddy's 1823 campaign concerning the discipline mill is a good example. A few years earlier, Quakers Isaac Collins and Stephen Grellet suggested the use of a treadmill, or discipline mill, to the superintendents of New York's almshouse and penitentiary. Copying the efforts of a London prison reform society, the city built a two-story building and placed three mills, which could accommodate sixteen prisoners each. While they were intended to grind corn for the institution's use, problems soon arose. Eddy responded in turn, reminding officials that the wrong people could misuse a good instrument.[62]

Eddy wrote a pamphlet accusing city officials of using the treadmill for degrading rather than reforming purposes. He argued that the mill ought to be used as it was in London, for pumping water or grinding grain. Used properly, Eddy contended, the mill would be of "real service" to the aims of "regular discipline." Unfortunately, Eddy wrote, officials allowed visitors to "gawk at criminals on the treadmill," treating them "as beasts in the market." Eddy concluded that officials failed to recognize the inmates' humanity or their potential for reformation. "Though a criminal," Eddy argued, "he is yet a man." The right disciplinary technology or prison architecture was not enough. Once again, men of benevolent character were necessary. "We are bound to extend to the criminal the same treatment to which we feel we should be entitled in his situation," Eddy wrote, "Every attempt to treat him as less then human is equally to outrage the feelings of nature, to disregard the obligations of social duty, and to violate the principles of Christianity."[63]

In his final years, Eddy witnessed the implementation of a prison discipline achingly close to the one he envisioned. Auburn's agent employed daytime collective labor and nighttime solitary confinement. The prison boasted a resident chaplain and opportunities for inmate education. The new system promised the order, fiscal security, and prospect of inmate reformation that Eddy sought for so long. He then saw officials use harsh corporal punishments to enforce Auburn's daily regime. When the public protested an inmate's death after an alleged beating, the system fell into scandal and disrepute. The new agent, Gershom Powers, made conscious use of language about religion and reformation to win back public approval for the prison. It is unclear whether Eddy approved of these developments. It is likely, though, that he remained skeptical. According to Eddy, most state appointees to prison management did not understand that patience and mildness were required in the work of inmate reformation. They did not see that "the work is slow." The example of the treadmill made it clear that even the new Auburn discipline and its deployment of religion was no guarantee for the prison's success.[64]

Changing Prison Religion

It remains unclear what role Protestant reformers played in the experiments that produced the Auburn system of prison discipline. Partisans' use of rhetoric about religion as a way to secure public favor and to promote the system's adoption around the country, however, is unquestionable. Doubters voiced their concerns. Inmate Horace Lane testified that he drew on the prison's religious resources, but never experienced saving faith and returned to a life of crime. Auburn's first resident chaplain lacked confidence in the prospect of many inmate conversions. Reformer Thomas Eddy remained skeptical of any disciplinary system controlled by the state that was subject to political interests.

But voices supporting a fusion of disciplinary interests—a combination of state power and religious messaging—won the day. Powers and Dwight applauded the system's order, financial soundness, and reformative potential. That support—voiced by state officials and prominent Protestant ministers—proved powerful in securing public affirmation. Dwight's approval, especially, meant that Agent Powers's regime qualified as reformative. He insisted that the church and the state had overlapping aims regarding the nation's criminal offenders.

The Powers-Dwight partnership reveals the way some citizens imagined religion's ability to help achieve national goals. Powers wanted a prison religion that bolstered the institution's orderly administration. Reformed convicts meant lower recidivism rates, thereby proving the prison's success. Dwight certainly supported Powers's goals, but he also had his own, values that reflected a large segment of the Protestant reforming community. He advocated a prison religion, a furnace of affliction, designed to increase the Christian populace and ensure the government's moral standing. Prison religion was a national project--or, as Auburn's next chaplain wrote in a popular Protestant periodical, the effort of "Presbyterians, Methodists, and

Baptists" to preach the gospel to inmates revealed their "bond of union in the common vineyard." They hoped to Christianize the nation through their ministry to inmates. But in the prison's furnace, their own religion was changed.[65]

The reformers' support, whatever the result of their efforts to effect mass conversion, contributed to Auburn's success. States around the union soon copied the model. When New York officials worried that another institution would be necessary, they also turned to the Auburn system for inspiration. In 1826, the state authorized construction of another prison—later known as Sing Sing—on the same design. Officials designated Auburn's former agent, Elam Lynds, to direct the new prison's construction and administration. Lynds, who had been removed from his position because of alleged rough treatment of inmates, led several dozen Auburn inmates to Ossining, New York, and began the first of Sing Sing's eight hundred cells. With the start of another prison regime under Lynds's direction, the public once again questioned the propriety of a discipline maintained by the lash. As New York's prisons became known around the world for inmate brutality, Dwight and his society of reforming Christians wondered how to respond. These clergymen were not alone in their interest in these questions. The rumors about America's prison discipline and religious populace prompted French commentator Alexis de Tocqueville to make a visit.

While signs of disagreement about the agent-chaplain partnership were already evident at Auburn, at Sing Sing they would come into full view. State disciplinary goals and Protestant national goals did not overlap. Indeed, prison agents pressed the practices of Protestant piety toward the ends of moral living and obedience to secular authority. And when Protestant ideas and practices did not have the desired effect, prison officials abandoned them and their promoters. The dynamics of religious disestablishment in the new nation became increasingly clear: claiming public space demanded a slow altering of the Protestant faith and practice that reformers deemed essential to the survival of the American prison project. Prison affliction took on new forms, not necessarily related to the prophet Isaiah's spiritual furnace.

4

The Furnace at Sing Sing, 1828–1839

In 1829 Sing Sing Prison's agent assaulted the resident chaplain and threw him out of the prison. The institution had no minister until a year later when a new head administrator took over. The new agent, Robert Wiltse, was also dubious about prison chaplains. In a report presented to the state legislature in 1834, Wiltse questioned the claims of inmate reformation boasted by prison ministers. "How much risk do they run of being deceived by hypocritical protestations?" he asked. Wiltse assured the legislature that "the hope once entertained of producing a general and radical reformation of offenders through a penitentiary system, is abandoned by the most intelligent philanthropists, who now think its chief benefit is the prevention of crime." In order to suppress lawbreaking, Wiltse argued, "criminals must be made to submit through corporal punishment." But chaplains' support for this new approach could not be counted on. Ministers, with their naive notions of redeemable human nature, hoped for inmate reformation. With their unrealistic perspective on criminals, Wiltse argued, chaplains underestimated inmate depravity and therefore endangered institutional security.[1]

In the Auburn discipline—at least as its originators theorized it in the 1820s—chaplains played a vital role in maintaining prison order and encouraging inmate reformation. To be sure, some observers had expressed concerns about the details of this partnership between state officials and

Protestant ministers. Even those with hesitations, however, agreed that the Auburn system had a reforming aim and that religion was vital to achieving it. In the 1830s, especially at Sing Sing, this partnership fell apart. The new prison's administrators, prompted by a host of new cultural concerns, recognized only two goals: prison order and profit were now the state's highest interests. Inmate reformation, they argued, was neither possible nor an appropriate goal for the state to pursue.

Sing Sing's first chaplain was thrown out after he questioned the agent's methods for achieving order and profit. The two men also disagreed about the possibility of inmate reformation. The chaplain's dismissal, however, did not mean state officials no longer employed religion in their prison disciplines. Robert Wiltse's career reveals that Sing Sing's agents, instead, promoted a different sort of religion inside prison walls. The 1830s witnessed a debate over just what kind of religion—and therefore what sort of chaplains and forms of Protestant piety—would be welcomed in New York's state prisons. It marked the beginning of a prison religion stripped of its Protestant particulars and focused on characteristics of American citizenship.

Why Sing Sing?

In the 1830s Sing Sing Prison served as a key site for debating American Protestantism's public character. Several practical concerns and cultural factors shaped the contours of this debate. Built to replace the increasingly decrepit and constantly overcrowded Newgate, Sing Sing rivaled Philadelphia's newest institution, the massive Eastern State Penitentiary. They were the flagship institutions representing two sides in the ongoing prison discipline debate. Sing Sing represented the Auburn system of congregate labor, whereas Eastern embodied the Pennsylvania ideal of separate confinement. Other states modeled themselves on these East Coast examples. The institutional building spree stretched across the young nation. In the late 1820s, Maryland built a new prison on the Auburn plan, while Massachusetts reorganized its institution along similar lines. In the 1830s New Jersey, Ohio, Missouri, Vermont, and Michigan also built prisons. States officials as far away as Louisiana and Mississippi had plans for prison construction.[2]

Historians at least partly attribute this wave of prison construction to rising concerns about crime and disorder. Scholars disagree about what constituted crime in this period and whether it increased or declined. Certainly, the general public perceived that lawbreaking, whether perpetrated by professional outlaws or the desperate poor, constituted a serious problem. Newspapers fueled the popular imagination, particularly the *New York Sun*, which ran a wildly popular column of "Police Reports" in the 1830s. Religious periodicals followed these trends closely, reminding readers that crime threatened the nation's moral fabric. "Crimes and criminals multiply," read an article in *New York Evangelist*. The editors supported prison construction but echoed a common Protestant refrain, "Religion alone, changing the fountain of human conduct, can effect real reform in the state of society."[3]

Citizens increasingly fixated on a particular sort of lawbreaking, namely illicit sexual activity. Historian Timothy Gilfoyle has pointed to a growing sex industry in the 1820s that would turn New York City into "the carnal showcase of the Western world" by midcentury. Other historians have tracked the sustained social commentary on prostitution in the 1830s. In 1831, for example, New York's Magdalene Society began its effort to eradicate prostitution. The city's tract society members began home visiting campaigns designed to rescue vulnerable citizens from an eventual life on the street or a life of crime. As historian Patricia Cline Cohen narrates, the city hosted extremes of wealth and poverty. Prostitutes symbolized a changing moral order and the difficult lives faced by the displaced or immigrant poor.[4]

These immigrant arrivals showed no signs of subsiding. Boston, New York, and Philadelphia served as entry ports for growing waves of immigrants. In the 1830s, New York City's population increased by 54 percent. By 1835 the city received more than thirty thousand Irish immigrants a year. Germans and English followed. The immigrants raised the hackles of established residents and increased competition for jobs with the resident working poor. Concerned about the new arrivals' differences, including their lack of education and commitment to Roman Catholic Christianity, New Yorkers cracked down.[5]

Officials responded to the public perception of a growing underclass of potential lawbreakers. In the 1830s, several cities began police reform in earnest. In New York, however, reforms came slowly. The city still had no professional police force by the 1840s. A "complex network of pickpockets, fences, opium addicts, and confidence men" flourished as city crime-fighting efforts staggered. City officials were successful, however, in lobbying for a criminal institution to replace Newgate's overcrowded chaos. In 1825 New York's Common Council authorized Sing Sing's construction just thirty miles north of the city. Convinced that the city's overwhelmingly

Irish immigrants were hardly "free, white persons" fit for self-government, officials also sought a prison agent who could discipline urban, immigrant criminals. To oversee their new prison, officials looked to a familiar name: Elam Lynds.[6]

Despite his dubious past, Lynds took the helm of Sing Sing's construction and management with utmost confidence. As noted earlier, Lynds had been removed as Auburn Prison's agent in late 1825 after a female inmate who had recently received a beating died suddenly. Lynds's political connections, however, allowed him to retain Albany's favor. He had friends within Martin Van Buren's growing political machine. Indeed, his position remained assured whenever the emerging party of Jacksonian Democrats wielded power. Commissioned to build the new prison, Lynds marched one hundred Auburn inmates to a site along the Hudson River. The crew constructed its living quarters and then set to work on the eight-hundred-cell prison. Like Auburn, Sing Sing had individual cells and communal workshops. It opened in 1828.

According to Lynds, Sing Sing required strict discipline to confront the tough, immigrant criminals within its walls. Having left the slums of the city and the disorder of Newgate Prison, these lawbreakers encountered a dramatically new world when they entered Sing Sing. They confronted Agent Lynds's particular approach to the Auburn discipline. Inmates labored silently in the stone quarries by day. They moved in a lockstep formation to and from their solitary cells. They ate alone without the benefit of utensils. Food was piled in buckets that sometimes went unwashed for days. Lynds enforced this routine through strict discipline. Even the slightest violation provoked the lash. At night, not a sound rose from the hundreds of cells. One observer noted that walking through Sing Sing at night was like "traversing catacombs." This funereal language captures Lynds's disciplinary intent: to subdue criminals so that their fear of misconduct squelched their own impulses. They lost all subjectivity and lived as the staff directed them. Or as literary theorist Caleb Smith has observed, antebellum inmates existed as ghostly bodies under the civil death dictated in law.[7]

Lynds's strict style occasioned furious debate about the Auburn system specifically and its rivalry with Pennsylvania as well. As historian David Rothman has noted, the conversation was "surprisingly fierce" given the systems' similarities. Partisans of Pennsylvania's regime of total confinement called New York's system of congregate labor corrupting. New York's defenders claimed that unmitigated solitary confinement drove inmates mad. While both disciplines were founded on rigid order and used various forms of corporal punishments to deal with rule breakers, each side claimed that its approach reformed inmates and that the other system made criminals worse.[8]

For years, the New York–Pennsylvania debate had focused on questions about inmates' proper treatment and the best reformative strategies. Which was the more humane way to discipline misbehaving subjects: immediate, though painful, corporal punishments or lengthy stints of solitary confinement? What were the best methods for securing good behavior? Partisans quarreled, claiming the other side advocated methods unfit for civilized society. Lynds's ascendance in the New York system, however, coincided with a change in this conversation. As historian Michael Meranze has argued, the resurgence of prison physical violence in the 1820s and its explosion in the 1830s signaled a deep concern with inmate intransigence. In Pennsylvania, Meranze has observed, officials refused the whip and implemented devices such as the iron gag instead. They argued that this was not a bodily punishment, but rather a tool for targeting the inmate's will. Meranze, of course, notes the irony of a focus on the will that involves inflicting bodily discomfort, if not torture. New Yorkers such as Lynds, on the other hand, had no qualms about seizing the body. Indeed, Lynds had to focus on the body because he questioned whether inmates had souls at all. Dubious about criminals' spiritual capacity, Lynds concluded that programs for inmate reformation were a ludicrous enterprise. And when a prominent prison agent denounced lawbreakers' reformative potential, religion's place in the prisons was suddenly disputable.[9]

Initially, the Reverend Louis Dwight and the Prison Discipline Society of Boston (PDSB) welcomed Sing Sing's construction. At the most basic level, the new prison meant an end to Newgate's overcrowding and filth. More important, Sing Sing signaled another victory for Dwight's efforts to promote the Auburn system. Dwight stood firmly for the Empire State. He reasoned that the lash's lawful application was a humane form of punishment. Stripes were immediate and not permanently damaging. They did not incite madness or cause ill health, something he believed unmitigated solitary confinement did. Dwight conceded that New York's inmates suffered because of lost freedom and difficult circumstances. Prison was surely a furnace of affliction, but its positives overwhelmed the negatives. In his first PDSB annual report, Dwight called Auburn Prison a "beautiful example of what may be done by proper discipline." Sing Sing's replication of this model boded well. According to Dwight, every prison that copied that model was destined for similar success.[10]

Part of Dwight's initial approval stemmed from his ability to select and support Sing Sing's resident chaplain. Having his own minister inside Sing Sing assured him that the use of corporal punishment—the extent and character of inmates' physical affliction—would stay properly calibrated for redemptive suffering. During Sing Sing's construction, Dwight nominated the Reverend Gerrish Barrett, a minister who shared his revivalist Calvinism. The post was Barrett's first after graduating from Princeton Theological Seminary in 1825. While Barrett certainly drew from the conservative Presbyterianism that dominated Princeton during his tenure, he took most of his theological affirmations from his earlier educational experiences. He attended Phillips Academy, a feeder school for Dwight's alma mater, Andover Theological Seminary. Graduating in 1821, Barrett bore the signs of Andover's New Divinity spirit. He valued revivals and missions. While he affirmed classic Calvinist tenets such as original sin, he also considered evangelistic work as the means God used to save the lost. He arrived at Sing Sing a young and optimistic pastor. The PDSB paid Barrett's salary and the young chaplain considered himself not just a state employee but also the church's missionary to inmates.[11]

Life at Sing Sing

Concerns about rising crime and soaring immigrant numbers surely influenced New Yorkers' decision to build Sing Sing. These and other factors also prompted Elam Lynds to enforce a particularly strict form of the Auburn disciplinary system. Sing Sing's architecture and daily routines followed Auburn's. Inmates labored silently by day and remained in solitary cells at night. But Lynds insisted that Sing Sing required stricter enforcement. The foremost historian of New York prisons, W. David Lewis, has noted that Lynds's fondness of the lash is not the only explanation. Architectural problems also contributed. Sing Sing lacked Auburn's recessed doors, which blocked the possibility of whispered inmate conversations. In turn, the guards had to be much more engaged to control the spread of messages down the lines of cells. Further, Sing Sing had no outer wall. New York legislators balked at the expense of such a massive structure. Guards, therefore, felt the need to be extra diligent against escapes.[12]

The most important factor, at least in the minds of prison staff, was the inmate population's ethnic makeup and urban experience. Sing Sing housed criminals from New York City. Many of them were newly arrived immigrants, along with a growing number of free blacks. Though Auburn's mix was not substantially different in ethnic backgrounds, the prisoners came from rural settings rather than urban ones. Even the most sensitive keepers and onlookers worried about Sing Sing's city masses. Dorothea Dix, the social reformer who usually decried any discipline beyond words of persuasion, saw something categorically different in Sing Sing's occupants. After a visit to the institution, she wrote, "Here is the most corrupt, the most degraded class of prisoners, of any prison north of the Mason and Dixon's line." Again, as Lewis has observed, Sing Sing's agent and keepers felt they had the worst criminals under the worst conditions. In turn, they used increasingly harsh measures to keep order among their charges.[13]

Broader cultural developments also impacted how prison officials—and the general public—perceived convicts. First, the increasing popularity of evangelical revivalism, with its focus on individual decisions for Christ, undercut older notions about the common human situation. When Calvinism dominated American theology, sin and guilt were communal matters. Everyone bore the stain of original sin. All needed God to save them from damnation. In this context, preachers accompanied criminals to the gallows and interpreted the event for all. The lawbreaker's death reminded everyone of his or her dependence on God's mercy. While Quakerism prevailed in a much smaller portion of the American population, it, too, posited a common experience. In the Friends' case, the common presence of the Inner Light demanded a sense of human connection. Every person, whether wealthy and white or impoverished and enslaved, carried the divine spark within.[14]

Protestant evangelical religion, as it was promulgated in revivals, threw these affirmations of common human condition into question. Although revivalists believed that all humans were guilty before God and that all had potential for salvation, they focused on individuals in need of grace and each person's responsibility to choose salvation. Revivalist preachers drew sharp distinctions between the saved and unsaved, those washed clean of their guilt and those still festering in it. Their ideas about the sufferings caused by unredeemed sin followed from their clear distinction between saved and unsaved individuals. Previously, bodily and mental afflictions were considered difficult, but routine experiences. A just God visited these pains on all sinful humanity. In the antebellum years, however, people began to disassociate pain from regular life, considering it, instead, an aberration. Pain became evidence not of common human experience but of "human transgression." Individuals were responsible for their deeds and bore the pain they suffered accordingly. As historian Elizabeth A. Clark has argued, pain was for those who "flouted the laws of human nature" and reaped the "consequence of their lawbreaking."[15]

As the ties that knit people together became weaker and the perception of pain and suffering transferred from the normal course of life to the abnormal, sympathy for prisoners became increasingly untenable. Indeed, the case for lawbreakers' humane treatment faltered with the growing popularity of abolitionist arguments supporting the fundamental right to be free from bodily violence on the basis of one's innocence. As historians have well documented, abolitionists followed on the coattails of revivalists and often copied their techniques. As newly evangelized Christians considered how they could spread the gospel and care for others, abolitionists presented the plight of innocent slaves to hearts newly overflowing with Christian concern. Beginning in the 1830s and culminating in the 1850s with Harriet Beecher Stowe's *Uncle Tom's Cabin*, abolitionists told tales of innocent, suffering slaves. While there is no evidence that abolitionists intended to undermine sympathy for other classes of people, their success surely proved that some Americans in the North accepted their claim that innocent people who experienced bodily violence demanded their sympathy. It easily followed that the guilty forfeited the same concern.[16]

Indeed, many factors undermined prison reformers' arguments that criminals were human beings deserving of humane treatment. As citizens sensed that crime was increasing, they became fearful. As immigrants flooded the country, those with longer residencies resented the newcomers for both their need and their potential to share in the nation's emerging wealth. The language of revivals persuaded many of the power of personal choice and the necessity of taking responsibility for one's sins. The image of the needy, thieving immigrant looked even worse against abolitionist portraits of innocent enslaved people suffering terrible violence. The Irishman counterfeiting or the free black stealing went against all that was sacred. They were different, poor, and guilty.

Some antebellum Americans resisted the use of corporal punishments on several populations, including criminal offenders. Historian Myra Glenn has reflected on the variety of cultural and institutional impulses that fueled anti–corporal punishment campaigns in the realm of schools and homes, the navy and penitentiaries. Nevertheless, she has noted that even the strongest advocates against whipping believed their claims were limited. "Most antebellum critics of corporal punishment harbored doubts about the efficacy of reforming all human beings." According to Glenn, they sensed that at least a small portion of the population "would remain incorrigible." Antebellum criminals, especially those emerging from the urban immigrant context of poverty, fit this description. In the popular mind, this tough approach to the most incorrigible was easily extended to all lawbreakers within prison walls. Criminals exhibited the most striking moral flaws of the antebellum underclass: laziness, drunkenness, tendencies to violence, and sexual immorality. As lawbreakers, they were different from everyone else and deserving of painful punishment.[17]

Reformation in Sing Sing

Chaplain Barrett followed the same instructions Louis Dwight had given to Auburn's chaplains. He offered himself as a partner in directing the discipline's smooth operation. The prison's agent and keepers subdued and ordered criminals and thus allowed the minister to offer a program of suffering aimed at redemption. Barrett organized inmate education and offered spiritual consolation to those brought low by Sing Sing's daily routines. At first, the tough conditions for both him and the inmates hardly gave him pause. The prison chapel was not finished, so Barrett led Sunday services in the prison's outer yard. In the evenings, he read scripture and prayed in darkened hallways. With no place to hold Sabbath school, Barrett whispered reading instruction through cell door grates. Because he lacked educational materials, Barrett taught inmates to read from the only book they had, the Bible. Despite these difficulties, both Dwight and Barrett imagined an agent-clergy partnership like Auburn's. They viewed Sing Sing as a dramatic improvement over Newgate's chaos and the only chance to redeem offenders who had languished there.[18]

Dwight and his PDSB chaplains resisted the cultural forces that questioned inmates' humanity and reformative capacity. Barrett articulated a theology of redemptive suffering that John Stanford introduced in New York prisons during his earliest years of service. The prison was a furnace of affliction that used prison sufferings to produce redeemed lives. In the evenings, Barrett articulated this message by teaching inmates to read and recite Psalm 88. In his 1829 report to the legislature, Barrett recounted one prisoner's heart-rending recitation of its verses: "Thou hast laid me in the lowest pit, in darkness, in the deeps. Thy wrath lieth hard upon me, and thou hast afflicted me with all thy waves. Thou hast put my acquaintance far from me; thou hast made me an abomination to them: I am shut up and I cannot come forth." In his selection of scripture, the chaplain offered an interpretation of inmates' daily experiences. The hardships of prison were the wrath of God. Criminals were cut off from all who loved them for breaking the laws of both heaven and earth. In Barrett's estimation, inmates deserved their punishments and the state justly prompted their sufferings.[19]

This furnace, though it prompted inmate pain, processed suffering into conversion and reformation. The prison was not solely a place of punishment and gloom. According to Barrett, Psalm 88 also included words of hope. "Wilt thou show wonders to the dead? Shall the dead arise and praise thee? . . . Shall thy wonders be known in the dark? And thy righteousness in the land of forgetfulness?" The minister answered the psalmist's questions with an enthusiastic yes. God not only punished offenders but also performed works of grace inside prison. As the chaplain, Barrett believed that he lifted up inmates who had reached rock bottom. He affirmed that New York State had an obligation to offer the gospel invitation to its subdued criminals.[20]

Psalm 88 perfectly articulated the theology of redemptive suffering that Dwight and the PDSB chaplains preached in the midst of a cultural shift concerning lawbreaking. American Protestants in the Reformed traditions had a long tradition of singing and praying the psalms. Any sinful person could speak the words of desolation contained in Psalm 88. Its use by Chaplain Barrett, then, affirmed that inmates shared in the common condition of sinful humanity suffering for their misdeeds. But prisoners' particular experiences mirrored the agonies expressed by the psalmist. They were separated from family and friends, troubled in heart, and physically afflicted. References to God's power to redeem seemed especially fitting. Barrett reflected on the psalm's particular power in the prison context. In an article in the *Boston Recorder and Religious Telegraph*, he reported on one inmate's recitation. "It never seemed to me half so impressive before," he wrote. The inmate's tones were "thrilling," he recalled, doing "more to open to my view the heart of the Psalmist." According to Barrett, wonders could be known in the dark, and righteousness could be proclaimed in a land of forgetfulness. Sing Sing then constituted a perfect furnace of affliction.[21]

Psalm 88, however, can also be read ironically. Was the psalmist accusing God of abandonment? "Shall the dead arise and praise thee?" What good was God's saving power after the body had been destroyed? Or as the psalmist inquired, "Shall thy lovingkindness be declared in the grave?"

Chaplain Barrett saw the psalm for its redemptive promise, but how did prisoners experience these words? According to inmate narratives, life in Sing Sing amounted to a living death. Acts of prisoner resistance surely signaled that some questioned the discipline imposed on them and the theology of redemptive suffering that supported it. Could lovingkindness be known in a world of walls, bars, and whips?

We know that the lash dominated the Lynds's era not only from inmate accounts but also from the agent's own words. In an interview given later in his career, Lynds reflected on the best way to maintain prison discipline. He argued that agents must have "absolute and certain power," something fussy legislators and an ignorant public sometimes questioned. Discipline demanded immediate punishment for breaking prison rules. The lash, he insisted, was the "most efficient" method of punishment. He also considered it the "most humane," especially in comparison to the strict solitude practiced in Pennsylvania. When pressed about the prison's disciplinary aims, Lynds focused on order and profit. He questioned the possibility of reform altogether. He told the interviewers that he did not believe in the complete rehabilitation of adult inmates. All society could ask for—and all that a prison could ever hope to produce—were inmates trained to obey orders and made fearful of disobeying them. In Lynds's penal imagination, bringing prisoners low was all that was necessary. Work to uplift was an utter waste of resources.[22]

A look at prisoner narratives from Sing Sing's early years reveals inmates' struggles with the institution's severe discipline. A burst of literary activity began in 1833, with new narratives appearing in 1835 and 1839. In these cases, ex-prisoners sought to expose the physical cruelties they both witnessed and experienced. They lambasted members of the staff, accusing them of torture. They upbraided the state for its negligence. They offered images of prison brutality to interested outsiders. In every way, they argued against Lynds's claim that his use of the lash was humane.[23]

Levi S. Burr, a veteran from the War of 1812, served a three-year term in Sing Sing and afterward addressed the state assembly about the abuses he witnessed there. He published his testimony in 1833. In the piece, Burr described the tools taken up to pummel inmates. Guards usually used the cat, a stick with strands of cord, each with sharp wires on the end. They also employed the cudgel, a cane applied to beat the head, back, arms, and legs of prisoners. Burr described starving inmates beaten for sharing food with others, prisoners used in the quarries as if they were beasts, and men freezing in their bunks during winter. The greatest cruelty, Burr argued, was the keepers' flouting of laws placing limits on corporal punishment. Burr saw a prisoner whipped with the cat 133 times on one occasion, so that he was "crying and writhing under the laceration, that tore his skin in pieces from his back." He reported that the keeper then delivered "a blow across the mouth with his cane, that caused the blood to flow profusely." The government at Sing Sing, Burr wrote, was "a Cat-ocracy and Cudgel-ocracy . . . where there is no eve of pity, no tongue to tell, no heart to feel, or will or power to oppose." With Lynds's permission, Burr claimed, keepers physically terrorized inmates.[24]

Aiming his wrath at the prison's administration, Burr confessed his "sickening contemptuous horror" for the agent who directed the keepers to "lacerate the body, spill the blood, and starve the subject." He compared Sing Sing to the French Bastille, urging citizens to rise up against the symbol of despotism standing among them. For Burr, treatment of Sing Sing's inmates seemed especially appalling given the historical connection between American prisons and the intent to reform inmates. In the work's preface, Burr wrote that he hoped to expose Sing Sing's cruelties so that readers would know that Agent Lynds undermined "benign sentiments of mercy" central to the state's punishment statutes and its citizens' religion. His focus on gory detail, which caused the public to question its high prison ideals, reflects the method of many antebellum personal narratives. In her study of writings by beggars, slaves, and convicts, literary theorist Ann Fabien has observed that writers piled on details to prove their story's authenticity. Burr marshaled these details to expose the hypocrisy of the Lynds regime.[25]

Another inmate, Horace Lane, also took up his pen in protest. As noted earlier, Lane served sentences at both Auburn and Sing Sing. He created a fictional dialogue between inmates recently released from each institution. In the narrative, the characters compare their prison experiences. The Sing Sing inmate reflects on work in the stone quarry, describing labor that tore at the body. He recalls "the severest agony" caused by pulling wheelbarrows laden with stone. In the months he spent hauling rocks, the Sing Sing prisoner declares that he had "never suffered so much." Worse than the labor, though, was the catalog of brutal punishments he and fellow inmates received. "The lash was severe," reports the Sing Sing inmate in Lane's dialogue. "I got my head cut open," by a keeper. Reflecting on the punishments he and his fellow convicts received, the inmate reports, "I could not help but cry almost all the time, and the more I cried, the more they beat me."[26]

A third narrative from a Sing Sing ex-convict echoed Burr's and Lane's accounts of mistreatment. James Brice was convicted of perjury and sent to Sing Sing in 1833. His narrative dwells on the violence he and other inmates experienced. He describes months-long periods when prisoners received so little food they felt close to starvation. He tells of a work-related injury that left one arm nearly crippled. His focus, however, is the prominent role of flogging in Sing Sing's discipline. In a direct address to the reader, Brice writes: "If you could but once witness a state prison flogging. The victim is stripped naked and beaten with a cruel instrument of torture called a cat, from neck to his heels, until as raw as a piece of beef." He told of floggings he witnessed in which inmates' backs were so mangled and infected that "they smelled of putrification." Brice reported his own flogging on two occasions. In the second incident, the keeper pressed a loaded pistol against Brice's chest and threatened to fire.[27]

Although ex-convicts' writings did not appear in print until a few years later, Chaplain Barrett began to hear inmate reports as early as 1829. Their details prompted him to wonder if the prison's harsh discipline jeopardized his work reclaiming lost souls. The stories shocked him. Rumors swirled that during winter months a prisoner's foot had frozen for the lack of blankets. Other reports mentioned inmates eating clay and grass out of hunger. The charges included not only mistreatment but also corruption. Convicts claimed that the prison's agent used public money earmarked for decent food and bought "offal beef" instead. The agent allegedly pocketed the difference.[28]

Believing the reports of these abuses, Barrett informed Sing Sing's Board of Prison Inspectors. Its members launched an investigation. Agent Lynds soon discovered the minister's action. According to Barrett's report, Lynds grabbed him, roughed him up, and threw him out of the prison. Clearly, the partnership between prison staff and Protestant clergy was compromised.[29]

Chaplain Barrett's 1830 whistle blowing was only the first in a long series of skirmishes about religion's place at Sing Sing Prison. Before the minister's tip-off, the prison inspectors trusted Lynds to run the prison well. Barrett's report, however, was too troubling. The inspectors demanded a full investigation and confirmed Barrett's accusations. They found ample evidence of prisoner mistreatment. Indeed, Lynds had defrauded the state in his purchases of "offal beef." The state prison commissioner who had raised doubts about Lynds during his rule at Auburn was especially indignant. After the agent assaulted and removed Chaplain Barrett, inspectors hoped that a keeper might assist their investigation. Lynds threw the keeper out as well. In light of these findings, the commissioner pressed the legislature for Lynds's removal.[30]

Dwight and the PDSB also decried the agent, but to no avail. To be sure, Dwight bristled at Lynds's humiliating removal of Barrett. In his next annual report, he called Lynds's use of power "despotic" and urged the agent's dismissal. His concern reached beyond his evicted chaplain to include the inmates left behind. The Democratic majority in the legislature, however, remained unmoved. Political associations and party loyalty trumped evidence of abuse and fraud. The state assembly found in favor of Lynds and named a new slate of inspectors sympathetic to the agent. Now Lynds faced no critical chaplain or keepers. The new inspectors asked no questions about the discipline and trusted the agent to run the prison. From the reformers' perspective, no one was there to ensure the proper workings of inmate affliction.[31]

Dwight bemoaned the breakdown at Sing Sing. The partnership he had brokered at Auburn did not survive the transfer to a new environment. While Dwight acknowledged Sing Sing's tougher crowd, he believed that his Auburn partnership—with its emphasis on reformation and clear limits on the extent of bodily suffering—was vital. A good agent oversaw the application of serious but not damaging affliction. He then made way for chaplains to do the work of rebuilding. But Lynds disrupted this pattern. His discipline was too severe. Under his command, prisoners simply suffered. Words of hope could not reach inmates in such conditions. Further, the convicts had no recourse when their inordinate affliction surpassed the legal limits on corporal punishment. "What refuge or redress is there for the mangled, sick, or starving prisoner," Dwight asked in his 1830 PDSB report. What was possible, he wondered, "when [the prisoner] is held to his task, and then lashed, when he cries out from weakness and hunger? I know he is a felon," Dwight continued, "but is he not also a human being?" Indeed, Dwight's concern that afflictions did not serve a redemptive end was closely tied to his sense of prisoners' basic humanity. Suffering as its own end was not a proper way to treat another person.[32]

While Dwight and some state legislators were at no loss for words, Lynds said remarkably little. He refused to address the accusations against him. He continued to perform the task he was charged to do: to keep order and industry at Sing Sing. It was Lynds's assessment that tougher routines were necessary because Sing Sing's prisoners—usually urban and immigrant— were more dangerous and less human. The agent's allies in the state house appeared persuaded. Despite evidence that Lynds starved and beat prisoners, defrauded the state, and bodily assaulted a Presbyterian minister, he kept his job. Secure in his victory over the inspectors, Lynds decided to take a break from prison life. In 1830, he resigned his post and moved to Syracuse to run a hardware store.[33]

If Lynds refrained from comment and Dwight and Barrett remained exasperated on the sidelines, inmates spoke directly to the question of redemptive suffering. In the face of prison leaders who questioned convicts' reformative potential, Sing Sing ex-convicts who wrote about their experiences affirmed redemptive suffering as inmates' only hope and the prisons' primary purpose. They advocated for the furnace of affliction that Protestant ministers had long promoted. The prison, they insisted, needed the right leadership and the right discipline to channel appropriate sufferings into energies directed toward redeemed life.

Levi Burr, for instance, contended that laws sponsoring humane punishment reflected the population's religion. Prison presented lawbreakers with a message about their crimes. Through the law and its penal institutions, Burr argued, the people "follow [the convict] with a Christian's mercy, call upon him to repent his transgressions, forsake the evil, and be forgiven." This process was hardly easy. Burr continued, the "time of penance" was difficult, but nothing like the "horrid place" Sing Sing was under Agent Lynds.[34]

Horace Lane's narrative comparing his terms in Auburn and Sing Sing made a much more dramatic case for redemptive suffering. His Sing Sing conversion experience convinced him that reformation was not just possible but was the institution's only acceptable goal. His words mirror those of Stanford, Curtis, and Barrett. "Affliction," he wrote, brought inmates "to the feet of Jesus." Sufferings could "improve the soul." He resisted Lynds's skepticism of inmate reformation. He scoffed at the notion that Sing Sing's punishments were humane. Though Lynds denied the possibility, Burr and Lane affirmed that God used appropriate prison sufferings for a greater end. Sing Sing's regime, however, was too harsh. Given the severe discipline they endured, the inmates considered their own reformation nothing short of miraculous. Inmate narratives, then, invoked the furnace of affliction as a mode of resistance. Arguing for this traditionally Protestant narrative of prison suffering provided a way to push back against new forms of envisioning religion that marginalized its redemptive capacity and emphasized its support for harsh regimes aimed at securing law and order.[35]

Ex-convict James Brice also turned to religion as both a coping resource and platform for critique. According to his narrative, he used daily devotional practice as succor for his misery. He tells his readers that he prayed no fewer than four times a day, not only for himself but also for his enemies in the prison administration. He attests to the comfort provided by religious literature, including a book of psalms, an Episcopal prayer book, and the popular tract, Baxter's *Call to the Unconverted*. While he focused most on the four gospels, Brice assures readers that he read the Bible "from Genesis to the end of Revelations" in his first three months of confinement.[36]

Brice's regular spiritual practice, however, could not overcome or make sense of his and other's physical afflictions. As a result, he marshals this failure to critique the prison's discipline. In his narrative's closing lines, he addresses his "fellow-citizens" directly. He attests to Sing Sing's "cruel sufferings, starvation, and abuse." To be sure, Brice admits that the job of Sing Sing is to "punish our convicts with the strong arm of the law." The prison was necessary to deal with a criminal who "willfully violates [the nation's laws]." But that arm had punished too strongly. "What is the object of punishment?" Brice asks. "Surely it is to reform the offender." Sing Sing's discipline had failed to meet this goal. Even more, it betrayed the nation's character. In a question that could have been taken from pamphlets published by Protestant reformers, Brice asks his readers if such practices can be "permitted in a Christian land, where the gospel is sounded."[37]

For the first time in New York prison history, prisoner narratives show inmates embracing the redemptive suffering preached by Louis Dwight and his PDSB chaplains. John Stanford preached it at Newgate. Jared Curtis preached it at Auburn. But with the advent of Lynds's discipline at Sing Sing—the beginning of a penal philosophy that underplayed, if not derided, inmate reformation—prisoners began defending the notion that their sufferings had to be for something. In the face of a changing cultural climate and an administration that scoffed at reformation, some inmates and Protestant reformers rallied behind the furnace of affliction in an effort to align prison discipline with traditions of Protestant piety and aspirations for the nation's millennial blessedness.

They fought an uphill battle. While new personalities in prison leadership steered away from a reformative focus, other factors contributed to a cultural climate where sympathy for inmates receded. Citizens sensed that crime was on the rise. Immigration surged. Political parties in power resisted reformers. Evangelical revivals encouraged new ideas about personal responsibility and social ties. Just as other reform movements gained purchase with the American public, prison reform stalled. Indeed, many citizens questioned prisoners' basic humanity, attacked prison disciplines based on redemptive suffering, and debated the place of ministers in establishing prison policies.

The Fear to Transgress

A new slate of prison inspectors, sympathetic to Lynds, appointed his nephew Robert Wiltse as Sing Sing's new agent. Though challenged periodically, Wiltse's regime lasted for a decade. Over the course of the 1830s, Wiltse took Lynds's strict discipline to new heights. He publicly advocated penal theories that questioned the possibility of inmate reformation. He reasoned that prisoners' guilt created a gulf between them and their law-abiding brothers and sisters. Mild means and redemptive words were no match for such debased characters. Severity in word and deed constituted the prison agent's only recourse.

Under Wiltse's administration, the whip could fall at any time. Prison staff and private contractors of prisoner labor could strike Sing Sing's inmates with any available weapon. Historian W. David Lewis has chronicled this period. According to legislative reports, Sing Sing keepers used whips, canes, cat-o'-nine-tails, red-hot pokers, and even pistols to subdue the smallest signs of inmate resistance. Labor continued to be grueling, as contractors demanded the mind-numbing and body-punishing tasks of moving heavy slabs of marble out of the prison's quarry. Inmates slow to work garnered lashes alongside pack animals receiving similar blows. Even mealtime proved dreadful as convicts received slop buckets with all their food mixed together. These vessels remained in cells overnight, drawing mice and other vermin. Life in Sing Sing clearly entailed no end of afflictions.[38]

Wiltse's regime received particular attention from Frenchmen Alexis de Tocqueville and Gustave de Beaumont. In 1831 they arrived in the United States on assignment from the French government. Charged with the task of making suggestions for the French penal system, the young men investigated America's rival prison disciplines during a particularly heated moment in the ongoing debate. Toward the beginning of their ten-month tour, they stopped at Sing Sing and Auburn. They interviewed inmates, prison staff, and state officials. They even searched out Elam Lynds in his Syracuse hardware store and spoke with him for several hours. Persuaded by Lynds's good stories and self-assurance, the two continued their voyage across the country. They saw dozens of prisons, jails, and houses of refuge from Massachusetts to Louisiana. In 1833 they entered the fray by publishing a highly anticipated report about their experience.[39]

Their book, *On the Penitentiary System*, laid out the differences between the two American systems. It also considered the possibility of implementing some of the systems' features in French institutions. The visitors did not side clearly with either system. Despite their appreciation for Pennsylvania's solitary confinement and restrictions on corporal punishments, they balked at the inordinate cost. They applauded the Auburn system's focus on labor and obedience because it offered inmates new habits they would need upon release. But Auburn institutions that used the whip liberally worried them. In a letter to a French colleague, Tocqueville extolled the labor, discipline, and health of Auburn Prison's inmates. He noted the institution's balanced budget. At the same time, he said the discipline was achieved not through "conviction" but rather through the "cat."[40]

At the same time the Frenchmen applauded American developments, they also expressed doubts about some of the foundational principles behind the institution. Namely, they questioned the possibility of inmate reformation. After seeing Sing Sing and interviewing Lynds, they wondered if inmate reformation was possible or recognizable. Offering up some of Lynds's reflections from their interview with him, the Frenchmen asked if chaplains could be deceived by inmate claims about reformation. They argued that the political system could not have individual redemption as its primary goal. Even as they respected some of the prison chaplains and applauded work to educate inmates, they also wondered about the state's ability to support these efforts.[41]

Ever the diplomats, Tocqueville and Beaumont avoided taking a stand, preferring to offer descriptions of each system, along with lists of pros and cons. They praised education, but articulated its limits. They worried about the lash, but appreciated the order and discipline of prisons that used it. These paradoxes get to the heart of the Frenchmen's observations about the system: the prison represented a "complete despotism" in the country with the "most extended liberty." Becoming "wicked" by breaking the law, they observed, meant that citizens forfeited the blessings of freedom. A few years later, Tocqueville took this line of thought even further. "In America, [a criminal] is an enemy of the human race and every human being is against him." As historian Rebecca McLennan has argued, this sentiment might have been overstated in the mid-1830s, but would later prove "prophetic."[42]

According to the Frenchmen, the prisons organized by New York's and Pennsylvania's systems certainly towered above southern institutions. They expressed horror at the New Orleans prison where they "found men together with hogs, in the midst of all odors and nuisances." This treatment, they insisted, was better suited for "ferocious beasts" and "rendered [inmates] brutal." But they were generally unwilling to promote one system unequivocally. Pennsylvania cost too much, New York had too strong sanctions in some places and too gentle chaplains in others, and the whole institution was decidedly out-of-sync in a democracy. Readers took their words in a variety of ways. The book received several flattering reviews. In New York, Sing Sing's Agent Wiltse put it to particular use.[43]

Wiltse cited some of the Frenchmen's conclusions in his effort to persuade the New York legislature that the Auburn system—and his strict implementation of it—best served the purposes of the state. Some officials still resisted. One congressman, who had served as a state prison commissioner, rebuked Wiltse for his inattention during a recent cholera outbreak and the severity of inmate labor assignments. His report to the legislature alleged that Wiltse treated inmates as if they were animals. They were struck with "blows by walking staves" and "used like oxen" in the quarries. Confronted with the charge that he disrespected prisoners' humanity, Wiltse simply refused to answer. Instead, he set his sights on convincing the legislature of the less-than-human status of inmates and the danger of those citizens who sympathized with such creatures.[44]

To make his argument, Agent Wiltse borrowed liberally from sections of Tocqueville and Beaumont's book. He decried prison disciplines that made inmate reformation a priority. Instead, he proposed a system designed for degraded subjects requiring physical pain to bring them into submission. He argued against undue sympathy for the plight of prisoners. Without full public support for the prison staff's authority, strict discipline could never be realized. And Wiltse was clear about who posed the threat. Reformers and ministers, with their misguided sympathy for inmates, threatened to cause a public safety disaster.

Wiltse argued that prison ministers undermined the necessary authority structure in several ways. Indeed, these chaplains had "deceived themselves." They held deluded notions of the "supposed good qualities of convicted felons." They missed inmates' "hypocritical protestations," despite the obvious incentives to feign remorse. According to Wiltse, the ministers' "mistaken sympathy" had serious implications and even caused them to question the use of corporal punishments. Wiltse pointed to the chaplains at Auburn in New York and Wethersfield in Connecticut as particularly troubling cases. They leaked misleading stories to the public, and their claims about inmate reformation invited public compassion for lawbreakers. Chaplain Barrett had done similar things at Sing Sing, and Wiltse delineated the consequences of such interference. False stories to the public undermined officials' capacity to maintain order and control life inside the prison. In a direct quotation from the Frenchmen's report, Wiltse claimed that the power of the officers "must be re-produced every day." The chaplains' meddling impeded this process. "Prisoners will not submit if they have public sympathy," Wiltse reasoned, "and if the discipline falls there will be a fearful catastrophe."[45]

Confident that reformation was neither achievable nor recognizable if it miraculously occurred, Wiltse proposed a different approach to prison discipline. No longer should society depend on improving inmate character. Reformation through conversion could hardly be expected. Instead, Wiltse argued for a more "natural way." Society should ask only that inmates be restrained and that they learn acceptable behaviors. "Even supposing that religion has not touched his heart," Wiltse argued, "his mind has contracted habits of order." This order, enforced with the lash, depended on the strictest discipline. Suffering for wrongdoing was not heavenly work toward redemption. Rather, it constituted the state's only tool for producing discharged convicts with a "fear to transgress."[46]

Wiltse's position signaled an unprecedented level of physical and psychological violence against lawbreakers. Although colonial-era criminals experienced physical penalties and sometimes death, most offenders faced short, painful punishments and then went on their way. Some bore obvious marks of their criminal past. Offenders sometimes had cropped ears, a branding visible on the body, or wore a conspicuous letter denoting their crime. But most people's criminal pasts were not so obvious. Most lawbreakers paid fines or experienced the intense but brief shame of a public whipping or period in the stocks. Wiltse's new regime, however, implied that the country could not abide lawbreakers until they had been utterly destroyed. The beatings of colonial days would now be stretched out over years and combined with separation from society. Such measures were necessary, Wiltse argued, considering the criminal population. Prisoners were of the "most desperate kind." Moral suasion and good influences did nothing to change them. "They can feel nothing but that which comes home to their bodily suffering." Obstinacy and breaking of rules, therefore, were met by "inflicting stripes upon their naked back with the cat." Separate from society and forced into submission, prisoners could reclaim their humanity only by surrendering their will. Only those chaplains willing to underwrite this discipline—with its dehumanization of lawbreakers and withdrawal of sympathy—were welcome at Sing Sing.[47]

Despite his railing against chaplains and arguments that physical pain was the only language inmates understood, Wiltse still hired ministers to serve at Sing Sing. He sought ministers to sanction the bodily afflictions that inmates suffered. Under Wiltse's direction, Sing Sing came under even greater scrutiny. The debate surrounding the new agent's discipline ranged broadly, from the statehouse to Boston pulpits, from local seminaries to the French government. The question of the prisoner's humanity and the purpose of physical afflictions stood at the center of these conversations. Increasingly, interested parties debated the role Protestant ministers and reformers should play in the prison system. State legislators fired the first volley in this skirmish by directing the search for a new chaplain rather than allowing Dwight and the PDSB to fill the post. Officials encouraged inspectors to find a minister amenable to the agent's approach. The Reverend Jonathan Dickerson fit the bill. The Presbyterian minister from New York City brought a theological emphasis different from his predecessor's, despite their outward similarities. Dickerson had no contact with revival-minded Calvinists. His thought showed significant influence from his teachers at Princeton Theological Seminary, namely Charles Hodge. In his classes and writings, Hodge campaigned against New Light, or revival-minded, Presbyterianism. Unlike the moderates at Andover, Hodge and other Princeton Presbyterians defended the firm lines of the Westminster Confession—total depravity, unconditional election, and limited atonement. Dickerson apparently drank deep at Princeton. He arrived at Sing Sing skeptical of newer evangelistic techniques such as revivals, voluntary societies, and educational reforms. All people deserved judgment, and only a few were blessed by God's election and grace.[48]

Chaplain Dickerson's particular form of Calvinism fit Wiltse's skepticism about inmates' potential for reformation. The minister assumed that criminals probably did not stand among the elect. Their lives evidenced their alienation. While he acknowledged that anything was possible with God, his work at Sing Sing reflected his opinion that redemption among such characters was unlikely. Dickerson performed his ministerial duties but with little hope of seeing the fruits of his labors. Indeed, he wrote of the difficulties posed by working with prisoners who proved such "great moral waste." He argued that many good people tried to use "moral means" to assist prisoners but that he remained "conscious that results must remain in a great measure bound up in secrecy until the revelation of the last day." In light of this tough crowd of prisoners who had little chance at redemption, Dickerson emphasized the necessity of admitting guilt. He wrote that Sing Sing's discipline worked so that inmates had a "deep and pungent sense of crime, as committed against God." Thus, he happily reported, inmates were submissive. They acknowledged "the justice of their sentences." They did not desire "deliverance or pardon." He cautioned against any hope that God or society might offer a reprieve. His theology found a fitting environment in Wiltse's approach to inmates.[49]

Indeed, the Reverend Dickerson began to see Wiltse's "humane, though firm and rigid discipline" as the "handmaid and assistant" to the gospel he preached. The discipline put inmates into a space in which they could be best acted upon. Such measures became necessary in order to reach prisoners with the message that God allowed affliction but was merciful because He might offer grace to a select few. The chaplain reported that by his moral instruction, Wiltse's "discipline is aided, strengthened, and sanctified." With the coequal efforts of Wiltse's order and the deliverance of the gospel, "the whole machinery will co-operate" with "amazing effects" on the inmates, Dickerson wrote. The partnership between state officials and clergymen had not ended but rather had taken on a new form.[50]

The Fate of the Auburn System

With no access to Sing Sing and a political and cultural climate that favored Agent Wiltse, Louis Dwight and his Boston reformers could do little to change the situation. But rather than reconsider the wisdom of the Auburn system or the penitentiary altogether, Dwight interpreted the Sing Sing debacle as one unfortunate episode within a generally sound system. He put all his hopes in Auburn Prison and other institutions where the trademark discipline was comparatively milder. He waged a public relations campaign to hold up Auburn's version of the New York system as superior to Sing Sing's strict interpretation. He pointed, especially, to the contribution of Auburn's chaplain as a sign of success upstate and insisted that Protestant chaplains played a vital role in maintaining the worthy program of redemptive suffering in American prisons.

According to Dwight, the Auburn system still flourished during the early 1830s, most notably at Auburn itself. He pointed to the chaplain he sponsored there, the Reverend Benjamin C. Smith, as proof. Born in Vermont, Smith attended Auburn Theological Seminary down the street from the prison and graduated in 1828. He served as Auburn's chaplain for the next twelve years. During his career at Auburn, Smith welcomed the opportunity to play a major role in Auburn's discipline. He not only saw himself as an integral part of the discipline but also recognized the prison staff and its disciplinary techniques as necessary for an inmate's conversion.[51]

According to reports he sent Dwight, Chaplain Smith established a routine of preaching, visits, and classes during his days at Auburn. While at seminary, he had served as a prison Sabbath school instructor. Now as the full-time chaplain, he organized the curriculum and the twenty or so students who came over from the seminary every Sunday. Smith preached in chapel, offered prayers throughout the week, and spent much of his time visiting and interviewing inmates. He assisted the agents in compiling data for biographical sketches of inmates about to be discharged. He presented these reports to the inspectors' board as proof of inmates' reformation. Especially under Agent Powers and later under his successors, Auburn maintained a reputation for order with infrequent resort to the lash. With the prison under Smith's watchful eye, Dwight believed that prisoners were treated humanely and the furnace of affliction was appropriately managed.

According to Dwight, Chaplain Smith was necessary to achieving Auburn's balance between justice and mercy. Prison officials directed the treatment and routines of the prisoners' bodies, and Smith made sure no inordinate suffering occurred. At the same time, he took charge of inmates' minds and souls. Both sides appreciated the partnership. In 1832 Auburn's inspectors acknowledged the "vigilance, skill, and energy, of all the officers of the institution . . . without which, the chaplain is as fully aware as we are, his utmost efforts would be unavailing." Smith, too, recognized that his successes were not his own. He reminded prison inspectors that "your system of physical coercion and discipline, merely, without its accompaniment of moral motives would only make bad men worse." On the other hand, he wrote. "Without such a system of strict seclusion and non-intercourse, religious motives would have no power to make bad men better." Smith needed the staff to restrain prisoners before he offered a message of spiritual transformation. Or, as he wrote of the prison staff's powers and the chaplain's mission later, "In the combination of both, lies the secret of their power."[52]

The PDSB approved of Smith's partnership with prison staff and praised Auburn Prison. When problems popped up, the staff, inspectors, and the legislature seemed to solve them quickly. For instance, in 1832 the number of inmates outnumbered the solitary cells. In response, the legislature authorized construction to accommodate the overflow. Concern for female inmates milling about in common rooms prompted the hiring of a prison matron. Chaplain Smith confirmed the wisdom of the system and its administration in his 1835 report on the prison's effects: of 449 inmates discharged from Auburn, 368 had shown some kind of improvement, with 229 of those "decidedly reformed." The prison turned a profit, and thousands of people visited it each year. Chaplain Smith reported to the PDSB that prisoners expressed gratitude for their arrests and confinement. He broadcast his successes in a wide variety of Protestant periodicals, ranging from the Baptist's *Christian Secretary* to the Unitarian's *Christian Register*.[53]

But Auburn Prison soon saw a major turn of events that jeopardized the relationship between the PDSB and prison officials. The institution began to struggle financially. Nervous prison inspectors worried that the state would close it if the deficits continued. To solve their problem, the inspectors fired Auburn's agent and asked Elam Lynds to come out of retirement. When the news reached Boston, Louis Dwight reacted. He had disapproved of Lynds's tactics at Auburn more than ten years earlier and even more so his practices at Sing Sing. Now Lynds was back and threatened the reputation of the PDSB's most treasured institution.

The PDSB report for the year following Lynds's return reveals Dwight's sense that Auburn had changed dramatically. The PDSB no longer paid Chaplain Smith's salary, most likely because Lynds did not allow it. Referring to Lynds's 1838 report to the state legislature, Dwight wrote that it was "the most unfavorable received in years." The reasons were clear. According to the Boston reformer, Auburn's environment made reformation impossible. Lynds used excessive force in order to achieve prison order. Dwight featured a PDSB-sponsored report by Charles Robbins, the former head of South Boston's House of Correction, who had visited New York's prisons since Lynds's return. Robbins saw both the cat-o-nine-tails and cowhide strips used to beat inmates in Auburn's workshops. Of both Auburn and Sing Sing, Robbins wrote, "I think there cannot be much reformation where there is much flogging done."[54]

As Dwight sounded the alarm, he ran into one problem. His man in charge of ensuring right treatment at Auburn, Chaplain Smith, praised the new agent. Smith never complained about Lynds and his tactics, no matter how violent. Smith's reports barely registered the change in command, except to dispel rumors. He noted the protests made by Auburn villagers but defended Lynds, mentioning that he had provided for religious education. Even though Lynds had stopped the Sabbath school, Smith assured legislators it was not out of hostility. He failed, however, to provide a reason in its place. Smith also defended Lynds's use of corporal punishment. He noted that there had been "agitations" that disturbed the "usual order and quietness of the prison." But Smith concluded that "it would be most unfortunate" if the public held to a "permanent repugnance to the use of such coercive means as are necessary to enforce obedience." For Smith, the issue was gaining the inmates' attention. "The motives of the gospel are efficient in proportion to the degree of the attention which they gain," Smith argued. Therefore, a prison run with the strictest regulations, even with coercion, offered the best chance. The prison was the ultimate mission field for Smith. The captive and restrained audience was the most receptive audience.[55]

Dwight assumed that an agent-chaplain partnership monitored by benevolent Protestant reformers practically guaranteed a prison's smooth and humane operation. He failed to foresee that the partnership itself, designed to guide and limit the use of corporal punishment, might take a different course. From an office far away in Boston, Dwight could not insist on his own interpretation of redemptive suffering. Clearly, he had to reconsider his consistent praise for both the Auburn system and Chaplain Smith. Dwight soon learned that inmates did not necessarily view their prison minister as highly as he once had.

A Peep into the State Prison at Auburn contains one inmate's catalog of the punishments received within New York's "terrible place of torture." Published in 1839, the narrative counters Dwight's assumptions about redemptive suffering in Auburn's furnace of affliction. To the Boston minister's surprise, the writer attests to tortuous practices that predated Lynds's return. He details inmates flogged for not working fast enough in the shops. He recalls an inmate receiving thirty-two stripes who died a few days later. "Was not this man murdered?" the author asks. The ex-prisoner also describes floggings of the mentally ill and of female offenders. The beatings caused consumption in many inmates and led others to attempt suicide. The narrative abounds with comparisons intended to shock readers with awful images of the prison's dismal reality. It is "but a Managerie [*sic*] for human tame beasts," with staff as cruel as the "negro drivers of the South," the convict writes. All in all, he claims it would be better for the courts to hand down death sentences than terms of confinement at Auburn.[56]

The author pointedly claims that extreme physical punishments undermined the prison's ostensible purpose to reform inmates. The effects of such physical treatment crushed efforts to reform. True reformation, the author argued, was impossible in such conditions and could only be faked in an effort to receive special privileges. He bemoaned the way some prisoners had tried to reform and met violence at every turn. Of one such inmate, he wrote that the "keepers had fairly flogged such notions out of his head." Of another, his profession of Christianity faltered when he realized that "hypocrisy was the governing virtue" among keepers who held "an instrument of torture in one hand and a Bible in the other."[57]

If the warden and keepers received the author's disdain, it was Chaplain Smith who received his most bitter criticism. According to his volume, the minister visited infrequently and met only those inmates who professed reform. But it was the chaplain's treatment of the sick, dying, and dead that provoked the writer's fiercest ire. The ex-inmate claimed that the minister sometimes neglected the prison hospital for five or six weeks at a time. He denied a dying prisoner of the Roman Catholic faith visitation by a priest. He often failed to contact next of kin when inmates approached death. As a result, many prisoners' bodies went unclaimed. To the author's horror, prison staff folded up corpses and stuffed them into whiskey barrels or old wooden boxes. These deceased inmates received no Christian burial. Some were even given over for dissection to local doctors.[58]

In words that echoed the sentiments of reformers such as Eddy and Dwight, the author proclaimed, "It is too abominable to think, in a Christian country, that for committing a small offense . . . [prisoners] should be flogged to death, and their bodies given over to dissection." His reference to small offenses was no understatement. Two counts of petty larceny earned citizens a stint at Auburn. The writer noted a fellow inmate whose first offense was pilfering three oysters. His second involved stealing underwear. This petty thief was sent to Auburn for two years. According to the writer, the offenses could be small but the stakes quite high. Auburn's discipline involved inordinate pain and suffering rather than any hope at redemption. Even the chaplain failed the prisoners by underwriting a system that prized their bodily suffering and offered nothing in its aftermath. While these buildings were envisioned as reformatories, the ex-convict wrote, inmates left them as "poor emaciated skeletons of their former selves."[59]

The Auburn inmate's narrative mirrors ex-convicts' accounts from Sing Sing in its descriptions of physical violence against inmates. Every ex-convict writer in this period deplored agents' approach to prison discipline and decried regimes in which reformation had no place. The narratives differ significantly, however, on the question of redemptive suffering. The Sing Sing accounts, particularly Lane's and Brice's, articulate classic patterns of affliction leading to reformation. The inmate relating his Auburn experience, however, found his physical suffering meaningless and indefensible. His narrative, unlike the Sing Sing accounts, includes episodes in which the chaplain contributes to an environment of unpardonable suffering. Burr, Lane, and Brice served time during Barrett's and Dickerson's tenure. Even if Dickerson offered tacit approval of the Wiltse regime, inmates would have known about Barrett's protest against severe discipline and Dickerson's effort to aid stricken inmates during a cholera outbreak. The Auburn inmate, however, connected Chaplain Smith with a regime involving harsh treatment of inmate bodies, both living and dead. The cooperation of a religious specialist in the harsh workings of the Auburn regime proved too much for him. His book connects religion to a prison regime designed only for order and financial security, with no possibility for fostering spiritual reformation. For this inmate, the chaplain's acts amounted to betrayal.[60]

Reformers and inmates alike decried the physical abuses common at both Auburn and Sing Sing in the 1830s. To Dwight's dismay, the partnership between agents and clergymen had fallen apart. He no longer chose and financed the chaplains. They did not keep a watchful eye on his behalf. Before the state legislature, agents declared that inmates were animals deserving no sympathy and only physical pain. The work of good ministers was derided and even identified as a danger to society. According to prisoner narratives, the chaplain Dwight once trusted had forsaken the cause. Rather than overseeing a process of redemptive suffering, he worked in tandem with an agent who terrorized.

Prison Reform

By the decade's end, Dwight concluded that the disciplines at Auburn and Sing Sing involved "improper treatment" and "barbarous punishments." Developments within the institutions, new agents' philosophies, and a changing cultural climate allowed for wide acceptance of excessive lashings and the deterioration of prison conditions. Despite Dwight's efforts, the notion of a lawbreaker's common humanity and the prison as a site of redemptive suffering came under fire. Indeed, by the late 1830s it was hard to say what role reformers and ministers could play inside New York prisons unless they supported harsh discipline. Order and profit prevailed. Reformation faded as a primary institutional aim.[61]

Even when reform impulses surfaced, effective change came from the state house rather than Protestant reformers' pulpits or pens. On 16 April 1839, New York governor William Seward delivered a blistering report to the state senate. A committed Whig, Seward had sympathies with reform-minded ministers. His message to the legislature included a long list of abuses at the state prisons, particularly Sing Sing. The inspectors neglected their duties and "surrendered control to [Wiltse]." The keepers had "unlimited power" to punish inmates. They neither kept track of the number of lashes they issued nor reported the punishments they meted out to their superiors. Mentally ill convicts received brutal lashings despite their conditions, including one "maniac" who was given one thousand stripes in just three weeks time. Inmates committed suicide because of cruelty. Keepers whipped some female inmates until they bled. Inmates were starved, and guards used illegal weapons ón their bodies. The report noted that prison keepers said harsh punishments were "indispensable" to the prison's order. Seward disagreed. Considering the discipline there, he concluded, Sing Sing Prison is "governed by the arbitrary will of one individual . . . [and] a discipline prevails there which is arbitrary, capricious, and unequal, and often as contrary to law as it is revolting to humanity."[62]

Louis Dwight concurred. He included Seward's address to the senate in his 1839 PDSB report and anticipated the response of the governor's critics. Dwight noted that many would say Seward's letter was purely political, an attack on Wiltse and Lynds for their Democratic connections. But Dwight, too, visited Sing Sing during the uproar. In a report on his visit, he attested to the abuses chronicled by Seward. He was convinced that "brutal punishments, poor fare, and neglect of the sick" constituted the prison's discipline. He congratulated the governor's efforts to expose these evils.[63]

Auburn, too, came under fire in Dwight's 1839 report. The prison ran its first deficit in several years, a sure sign of mismanagement, he thought. Other serious concerns surfaced as well. Against the wishes of Chaplain Smith, Lynds canceled the Sabbath school. He gave the excuse that worship services and the classes afterward required more keepers on duty. He could not see why the state should shoulder the extra expense. Beyond these concerns for Auburn's educational and religious program, Dwight criticized Lynds's administration of daily prison routines. The agent believed that "the lash is the chief good of prison discipline." This was dangerous, Dwight wrote, because "out of this principle has risen alarming cruelty in punishment in the Prison at Auburn and Sing Sing." Both government officials and citizens would be "shocked by the disclosure of the abuses."[64]

Dwight could do little to change matters, but Governor Seward could. By the end of 1839, he had Lynds and Wiltse fired. The legislature named new inspectors, who, in turn, named new agents. During the transition, two new chaplains arrived as well. The Reverend Thomas Townsend, a graduate of Auburn Theological Seminary and a Presbyterian minister, took the post at Auburn. At Sing Sing, a Methodist elder named John Luckey began his work. Both men enjoyed new freedoms under regimes marked by milder punishments. As the crisis ended and new staff ascended, Dwight took stock of what had happened. How had he missed the abuses? How had government officials recognized an agent's rampant cruelty before his own prison society did? Had his early trust of Auburn's first agent blinded him to the prison's risks? Dwight entered the 1840s with profound hesitation. The partnership he initiated in the 1820s had failed. He now wondered what role chaplains played in prisons increasingly focused on inmate suffering as an end in itself.

Of course, the earliest American prison experiments had relied on a theological articulation of the lawbreaker's sin and need of redemption. For the Quakers who created Newgate, crime signaled the human failure to realize the Inner Light. Prison made the way, through decent environment and ordered routine, for redeemed living. While they did not call it suffering, it was at the very least a difficult process of refining. The process burned away the old habits and formed new ones. As with the most dramatic transformations, it was bound to hurt. Thomas Eddy's inability to recognize the pain in even his "mild" system proved to be his downfall. Revival-minded ministers from the Calvinist traditions filled the role of religious expert once the Quakers were removed. They, too, envisioned the prison as a place where inmates realized their guilt through suffering but found a path through it to redemption. Stanford, Dwight, and Barrett subscribed to this theory. In both of these visions, suffering played a role as a fitting part or natural consequence of the prison situation that served a greater end. Inmates' affliction remained incomplete without proper redirection toward a spiritual good.

In his 1834 testimony, Agent Wiltse had offered a new theological articulation of prison suffering. To be sure, he emphasized the need for a more "natural way" to understand the prisoner's experience. He dismissed supernatural conversion as something society could expect, let alone measure. Indeed, Wiltse insisted that the agent and his lash occupy the primary place in the inmate's mind. Submission to the agent's rule was vital. Returning to society subdued and fearful to transgress society's laws was paramount.

While Wiltse argued that his approach was natural as opposed to super-natural, he continued to engage the chaplains as religious resources. Indeed, Wiltse wanted to get rid of the supernatural only insofar as chaplains claimed the possibility of inmate reform through God's grace. While the agent claimed that inmates understood nothing but bodily pain, he sought out chaplains willing to fill inmates' ears with refrains about sin and guilt, God's anger and judgment. Wiltse did not cut out religion, but he appropriated it for his own purposes. Suffering became a means to a different end, and he wanted chaplains with theologies heavy on judgment and light on mercy. Some ministers complied, offering inmates bleak messages.

According to at least some ex-prisoners, chaplains participating in these regimes were a mockery. While Barrett had found hope in Psalm 88, the psalmist's claims sounded different after his departure. "Shall thy lovingkindness be declared in the grave or faithfulness in destruction?" the psalmist asks. "Yes," Barrett would answer. But now, the psalm's irony was apparent. What would love matter to one in the grave? What is faithfulness to a person utterly destroyed? The violence overwhelmed. Protestant reformers and ministers who promoted this theology and allowed it to underwrite prisoner abuse garnered inmates' contempt. A woodcut in one prisoner narrative suggests the negative power of the association. Featuring a keeper lashing an inmate, the caption reads, "Christian Reformation!!"

After the seeming successes of the 1820s, events at both Auburn and Sing Sing in the 1830s had a devastating effect on Louis Dwight and his PDSB. New Yorkers, it seemed, valued order and profit, not reformation. With their entire purpose questioned, it was unclear what Protestant reformers and ministers such as Dwight had to offer New York State prison officials. Theirs was an old-fashioned piety. It preached human connection. It ascribed sin and guilt to all. It insisted on an older pattern of long, quiet suffering before a moment of realization and acceptance of grace that transformed one's life. They could not compete with a society fixated on the fear of crime, committed to individual responsibility, and consumed with questions of pain, innocence, and guilt. No one wanted the furnace of affliction they advocated. Elam Lynds had called for a prison that was a hell on earth. Its flames produced submissive inmates who followed laws out of a fear to transgress. It paved the way for a religiosity of citizenship that reformers eventually embraced.[65]

Slowly, Protestant reformers adapted their public ministries to this new reality. Some dedicated themselves to persuading young people to stay out of this earthly hell. Gerrish Barrett's career is a good example. In 1829 Elam

FRONTISPIECE.

CHRISTIAN REFORMATION!!

Woodcut illustration from *A Peep into the State Prison at Auburn, N.Y.* (Collection of The New-York Historical Society. Negative #81590d)

Lynds had assaulted and thrown out the young minister. Afterward, he served as chaplain at the Connecticut State Prison at Wethersfield for nine years. He also periodically served Dwight and the PDSB as a traveling investigator of the nation's prisons. While he always bemoaned negative findings in the prisons, he spent a great deal of energy cultivating a ministry to young children he hoped to keep away from the prison. In 1839 the American Sunday-School Union published Barrett's tract, *The Boy in Prison*. He related to his readers the story of a good young man who had taken the dangerous path to greater and greater sin. First, he stole. Later, he lied. Finally, he took to a life of theft with a gang of thieves. He eventually found himself in the horrors of Wethersfield prison. Barrett wrote of the shackles on the boy's feet, his long days of labor, and the course food that was too awful to eat. But worse, Barrett wrote, was the solitude. The boy sat alone for hours on end, often lying awake at night to consider the "condition" to which his sins had brought him. Barrett attested that the young man asked him to write the pamphlet as a warning for Sunday school students. They needed to know, he said, "how bad it is to sin."[66]

Barrett's piece echoed classic tropes in Protestant tract literature. Avoid wrongdoing, it cried out. Beware the wages of sin. But a comparison with John Stanford's earlier tracts reveals a change in the Protestant prison reformers' approach. Stanford, who had written prison tracts in the 1810s and 1820s, admitted that prison was awful. But Stanford worked from the perspective that some people were going to end up in prison and that it was his job to help them make the most of it. He would guide them through the furnace of affliction. Barrett took a different tact. He warned people to avoid the things that would result in incarceration. Prison was awful. It destroyed. It sunk one deeper in corruption. It was hell on earth with no redeeming value.

As Lynds and Wiltse's strict prison discipline became the norm in New York prisons, reformers were presented with two options: make adaptations that allowed them access to the prisons or resist the recent changes and protest prison conditions from the outside. Those who stayed within found themselves in a growing conversation about religion that focused on values of American citizenship. Their particular Protestant practices were up for grabs. They, too, were being remade in the furnace of affliction.

5

The Furnace Transformed, 1840–1847

In 1843 Sing Sing's resident chaplain went to the head prison inspector to plead the case of a suicidal inmate. The inspector, a New York judge named John Edmonds, usually supported Sing Sing's notoriously severe regime. He led an inspectors' board aligned with Albany Democrats, who traditionally favored tough prison discipline focused on order and profit. According to the chaplain's memoir, the inmate in question deliberately provoked keepers, hoping to incite a fatal beating. He sought immediate death over the "slow death by the cat[-o'-nine-tails]" he would endure if he served out his sentence. To the chaplain's surprise, Inspector Edmonds appeared moved by the story. Edmonds visited the inmate and stopped the keepers from lashing him. The prisoner apparently responded, becoming a diligent laborer in the workshop. In light of this change, Edmonds questioned the prison's harsh discipline. He pressed Agent Lynds to modify his regime. When the agent refused, Edmonds called for his removal. In 1844, New York officials relieved Lynds of duty for the last time.[1]

The chaplain's successful alignment with the inspector might have signaled Protestant reformers' advance in the antebellum public sphere. By persuading Edmonds, the minister helped unseat Lynds, one of the most entrenched figures in state corrections. The victory, however, was short-lived. In fact, John Luckey's enlistment of Edmonds led to a new series of conflicts over religion's place in the prisons. It prompted Edmonds to found a new voluntary society dedicated to prison reform. To be sure, his organization, the New York Prison Association (NYPA), shared goals with Protestant reformers who had worked in the prisons for decades. The NYPA advocated a less severe prison discipline. It boasted the importance of inmate reformation and the vital role religion played in securing it. The difference, however, lay in its focus on religion primarily as a vehicle for promoting citizenship. NYPA leaders sought spiritual transformation for the primary purpose of securing civil society.[2]

The difference between the NYPA leaders and more traditional Protestant reformers became clear a few years later when Inspector Edmonds helped orchestrate Chaplain Luckey's dismissal from Sing Sing. The inspector parted ways with Luckey in a dispute over disciplinary methods in the prison's female department. A new matron instituted practices, including lectures on phrenology, that Luckey found antithetical to Christian reformation. When the argument reached the editorial pages of New York newspapers, Edmonds had Luckey fired.

The chaplain's removal, along with events at Auburn Prison, signaled a transition for Protestant reformers working to shape New York prison discipline. For years, they understood their opponents to be state officials aligned with the emerging Democratic Party, a group known for laissez-faire principles, tough prison policies, and suspicions of religious reformers seeking to influence public life. Reform impulses in the 1840s, however, transformed the landscape of prison activism. The Protestant reformers still faced opposition from notorious agents and their political allies. But they also found themselves at odds with a new set of prison reformers— other citizens focused on inmate reformation and committed to religion's important role in that transformation. Though they sometimes worked together, differences emerged in their sense of religion's primary purpose, the way religion prompted reform, and ultimately religion's capacity to explain and confront human misbehavior. As the NYPA rose to prominence, the Protestant reformers' vision of the furnace of affliction was slowly transformed. A religiosity of citizenship replaced the older pattern of suffering and redemption.

The Spirit of Reform

Chaplain Luckey's eventual dismissal seemed unlikely in the early 1840s, a moment in which state officials and prison reformers ushered in a new focus on humane treatment and inmate reformation. With that burst of reform, Louis Dwight and other Protestant ministers once again affirmed the course prisons were taking. The early part of the decade especially witnessed deft responses to several crises. As immigration surged, a burst of city agencies and private voluntary societies responded. As financial crisis threatened the state, municipalities increased aid. As crime rates rose, cities reconfigured policing and built new disciplinary institutions. Important for advocates such as Louis Dwight, elections swept in politicians who shared the ministers' affinity for institutional approaches to social disorder. Reform was in the air.

As noted earlier, the Whig governor William Seward began steps toward prison reform when he entered office in 1838. He had fired Sing Sing's Agent Wiltse and radically altered the prison's disciplinary regime. The new agent placed strict limitations on the use of the lash. He required keepers to report punishments to their superiors and mandated supervision for any lashings administered. He also reinstated the Sabbath school and allocated funds to start a prison library. He visited inmates on Sunday afternoons, stopping by cells for conversation and delivering books. By early 1842, the new agent allowed prisoners to receive and write letters and have visits from relatives. He supported a temperance crusader's visit. Mentally ill prisoners received better treatment. Inmates could also request pardon, something former agents had prohibited.[3]

The new agent also expanded the chaplain's role. He repealed rules that limited conversations between ministers and inmates to dogmatic issues. He encouraged chaplains to consider the positive influence of inmates' family and social networks and the possible negative effects of city life. Under his leadership, chaplains urged relatives and friends to write to inmates and promise them support upon release. The agent, with the chaplain's support, proposed a state farm for inmates and a benevolent society specifically charged with supervising the "morals and employment" of released convicts. Because no such structures were yet in place, the agent also encouraged chaplains to accompany discharged prisoners to the city. He asked ministers to help inmates find boardinghouses and jobs as a defense against the "attacks of their former associates."[4]

Historians have attributed the Seward administration's changes to a burst of humanitarianism. Indeed, leaders such as Seward believed in a "higher law" that required the humane treatment of all people, including immigrants, the enslaved, the mentally ill, and the imprisoned. As energies surged behind antislavery and antigallows campaigns, politicians such as Seward had some popular support for progressive causes. Nevertheless,

Seward and other recently elected Whig leaders' commitment to issues such as prison reform did not necessarily imply popular approval for all of their professed causes. In the midst of continued financial stresses that prompted Whig electoral victories across the country, Seward eked out a reelection victory in the 1840 governor's race. He continued his battle against the laissez-faire policies of Democratic leaders and supported the increasingly popular Whig notion that the state should take a firm hand in containing social disorder.[5]

For Seward, New York City provided clear evidence of the nation's instability and the need for government to take control. The financial crisis that swept Seward and other Whigs into office had a profound effect on urban life. Demand for poor relief overwhelmed both private philanthropic organizations and municipal efforts. Unemployment stirred up nativist leanings. Ethnically based street gangs spread beyond their former territories of Five Points and the Bowery. And while the first years of the depression had some effect in quelling immigration, by the early 1840s the numbers picked up again. Up to forty passenger ships—each carrying a thousand immigrant Irish, German, and English—made port in Manhattan every day.[6]

With the tough economy and a surfeit of needy citizens without access to relief, crime rates went up. New York City's Common Council noted the increase in complaints for robbery and mugging. Property crimes continued to make up the vast majority of criminal cases, with larceny, robbery, and forgery accounting for more than 85 percent of sentences. Concerned about urban unrest and potential prison overcrowding, municipal authorities overhauled city policing, and the state senate began plans for a new correctional facility far upstate in Clinton County.[7]

In the midst of such unrest, Protestant reformers such as Dwight found common cause with Whigs and their approach to social problems. They made headway with state officials in the early 1840s because their prescriptions for lawbreakers cohered with Whig sensibilities about ordering and disciplining the country's unruly citizens. In particular, they shared a commitment to humane institutions and the important work of prison chaplains.

With the Seward administration's backing, the Reverend John Luckey arrived at Sing Sing in May 1839. He could not have appeared at a more dramatic moment. The governor's investigation was underway. Agent Wiltse was in the last few months of his tenure. While he served under Wiltse for only a few months, Luckey's ministry was dominated by the effect of the Wiltse regime on Sing Sing's inmates. The minister's memoir includes many stories of prisoners permanently altered by corporal punishment. One episode included an Irish prisoner whom Luckey found a "used up man" after being "absolutely brutalized" by nearly weekly floggings during his term. By the time the inmate was pardoned in 1840, after serving twenty years, he had forgotten how to use a knife and fork. He had not walked normally for so long and was so fearful of breaking prison routine that he could not stop himself from lockstepping down New York City sidewalks. Luckey and the ex-convict's lawyer looked on with wonder at the spectacle. The lawyer turned to the chaplain and remarked that the poor man "had his brains knocked out at the prison."[8]

While Luckey witnessed several sad cases, he relished the opportunity to be part of Sing Sing's fresh start under a new agent. He appreciated the agent's commitment to Sabbath school and the prison library. He flourished under the expanded spectrum of ministerial possibilities, including visiting inmate families, bringing in temperance speakers, and assisting inmates in their transition into life after prison. But most of all, he relished the "mildness" of the new discipline. Keepers used the lash infrequently. Mentally ill convicts received gentler treatment. With such broad latitude to address prisoners' needs and a milder disciplinary climate, Luckey felt that reformation was more likely.[9]

Some historians attribute Luckey's preference for a milder prison discipline to his Methodist sensibilities. They contrast his Methodist theology, both evangelical and Arminian, with strict Calvinist traditions. But on close inspection, Luckey advocated a spiritual journey for inmates similar to predecessors such as Stanford, Curtis, and Barrett. Luckey did not advocate emotion-laden, revivalist Christianity. He never attempted to turn Sing Sing into a tent meeting. Instead, he preached a message of suffering, conversion, and regeneration in a subdued and organized prison environment. He offered a vision of Methodist Christianity common in New York in this period, one that emphasized industriousness, morality, and self-discipline. Methodists such as Luckey had some differences from their Calvinist counterparts. He certainly posited humans' free will. But as historian Daniel Walker Howe has pointed out, both Calvinists and Arminians in this period "taught that God extended grace to human beings, which they were morally responsible for accepting." The differences, Walker observes, were more noticeable in terms of doctrine rather than daily practice. Luckey, like his Calvinist colleagues, preached a story of judgment and mercy they hoped would inspire change in inmates' lives.[10]

While Luckey's theological understanding of prisoners' situations co-hered with his predecessors, he drew on Methodist practices—particu-larly the class meeting—to shape his day-to-day ministry. From the time of John Wesley, Methodists in Britain and later in America gathered in small groups to "help each other work out their salvation." Classes met to pray and discuss spiritual progress. Class leaders visited members, offered words of advice, performed administrative tasks, and brought the disor-derly into line. These steps were necessary as Methodists affirmed original sin in every person and the continuance of some sin even after justification by faith. The person trying to be faithful prayed for the grace to perform good works, which Methodists believed were the "evidence [of one's] desire of salvation." Over the course of the nineteenth century, Methodists contin-ued to affirm a path that involved sin and suffering, repentance and grace. This path resulted—they hoped—in a new and sanctified life through the Holy Spirit's power.[11]

Although historians have found that Methodists moved away from class meetings and toward camp meetings in the early nineteenth century, Luckey's ministry more closely resembled the former. He visited prisoners regularly. He listened to them in order to "advise, reprove, comfort, or ex-hort," where necessary. He rebuked them for their disorderly pasts. Finally, Luckey tried to convince them of their need for prayer. From Methodist societies, Luckey had a set plan for dealing with those unrepentant in their sin. He asked prisoners to acknowledge their fault and undergo "proper humiliation." Clear evidence of suffering and repentance was crucial. Methodists expelled the intransigent who showed "no sign of real humilia-tion." For Luckey and other Methodists, every person was a sinner in need of grace. Criminals resisted the laws of God and country. Therefore, they needed to acknowledge their crimes, feel the shame of their deeds, and be brought back into fellowship with others hoping to walk the straight and narrow path.[12]

Luckey's ministry mirrored class meetings in his invitation to disciplined living. As historian John Wigger has observed, Methodist "spiritual" ide-als overlapped with "American values of hard work and worldly success." Rapid Methodist expansion relied on this optimistic message that ordinary people could improve themselves. Luckey translated this message into a particular form at Sing Sing, concentrating less on worldly success than on his ongoing hope that inmates would renounce vice and embrace godly living.[13]

Luckey revealed his understanding of this traditional path to salvation through his Sunday morning chapel presentations. He read letters from discharged convicts to the prisoners gathered for worship. The letters, some of which Luckey published in his memoir, reveal his theology of imprisonment. First, Luckey assured inmates that their affliction in prison worked for good. In one letter, a discharged convict confirmed that time in Sing Sing "was one of the best things that ever happened to me." Another reported how glad he was to be "arrested in my wild course." Second, Luckey used the letters to remind inmates that Jesus saved. Discharged convicts reported that they read the Bible, learned new professions, and received the mercies of God after their release. But all these things paled compared to the hope of heaven, as one inmate letter put it, "through the merits of a crucified Saviour." Finally, Luckey read letters that illustrated the possibility of reformed living. Several contained prayers that inmates who were listening to the message would benefit from their affliction. Luckey read one letter in which a reformed convict wrote of his long prayers "that my fellow prisoners might come to serve the Lord also." Through the letters, Luckey urged inmates to use the afflictions of prison to experience God's mercy and prompt moral reformation.[14]

Protestant periodicals boasted of Luckey's successes under the milder prison discipline. In 1840 *New York Evangelist* attested to significant tract distribution and inmate conversion at Sing Sing. *Boston Recorder* praised Luckey's "faithfulness and unwearied exertions." Another *New York Evangelist* article detailed Luckey's Sunday schedule, recounting his sermon on the prodigal son, prayers with sick inmates, and afternoon visits to individual cells. The writer detailed several inmate stories, including testimonies of their thankfulness at having been brought to prison and their gratitude for coming there to learn the word of God.[15]

As Luckey flourished under the new agent's administration, Louis Dwight, too, was basically pleased with Governor Seward's reforms. His 1841 PDSB report extolled religious instruction at both Auburn and Sing Sing, citing the "good conduct" after discharge of inmates from the former and the "one-hundred fifty convicts . . . brought to experience the beneficial effects of gospel truth" at the latter. While worship services and Sabbath school were central for Dwight, so too was the change in punishments for disobedience. The minister quoted both institutions' inspectors to document the positive changes. Of Auburn, Dwight reported that, "we do not have the remotest apprehension of any unnecessary severities being either practiced or allowed." As a result, inspectors witnessed an "unusual degree of harmony and good feeling existing among the officers and guards."

Sing Sing also warranted a positive report. Quoting the inspectors, Dwight noted that "the extreme severity of punishment is essentially done away with" and this "salutary change" worked for the "benefit of the convicts in every respect."[16]

Beyond his praise for Seward's reforms, Dwight offered a meditation on the dark days that preceded them. Considering inmate experiences in the 1830s, Dwight admitted that something had gone terribly wrong. Cruelty had won out over corporal punishment's moderate use. Retribution for law-breaking superseded the impulse for inmate reformation. Considering the past decade, Dwight devoted a large portion of his report to one question: Did the Auburn system depend on stripes? Could he continue to argue for the humane use of the lash given recent events at Sing Sing and Auburn? Tyrannical agents, he admitted, set the "hearts of prisoners" at "enmity with society." In an ironic choice of words, Dwight wrote that agents relying on the lash struck a "deadly blow" to the hopes for the American prison. Dwight acknowledged that shameful practices had occurred in the prisons, even while his own society had aims of making the system the best in the world. He had learned from the experience. "Absolute power, unlimited power, despotic power," he wrote, "are entirely inadmissible in the American Penitentiary system."[17]

Despite its potential for "despotic power," Dwight reaffirmed the Auburn system. Even with its lockstep and the occasional use of the lash, even if it had been taken to awful extremes, he insisted it was the best prison discipline available. It offered labor and solitude. It was stern, but allowed for hope. Dwight believed that the right men could make the Auburn system work. As prime example, he pointed to Gershom Powers, Auburn's former agent. When Powers spoke in chapel, Dwight wrote, "half the men were in tears." It would take men like Powers to run a prison with the goal of inmate reform and only minimal use of the lash. Stripes ought to be "a very small part, or no part, of the system," Dwight argued. Though New York's prisons had missed the mark, others had not. Indeed, he noted that Boston's House of Correction had run on the Auburn system for six years without using the lash. Dwight concluded that recent events at Auburn and Sing Sing were an aberration. The Auburn system remained the best. It protected the public and fostered reformation in its effort "to subdue, to silence, to instruct, to restrain, to render submissive and pliable, to keep in safety" those who broke the law. It was the only hope for punishing wrongdoers and, at the same time, reclaiming them to God and community.[18]

Dwight continued to advocate for the Auburn discipline, including its provisions for chaplains and religious education, in his annual PDSB reports. Throughout the 1830s and 1840s, Dwight cheered prisons in Maine, Massachusetts, Connecticut, Vermont, Ohio, New Hampshire, and Washington, D.C., for their appropriations reserved to pay chaplains' salaries. Despite the spread of the prison chaplaincy, Dwight lamented the number of institutions with inadequate resources dedicated to religious education and spiritual formation. He criticized Kentucky's reliance on keepers to provide religious instruction. He attacked prison agents in Georgia, Tennessee, Maryland, and New Jersey for relying on local clergy to run Sunday services instead of hiring at least a part-time chaplain. The Auburn system, with its chaplain partnerships, was clearly advancing, but the race was not yet won.[19]

Dwight's reaffirmation of the Auburn system—imagined specifically as a furnace of affliction—makes sense in light of the early 1840s New York reforms. Bad agents at Sing Sing and Auburn had been removed. New prison officials instituted dramatic reforms. Prisoners had access to books, Sabbath school classes, and letters from family. Chaplains were released from strictures limiting their inmate conversations to religious dogma, primarily questions of sin and guilt. Most dramatically, the governor established a prison administration that reduced by half the number of prison lashings for disobedience. In 1841, Dwight had reason to hope that the New York prisons once again occupied their place as a national example. Events of the 1830s seemed like an anomaly, a moment when bad men took a good system in the wrong direction.

Reform Remade

Governor Seward's reforms lasted only as long as he remained in office. Like so many other moments in New York history, a transfer of power in Albany meant changes in the state's prisons. With the economic depression lingering and resentment against Whigs growing, New Yorkers elected a Democratic governor in 1842. He named a new slate of prison inspectors, including John Edmonds, a New York City lawyer and judge. Edmonds, in turn, did what most of his Democratic predecessors had done. He hired Elam Lynds as Sing Sing's chief disciplinary officer.

Lynds restored the tough discipline he had established earlier at both Sing Sing and Auburn. The number of floggings soared. Chaplain Luckey wrote that keepers used a "knock down and carry out" system to keep order. Lynds also ended the privileges allowed in the last few years. He prohibited family visitation, letters from friends, and singing in worship. He dismantled the prison library. He stopped the Sabbath school and curtailed Luckey's interaction with prisoners. Officials cut the prison staff. Despite an increase in the inmate population, the budgets for food, clothing, and hospital supplies shrank. Edmonds and the board of inspectors supported Lynds's tough approach. In their 1843 report to the legislature, the inspectors wrote that "to talk of the power of moral suasion in a company of felons, is to talk nonsense." Edmonds recognized his conflict with the staff who remained from the former agent's tenure, especially Luckey. In the same report, he acknowledged the acrimony. "Your committee," Edmonds wrote, "are constrained to differ in toto with the Chaplain of this Prison." It looked like the same old debate between the Protestant reformers and a set of prison officials backed by Albany Democrats.[20]

Luckey bemoaned the return of Lynds and the support the agent received from the new inspectors. In his memoir, he referred to the period as a "bloody time" and a "reign of terror." Mentally ill inmates, in particular, suffered under Lynds. On one occasion, Luckey pleaded with Lynds not to flog a "maniac." The agent responded with "withering sarcasm," remarking that chaplains were "benevolent dupes." As noted earlier, Luckey counseled a suicidal inmate who hoped to be flogged to death rather than serve out his sentence.[21]

From his desk in Boston, Louis Dwight tried desperately to keep tabs on Auburn and Sing Sing. In his 1843 PDSB report, he noted that a newly elected legislature had appointed Elam Lynds as principal keeper. Dwight begrudgingly acknowledged that Lynds had some administrative talents. He could run an orderly prison, marked by "cleanliness, order, obedience, and industry." But the old problems remained. Dwight recommended that Lynds adopt more mild punishments and add "moral means" of inmate reclamation and reformation. Without these changes, he concluded, "there will be bloody work" at Sing Sing.[22]

While Dwight's evaluation of Sing Sing had little effect, Luckey's stories of suicidal inmates did. His experience with the prisoner hoping to die quickly instead of slowly by the lash proved to be a catalyst for change. Luckey went to Inspector Edmonds, who "was beginning to have his eyes opened to the cruel, unjust, brutalizing 'discipline' then in full operation." As noted earlier, the inspector began to connect milder discipline with improved prisoner behavior and morale. He concluded that Lynds inappropriately neglected prisoners' moral and spiritual welfare. Edmonds persuaded the rest of the inspectors that a milder discipline ought to be restored.[23]

With Edmonds's change of perspective, a new pattern of reform activity appeared in New York's prisons. The results were dramatic. State officials fired Elam Lynds for the last time. Nevertheless, Edmonds still faced Democrats in control of the governor's seat and the legislature. When he petitioned the state to mandate a milder discipline and aid for discharged prisoners, the legislature balked. Edmonds turned instead to the public. In December 1844, he placed an advertisement in a New York newspaper calling for citizens to assist discharged prisoners. The first meeting of the New York Prison Association soon followed. Within a few weeks, the association opened an office for the aid of discharged convicts. Members soon lobbied for incorporation and drafted reports on potential changes to the penal code and prison discipline. A new age of legal reforms was at hand.[24]

In light of the situation, the NYPA's focus on legal intervention and lobbying can hardly be criticized. It did not have the luxury of discussing the ideal prison in the abstract. Instead, the NYPA faced a system intimately tied to state politics and responsible for prisoners' unceasing brutal treatment. Inmates were not the only ones who felt the discipline's negative effects. Discharged convicts brought their experiences with them upon release. In the mid-1840s, Sing Sing alone released between 200 and 250 prisoners a year. Most returned to New York City. Many had been underfed and beaten frequently. As Edmonds claimed after his experience with the prison's inmates, convicts treated with kindness responded likewise. In the face of a prison regime that changed every election and doled out more than one hundred stripes a day, only immediate legal and political intervention could solve the problem.[25]

Edmonds and NYPA members quickly became the major players on the New York prison scene, offering sharp critiques of the prisons' politics and practices. The association's members emerged from the ranks of lawyers, judges, and community leaders. They sought a fair penal code that was efficiently implemented. In their first report, NYPA members spelled out how they proposed to achieve prison reform. They sought the "amelioration of conditions of prisoners" through inspections of the cleanliness, employment, legal representation, classification, and education in the prisons. They urged the "improvement of prison discipline and government of prisons" through the "supervision of the internal organization and management." Finally, they assisted "reformed criminals" after their discharge. With the hope of "sustaining them in their efforts at reform," NYPA members found clothing, lodging, and employment for those recently released. As the historian M. J. Heale has noted, these were moderate rather than radical goals. Members blanched at inordinate inmate suffering. They assisted those left destitute outside the prison's gates. Nevertheless, they did not seek significant change to New York's penal philosophy. Rather, they wanted the system's smooth and judicious operation.[26]

For the NYPA, the fair application of the established criminal justice system encouraged inmate reformation. The problem was that many officials made the experience harsher than it needed to be, sometimes in ways that were clearly illegal and at other times by holding to the letter rather than the spirit of the law. Association members contrasted their positive approach to former days—in this case, the 1830s—when "the thought of reforming the violator of law and order, scarce occupied the attention of the most benevolent." They clearly disagreed with the tactics and philosophy of prison officials of recent memory, such as Elam Lynds and Robert Wiltse. They considered themselves part of a wider movement of "prison associations and prison discipline societies" making a "change" toward more humane routines. As in their first report, members affirmed what good conditions and education could do for the inmate. They advocated "kindness," not the lash.[27]

For the NYPA, religion was vital to the prison's improvement, particularly its reformative aims. Their reports referenced ministers' work in prisons across the country. They praised states that provided religious services on days besides Sunday, as opposed to many states that hosted services only one day a week if they had them at all. They saw chaplains as integral components to inmate reformation, as part of "bringing all practical, moral, and religious influences to operate upon [prisoners'] minds."[28]

Despite mutual commitments to reformation and religion, NYPA members and Protestant reformers had different notions of what reformation involved and how religion prompted it. In their reports, NYPA members did not articulate reformation in spiritual or religious terms. They defined it as the transformation from lawbreaking to law-abiding behavior. For these new activists, reformative incarceration involved making criminals into "respectable and useful men." To be sure, NYPA members did not explicitly condemn traditional notions of reformation, ideas shaped by Protestant reformers and ministers' narratives of sin and grace, suffering and redemption. Their major enemies were state prison officials who argued that reformation was not possible. Nevertheless, their difference on this question mattered.[29]

Their expectations for chaplains revealed how their notions of reformation and religion differed. NYPA members certainly noted recommendations made by prison ministers. They quoted an Auburn chaplain who recommended the "essential" experience of guilt before moving on to "repentance which lies at the foundation of all thorough reformation." But their own prison discipline committee made different suggestions. They rejected Wiltse and Lynds's idea that most prisoners were unredeemable. At the same time, they expressed concern about spiritualizing bad behavior. NYPA leaders wanted inmates to see that breaking the law warranted punishment, but "not as necessarily incurring eternal infamy." Chaplains were not to push narratives of God's judgment and mercy but rather to contribute to the educational mission of the institution. An NYPA committee recommended that chaplains "expand" their work to include all "ordinary and moral instruction." The minister's duties involved "not just religious education," they argued, but a central role in the "new vigilance in prisons." They needed chaplains to play a vital part in producing the "quiet, industrious, machine-like prisoner."[30]

While prison chaplains had always been involved in "ordinary and moral instruction," the difference between Protestant reformers and NYPA leaders soon became evident. The NYPA's openness to a broad reform agenda did not always sit well with its Protestant colleagues. Chaplain Luckey provides the most dramatic case. As mentioned earlier, Luckey approved the broad reforming program instigated by Governor Seward in the early 1840s. He also served as a key influence in John Edmonds's move to start the NYPA. His difficulties began when Edmonds and the NYPA named a new matron for Sing Sing's female inmates. Eliza Farnham brought a new, psychological approach to discipline. She relaxed the rules in the women's quarter, allowing for inmate conversation and popular novel reading. She also advocated theories of phrenology among prison staff members. As historian Janet Floyd has observed, Farnham brought new ideas to an institution in which routines were not yet entirely fixed. While she surprised many with her literary choices and advocacy of phrenology, her work signaled an openness to new formats for achieving inmate reformation.[31]

Farnham's methods soon prompted a conflict over what sort of practices and materials supported inmate reformation. Farnham, it was rumored, argued against preaching only Christian theology to inmates and stopped an assistant who tried to convert Catholic prisoners to Protestantism. She invited an artist to make drawings of inmates' heads for a phrenology book. Chaplain Luckey and his wife, Dinah, found Farnham's practices unChristian. Luckey took his concerns about the matron's "liberal" methods and lukewarm Christianity to Edmonds and the prison inspectors. Edmonds and the NYPA, however, sided with Farnham. When they rebuffed him, Luckey transferred his campaign to local ministers and the public more broadly through an opinion piece in the *New York Sun.*[32]

An NYPA investigative committee asked for myriad details about the matron's and the chaplain's differing ideas about inmate reformation. According to former keepers in the women's wing, Farnham allowed public reading of Dickens's novels, the Bible, works by phrenologist George Combe, devotional pieces, travelogues, and her own memoir. The focus on novels and nonreligious literature proved maddening to some, including Luckey's wife, who testified against the matron. Mrs. Luckey claimed that she never heard the Bible read and instead heard mostly Dickens. The focus on novel reading, she claimed, kept inmates away from their labor, something she considered essential to reformation. Quiet labor, bolstered by the reading of religious literature, prompted reform. Farnham's regime, which deemphasized silence and allowed nonreligious literature, had problems. A prisoner who came to the prison "deeply penitent," Mrs. Luckey claimed, changed after "reading novels for the last three months." She had turned, the minister's wife argued, into someone unconcerned about her eternal soul and captivated, instead, by fiction-fueled notions of becoming "rich" and a "fine lady."[33]

The NYPA sided with Farnham. Luckey's concern about traditional contours of Protestant experience paled against Farnham's willingness to enlist a broader reforming arsenal in the interest of producing a virtuous citizenry. She won the battle over inmate education. Luckey lost his job. Concerned Protestants added their voice to this battle over the proper role of religion in the prisons. The *New York Sun* printed editorials supporting the minister. An anonymous article in the *New York Observer and Chronicle* decried Luckey's ouster and registered sharp dissent from Farnham's use of phrenology and popular novels. The state, the columnist argued, was using the wrong means in its effort to secure inmates' moral character. Contrasting the prisons with public education, the writer argued that the schools were too diverse to sustain a state-sponsored religion. The prisons were a different case. "Here is an institution supported and fostered by the State, where the moral culture of its inmates ought to be made the subject of intense attention, where the wisest and best means ought be adopted to exert a permanent reforming influence." The problem for the Protestant reformers was not that the state hired people concerned about moral reformation but that the people they hired did not make particular Protestant practices a central part of their reformative program.[34]

Luckey's dismissal signaled the rift between NYPA members and the ministers long associated with prison reform. Indeed, the NYPA emphasized lawbreaking as an offense against the state, not God. Members argued that the prison ought to punish for punishment's sake. As an association subcommittee wrote, "The idea of punishment for wrong-doing should not be dissociated from the disciplinary process to which the criminal is subjected. He has violated the law . . . and its majesty can only be vindicated by the infliction of penalty." For the NYPA, suffering and mortification was needed to appease the law. It brought the prisoner low and taught inmates to revere the legal code.[35]

The NYPA's perspective on reformation also differed from clergymen's. If criminals suffered for breaking the law, they reformed in order to obey it. NYPA members argued that inmate reformation was the most important end of prison discipline. Criminals needed education and job training. After serving their sentences, they needed resources to navigate the outside world. But the NYPA's recommendations were primarily national. It did not focus on inmates' spiritual redemption. The NYPA wanted law-abiding citizens.[36]

The differing wings of the reform movement did not often have the luxury of dwelling on their differences. Indeed, punishments in Sing Sing's men's wing were becoming increasingly brutal. In 1846 an NYPA committee interviewed more than five hundred inmates. Its report, which included accounts of "several instances of inhumane treatment," reportedly shocked the legislature. The stories ranged from prisoners threatened with bayonets to those shot at by keepers and beaten beyond what was legally permissible. According to NYPA members, Auburn Prison also had serious problems. Wooden, rather than iron, beds were "complete nests for vermin." Clothes drying in between cells created a "stench and vapor" they believed to have prompted the previous summer's outbreak of prison fever. Association members also found evidence of fraud. A contractor supplied "bad meat," although the state had paid for decent cuts. After these visits, NYPA members concluded that prisoners needed further protections from wretched conditions and illegal punishments.[37]

The dramatic accounts of their 1846 visits prompted prison officials—and the Democratic administration behind them—to respond in defiance. When an NYPA committee returned for a follow-up inspection in 1847, Sing Sing's agent refused it entry. So began a long and heated battle between NYPA members and prison officials and inspectors. Year after year, prison agents blocked association members trying to enter the prisons. In their annual reports to the legislature, the reformers pointed to their right to inspect by virtue of their incorporation. Without their specific attention to interviewing every inmate privately, NYPA members felt sure that the legislature and public would now be "blinded as to the existence of abuses and seduced into general and unmeaning commendation." They excoriated state officials for tolerating a situation in which inmates had no recourse for mistreatment. They had no access to a prison they assumed would be characterized by harsh treatment.[38]

Sin, Crime, and Sanity on Trial

If the definition of reformation was changing in disputes about Sing Sing, the causes of criminality were debated at Auburn. In defense of convicts accused of murder, lawyers laid out some of the first insanity defenses in United States history. While the history of this legal defense lies outside the scope of this work, the first trial at Auburn is important because it prompted new accounts of human criminality and responsibility. The trial of a prisoner accused of killing another inmate involved meditations on prison brutality and moral mania that excluded traditional Christian categories altogether. The case reveals the way traditional Protestant concepts no longer appeared useful as doctors and psychologists developed modern notions such as moral insanity.[39]

On a Sunday morning in March 1845, Auburn inmates emerged from their cells into a line lockstepping to Sabbath services. Within moments, chaos ensued. One convict, Henry Gordon, hollered and weaved out of line. A pair of scissors slid across the floor. Keepers pushed inmates back into cells. Noting Gordon's distress, the staff dispatched him to the prison hospital, where he soon died from a deep abdominal wound. Prison officials quickly coalesced around another convict, Henry Wyatt, as the likely culprit. Locked in his cell, Wyatt received multiple visits from staff demanding information. When he refused to speak, officials placed him in Auburn's dungeon for four days. The next February, Wyatt was taken to court and tried for murder.

The trial involved a local celebrity, former governor William Seward, who had initiated a series of prison reforms in the early 1840s. Back in the village of Auburn, Seward took up Wyatt's legal defense. His approach never involved denying Wyatt's commission of the crime, although he examined witnesses in ways to undermine officials' certainty that Wyatt was the only possible offender. Instead, he constructed a defense based on the cruel treatment Wyatt experienced at Auburn and the moral insanity that it caused. Seward's defense eliminated traditional notions of sin and crime, responsibility and penalty. In order to build his case, he avoided any input from the institution's chaplain.

Seward, along with the district attorney, questioned several prison keepers and inmates. While they tried to re-create the events of that Sunday morning, their questions touched on a broad range of prison experiences. Seward sought to establish Wyatt's experience of corporal punishment and mental despair. He cross-examined a keeper about Wyatt's experience of flogging and the physical details of the cat-o'-nine-tails used to execute the punishment. Early in the trial, he defended this line of questions, arguing that it showed that "the prisoner has been flogged and tortured with an inhuman instrument of torture, and that the prisoner was driven to desperation, and that a homicide was a result." In his exchanges with inmates and keepers, Seward garnered testimony that Wyatt had been flogged anywhere from fifteen to ninety times for attempting to escape the prison. Others testified to Wyatt's depression, noting that he remarked he would rather die than serve his ten-year sentence. After the altercation with Gordon, Wyatt was placed in irons, spent four days in Auburn's dungeon, and tried to commit suicide.[40]

Seward questioned the prison's head keeper and local physicians to establish a connection between physical brutality experienced in prison and Wyatt's moral insanity. During questioning, Seward pounced on the keeper's claim that "Wyatt was treated with kindness." With reference to the keepers' lashings of Wyatt and other inmates, Seward held up the punishment log "for the purpose of showing that witness is incapable of judging as to what is proper punishment."[41]

Seward then mounted a defense based on the latest developments in psychiatry. He relied on expert testimony from a forensic medicine professor and a manager of the state's asylum for the mentally ill. Diagnosing Wyatt with "moral mania," the witness claimed that his moral insanity came from feelings that had become diseased, possibly from injury, and this resulted in homicidal impulses. A second expert witness claimed that "the disease of moral insanity has only been recently known and recognized as a distinct moral disorder." Considering Wyatt's crime, he continued, "An individual laboring under this form of recognized insanity [is] not a moral being, and not responsible."[42]

Seward clarified why he did not call Auburn's chaplain, the Reverend O. E. Morrill, to the stand. He noted that Morrill, a Disciples of Christ minister, had conversations with Wyatt, which were inadmissible in court. The legal status of clergy-inmate conversations notwithstanding, Seward had additional reasons to keep Morrill out of the witness stand. Morrill could not have supported the insanity defense. He might have agreed that Wyatt was treated harshly. He wrote to the prison's inspectors that inmates' ill treatment produced only bad results. Nevertheless, Morrill preached a traditional message of suffering and redemption, guilt and forgiveness, a theology undermined by Seward's insanity defense. Morrill reported to prison inspectors that inmates responded to his sermons and lessons. They exhibited "intense anxiety and interest." Their weeping in chapel served as an index to the number of "sorrowful and repentant hearts." Morrill focused his redemptive program on Henry Wyatt as he awaited trial. In a report to *Prisoner's Friend*, he described visiting the convict with a former gambler, turned moral reformer. The visitor told Wyatt to read his Bible, pray, repent, and believe in Jesus. He exhorted the inmate to "seek religion." According to Chaplain Morrill, Wyatt wept. The minister viewed the encounter as a successful moment in his program for inmate conversion.[43]

Chaplain Morrill's focus on sin and redemption did not imply that he wanted Wyatt to hang. Indeed, the minister asked Seward to take the case. When another man began to publish accounts that Wyatt had confessed not only to Gordon's murder but also to six others, Morrill wrote in Wyatt's defense. Seward's insanity claims, however, undercut the minister's traditional Protestant message about sin and its punishment. It departed from the standards of behavior and consequences for evil so clearly delineated by God and communicated through the Bible. With Seward's insanity defense, the Protestant reformers and chaplains had an advocate for prisoners' humanity and a defender of their humane treatment. This agreement was inherently unstable, however, because it masked significant disagreement about the nature of human sin and responsibility.[44]

The Religion in the Reform

Despite two bursts of reform activity in the 1840s, the New York prisons continued to be brutal places for inmates. When a Whig governor came into office in 1847, few of his colleagues showed much concern about prison issues. That year some legislators pushed through a bill outlawing whipping, but prison officials worked around the law, by either using the lash illegally or relying on alternative forms of corporal punishment. Physically severe regimes continued.[45]

Prison agents increasingly used the shower bath to discipline unruly inmates. As one of Sing Sing's resident physicians reported, prison officials took an inmate stripped of clothing, placed him in stocks with "feet and hands securely fastened, and his head contained in a sort of hopper, the bottom of which encircles his neck so closely that the water will not run off." The water, kept at a freezing temperature, dropped a foot and a half onto the inmate's head. "The suffering induced, the danger incurred," reported the doctor, "must appear momentous in the extreme." The physician went on to describe inmates' responses to the punishment, including convict number 5066, who was brought to the prison hospital after being showered twice. He arrived in "a perfectly unconscious state, with convulsive twitchings of the muscles. His mouth filled with frothy saliva," the doctor wrote. While that convict recovered from the experience mentally sound, many did not. The physician reported that convict number 4959 emerged from the shower bath "an insane man, hopelessly incurable," and number 5669 came out "with a mind totally destroyed" and died three months later.[46]

While the shower bath was the most used punishment after the lash, some keepers also employed the yoke. According to the same Sing Sing physician, the yoke consisted of a forty-pound bar with a "movable staple in the centre to encircle the neck, and a smaller one at each end to surround the wrists." Once the keeper tightened the screws around the neck and hands, inmates could not stand up straight because of the weight bearing down on the top of their spines. The prison doctor reported that most prisoners bent forward in "continual writhing," with their nerves "benumbed" and their hands "purple" and "swollen." While the doctor could not imagine that even the healthiest inmate could stand the yoke for more than thirty or sixty minutes, he reported that the average punishment involved wearing the instrument for two hours. Most inmates required medical attention and were unable to labor for days or weeks after being yoked.[47]

Chagrined by agents' abilities to circumvent the antiwhipping law, Louis Dwight gave up on New York State. Its institutions hardly figured in his annual reports from 1845 to 1848. Instead, Dwight looked to other states, such as Connecticut and Massachusetts, that hosted more amenable examples of the New York discipline. In these states, he argued, the Auburn system was instituted without harsh physical punishments. With these examples in mind, Dwight overlooked New York's disappointments. He continued to champion the Auburn system when it was implemented according to his theological commitments. The perfect discipline—a furnace of affliction—used difficult labor and strict solitude to bring the prisoner low. It then furnished instruction, leadership, and an orderly and healthy setting in which the graceful work of God could be realized. With the "help of God," Dwight wrote, a good prison discipline used suffering to achieve a redemptive end.[48]

Divine help was necessary, in Dwight's estimation, because most U.S. prisons had more negative elements than positive. His list of the necessities for good prison discipline included thirty-five items. Even institutions that reached some of Dwight's goals were threatened by every way in which the system fell short. Indeed, good discipline involved getting things just right. Legislators thwarted good prison officials. Local artisans protested the unfair advantages of prison manufacturing fueled by inmate labor. Solitary cells had less edifying effects when coupled with poor food and health care. Chaplains could not make their maximum effect when inmates worked so long and so few monetary resources went to education and uplift. Even convicts committed to reforming lacked resources and experienced social isolation upon release. No institution approached a perfect mark on Dwight's scorecard. Prison imperfections were of great consequence. To get any part of the furnace wrong jeopardized the entire enterprise.[49]

Even if the furnace was perfected in the prisons, there were bigger problems. Vocal supporters of capital punishment argued for increasing the number of capital crimes. Most county jails remained unreformed. Houses of refuge for juveniles were only getting off the ground. Too many insane inmates were in prisons rather than mental asylums. And in some states, debtors still served time beside violent felons. These disappointments were only amplified by the construction of additional imperfect institutions across the country. Worst of all, even citizens committed to reform failed to achieve unity. Agreements about mild discipline and inmate reformation covered up deeper discord over what constituted discipline and reformation. Dwight's experience makes clear that the reform movement included multiple, sometimes discordant, voices. As historian W. David Lewis has observed, while the energies for reform might have reached their peak around 1844, the period was "marked by acrimony and debate."[50]

Louis Dwight's concerns reflected the continued debate about religion in the prisons. The questions still centered on the severity of prison discipline and the prospect of inmate reformation. John Edmonds and other NYPA members reflected the country's Protestant majority. They sensed that Christian faith demanded more concern for prisoners and criminal justice than was typically shown. "Other objects of benevolence [besides prisoners], appealing more cogently to the heart, or presenting apparently stronger attractions, find abundant and ready sympathy with the Christian public," they complained in an annual report. Referring to Jesus's commands to serve others in Matthew 25, the NYPA called "Christian charity" to convicts an "essential duty." Protestant reformers and ministers certainly shared the NYPA's sentiment. Louis Dwight opened sessions of the PDSB with the same biblical allusion. Chaplain Luckey published inmates' stories to incite similarly spirited charitable work with discharged convicts.[51]

The scripture quotations, the incessant references to reformation, and the continued focus on prison chaplains, however, obscured fundamental disagreements over religion's place in New York's prisons. As theorist of religion John Lardas Modern has observed, the episode between Luckey and Farnham epitomized this conflict. In the debate that pitted Luckey's traditional Protestantism against Farnham's phrenology, the question of dealing with criminals' sin took on importance beyond the spiritual. As Lardas Modern has written, sin became a political problem. Farnham's victory shows that God had been displaced in the prison's public space. Sin was now a physical or social problem to be addressed by the political community, not a theological issue addressed by religious specialists. Lardas Modern has shown activists such as Farnham relied on the traditions that inspired Luckey's evangelical benevolent activity but then remade this activity in ways that excluded traditional reformers. Both Luckey and Farnham envisioned righteous citizens. Both dreamed of a virtuous, democratic republic. But Luckey's more traditional religious notions were out of step with the emerging prison reform ethos. He wondered how Christian classics such as Baxter's *Call to the Unconverted* could be discarded in favor of Charles Dickens and phrenology. His experiences show how religion's role in reformative incarceration had been transformed. Edmonds and the NYPA articulated a vision of religious life that the public more readily embraced, a vision focused not on redemptive suffering, but rather on prisoners' potential for citizenship.[52]

An 1847 article in the premier newspaper for prison reformers documents the movement away from traditional Protestant practices toward a moralism directed at civic life. The piece, aptly titled, "The Office of Prison Chaplain, or Moral Instructor," reiterated the importance of prison ministers. In fact, the writers declared that any decent prison discipline involved inculcating "moral and religious truth" to inmates. But this learning took on different forms than traditional Protestant reformers imagined. "Dogmatic theology," the authors insisted, "has no place" in the prisons. In contrast, "the plainest and simplest principles of truth need to be set forth with perspicuity." While the pulpit had some importance, the writers admitted, "private personal conversation" and "elementary teaching" constituted the chaplain's most important duties. The authors expressed their hopes that inmates would show "sincere repentance for all their past offenses." But their definition of repentance is unclear. Toward the end of the article, the writers emphasized their national aspirations for the prison chaplain's work. The "end of penal suffering" was not spiritual conversion, they insisted, but the inmate's embrace of "the privileges and enjoyments of an upright and virtuous citizen."[53]

In the years leading up to the Civil War, some Protestant reformers continued to struggle against a system that defied their influence. Some argued that the Auburn system could be a perfect furnace of affliction, producing reformed inmates who followed Christ and a society closer to its Christian ideal. Others, however, turned a new leaf. Recognizing that the prison had become a living hell, these reformers and ministers concentrated on ministering to the broken bodies and souls that languished in prison and returned to society indelibly affected by their sentences. These chaplains preached Christianity as a release from the prison's pain. They asked Christian citizens to help these poor men and women. These reformers turned to what we might now call social work. They offered material aid to those broken by their prison experience and then sent them back out to make their way in the world.

6

The Prison as Hell, 1848–1860

On a visit to the state legislature, Quaker Isaac Hopper almost got himself thrown out of the capital. Like many Friends, he refused to show deference to government officials. When he declined to remove his hat, the assembly's guard threatened to eject him. Hopper explained his position to the guard and took his place in a hearing about the state prisons. His visit, however, continued to provoke responses. His traditional clothing, plain speech, and adherence to old customs reportedly amused lawmakers. They "regarded [him] as a curiosity." His conspicuous attachment to the Friends tied him to another world, one legislators associated with church instead of politics.[1]

In some respects, New York Prison Association (NYPA) members shared the lawmakers' perspective on Hopper's distinctive identity. Led mostly by lawyers and judges, the NYPA assigned legal professionals to committees working on prison discipline and reform. It assigned the conspicuously religious Hopper to work with discharged inmates. The association's leaders noted his "peculiar tact in managing wayward characters." They viewed his Quaker background and long experience assisting runaway slaves as particularly fitting for the Office for Discharged Convicts. Hopper, too, pointed to his religious tradition as inspiration for his prison work. In a report to the NYPA, Hopper envisioned a day when all people would be looked upon as "brethren" and the erring would receive a "peculiar sympathy and regard." He claimed that the "spirit of Jesus" made such a position possible.[2]

Hopper's work with ex-convicts involved hearing their stories, which increasingly included accounts of physical mistreatment. Over the course of the late 1840s and early 1850s, Hopper and some of the remaining Protestant chaplains and reformers saw nothing Christian in New York prison discipline. It was no garden. It was not Isaiah's furnace of affliction. Instead, the prisons were hell on earth: inordinate suffering with a punitive rather than redemptive aim. For Hopper and these ministers, the spirit of religion demanded that Christians respond to the prison's evils. He called for Christian outreach to inmates' bodily and spiritual sufferings.

Even as the Protestant reformers and ministers decried prison disciplinary practices, the presence of these activists allowed partisans to claim the institution's ongoing religious character. They could point to chaplains' work and reformers' service to garner public approval, even as the prison hosted acts of horrible cruelty and legal reformers focused on making upright citizens rather than converted Christians. Indeed, Protestant activists had little influence in protracted arguments about the course of prison discipline in this period. Their activity coincided with a dramatic worsening of prison conditions and a period in prison history in which "religion" worked primarily to support strict sanctions designed to produce virtuous citizens. By staying inside the prison and continuing to work with legislators and more secular reformers, the Protestant prison reformers contributed to institutions with all the trappings of religion but no Protestant particulars.

Changing Times

Hopper and the New York prison chaplains witnessed deteriorating prison conditions. Huge waves of immigrants, along with many Americans' negative reaction to them, accounted for some of these developments. As the eastern seaboard cities bore the brunt of immigrant arrivals, frontier towns also received some of the overflow. Urban conditions deteriorated. Crime increased. Institutions created for social welfare were pushed to the limit. New York's prisons felt the impact of these changes. Even though the state boasted four prisons by 1850, they were overcrowded. Officials used harsh tactics to maintain control in institutions brimming with people, many of whom were new to the country.[3]

Immigration put exceptional pressures on New York City. The city, which counted just over 300,000 residents in 1840, grew to more than 800,000 by 1860. During those two decades, New York received an average of 157,000 immigrant arrivals per year. In 1854 alone, the city accepted 319,000 European newcomers. Even if many immigrants moved on to other parts of the country, the city was dramatically transformed by the unprecedented surge of Irish, German, and English émigrés. By 1855 more than half the city's residents had been born outside the United States.[4]

The obvious effects of the immigration surge included growing slums and increased ethnic tensions. Tenements filled and overflow crowds set up shantytowns on the city's outskirts. The homeless population shot up. In 1853 the police force sheltered more and more people, including twenty-five thousand homeless residents in one six-month period. The new urban mix proved volatile in crowded districts where residents crammed into tiny apartments and roamed chaotic streets. An expanding saloon culture hosted the violent work of neighborhood gangs. Ethnically identified groups fought pitched battles, sometimes against each other and at other times in conflict with native-born crowds.[5]

If politicians were not fixated on urban conditions, reformers were. Concerned Protestants sought to serve the needs of new arrivals and exert control overly frenzied city life. Evangelical missions cropped up all over the city, seventy-six by the late 1850s. Reformers urged the building of new institutions or the expansion of older ones. The city sent thousands of destitute residents to the poorhouse on Blackwell's Island. Nearby stood a lunatic asylum, which held a population in which three-quarters of the inmates were foreign born. Thousands of the sick ended up in Bellevue Hospital, an overcrowded institution reportedly overwhelmed by rats and lice. Paupers and vagrants also made their way to Blackwell's Island, to either the workhouse or—if they were considered "debased" or "depraved"—an adjacent penitentiary. Street children, who by the 1850s numbered between five thousand and ten thousand, ended up in the House of Refuge or the new juvenile asylum. Still others were sent by the thousands out of the city to be taken in by rural midwestern families.[6]

Despite this burst of activity to deal with immigrant expansion and the pressures it placed on the city, reformers could not contain the chaos. Indeed, crime increased in the 1850s. As historians have observed, immigrant arrivals transformed the labor environment. New residents fought with each other and with native-born citizens for work and wages. As in other antebellum decades, a struggling labor market fueled a rising tide of crime. Petty larcenies—including people pilfering food—increased. The immigrant surge also brought organized crime networks made up of professional lawbreakers. River pirates trolled the waterways. Gangs extorted money from the less powerful. Violent crimes also increased.[7]

As a result, New York's prisons held more petty offenders and more people guilty of serious crimes. By 1852 approximately 12 percent of inmates had been convicted of murder or manslaughter, rape or "intent to kill." This segment of the inmate population had increased since the prison's early years, when less than 2 percent of inmates had harmed people. At the same time, New York's prisons still held a vast majority of inmates convicted of property crimes; those found guilty of larceny, burglary, counterfeiting, or forgery totaled 82 percent. As state officials focused on the growing number of violent offenders, their increasingly harsh methods left a lasting imprint on the overwhelming number of small-time criminals as well.[8]

Overcrowded conditions added to prisoners' daily miseries. By 1850 the state had more inmates than single cells. After long days in Sing Sing's stone quarry or Dannemora's iron works, convicts returned to cells they shared, even though these spaces were built to hold only one person. Opportunities for education also declined. Depending on the season, New York inmates worked eight to ten hours a day, six days of the week. Only Sunday contained enough free hours for extended instruction. Reformers, in turn, complained that profits trumped reformation. One wrote that Sing Sing's female inmates had no time for lessons because of their labor and that the chaplain there complained for want of books and teachers. Others estimated that only one-hundredth of the state's annual prison expenditures went to improve "the mental or moral condition of the prisoners." While state officials lauded education programs in the prisons, reformers focused on their inadequacies. In 1849 only one in four inmates at Sing Sing received any form of common education. At Auburn, the ratio was one in three. In sum, New York's inmates worked long days, stuffed themselves into overcrowded quarters at night, and rarely had an opportunity to learn.[9]

Breaking prison rules invited severe penalties. Even though the legislature had outlawed whipping in 1847, prison agents and keepers continued to use the lash extralegally and devised new punishments that did not conflict with the law. Some tried deprivation through solitary confinement with limited food, water, and light. Others used the freezing waters of the shower bath and the heavy burden of the yoke. Prison historian W. David Lewis has found that Sing Sing inmates also experienced the pulley, in which they stood on one leg while their arms and other leg were raised by ropes. Other prisoners received a treatment borrowed from the military called bucking. They sat with their hands around drawn-up knees. Keepers inserted a stick between the knee joints and the elbows. A *Harper's Weekly* article described the "spitted" inmates as helpless to defend themselves from being rolled around the floor by keepers. Whether subject to legal punishments such as the shower or the lash that had been outlawed, prisoners experienced harsh penalties for resisting daily discipline.[10]

Political changes also exacerbated the prisoners' situation. Throughout the 1830s and into the 1840s, partisan affiliation predicted legislators' approach to prison reform. Democrats typically sided with prison agents committed to tough discipline. In particular, they tended to support the regimes established by Elam Lynds and Robert Wiltse. Whigs, on the other hand, had a tendency toward reform. Most notably, Governor Seward instituted reforms aimed at ending the inordinate prison lashing common in the 1830s. His replacement by a Democratic governor in 1843, however, signaled a return to harsh prison conditions. These partisan differences continued, although no subsequent governor took Seward's strong stand. New York's political upheavals of the late 1840s and through the 1850s prompted some prison discipline change. Democrats continued to support tougher regimes. Whigs, and eventually Republicans, tended toward milder disciplines. But none took up the issue in earnest. With the exception of periodic crises and scandals, few politicians took a decided interest in prison reform. Most stayed within their party alignments, even as prison agents experimented with new bodily sanctions.[11]

Prison profitability, on the other hand, continued to occupy state officials. Fluctuating markets and the protests of free laborers made the prison agent's financial job increasingly difficult. In 1842, under pressure from workers, state officials passed a law that restricted prison production to items for "state-use" only. Turning a profit became nearly impossible, although politicians continued to insist upon it. In 1856 the New York prison system saw the first of many years in the red. Indeed, the tough economic environment, along with urban conditions and institutional overcrowding, made prison life odious. Punishments were awful and no political party evidenced significant interest in reform.[12]

The Redemption of One Individual

The New York Prison Association had formed to combat abuses stemming from profit-seeking and illegal practices of disciplinary control. From its incorporation in 1844, the NYPA insisted that prisons operate in strict compliance with the law. Members regularly visited New York's institutions to ensure that prison agents and keepers did not cross legal boundaries. These visits were sometimes tense, if not hostile. Agents did not appreciate their meddling. Outside of the NYPA's work of inspecting institutions and commenting on disciplinary issues, members also wanted to assist discharged convicts. They assigned this task to their colleague and well-known Quaker humanitarian Isaac Hopper.

Hopper, known for his work with runaway slaves, coordinated the NYPA's work with ex-prisoners. He identified Quaker testimonies as the source of his concern for the poor, the enslaved, and the imprisoned. His biography attributes his 1792 application for membership in the Philadelphia Monthly Meeting to a spiritual experience he had as a young man. While Hopper disagreed with some aspects of the Society's life in America, he respected many Quaker traditions. He dressed plainly. He used plain speech. His social commitments often compromised his tailoring business, so he did not gain the wealth of many other Friends. Hopper played a variety of roles in Quaker communal life, including a stint as an overseer, or a member who "treated" with members of the community who disobeyed the rules. From his social commitments to the details of his daily life, Hopper reflected the Society and its testimonies.[13]

Hopper ran a New York bookstore that distributed Quaker and antislavery literature. Earlier in his career, he had assisted dozens of runaway slaves. Hopper and his family hid them from slave catchers, directed them to stops on the Underground Railroad, and defended them against legal challenges. While he is best known for his antislavery work, Hopper also labored on behalf of prisoners and the poor in Philadelphia and later in New York.[14]

Hopper's interaction with prisoners stretched back to his teen years. His uncle, a Philadelphia Quaker and prison inspector, took Hopper along to hear the first sermon preached at the Walnut Street Jail. The young man looked on as the Reverend William Rogers and Episcopal bishop William White delivered their sermons to inmates. Hopper's work with prisoners started soon after. He later recalled his experience with two young men sentenced to hard labor in a Pennsylvania prison. Hopper applied for pardons for them. He had them separated from older criminals in the jail. "I tried to speak to them," he reported, "as a kind father would speak to erring sons." After their release, Hopper invited them to his home to hear Scripture and instructional books. He reported that both went on to lead respectable lives.[15]

With his background assisting escaped slaves, the poor, and the imprisoned in Philadelphia, Hopper was a natural choice for the NYPA's first position with discharged convicts. Typically, prisoners left Sing Sing with three dollars and the clothes they had worn when they entered prison. Auburn prisoners had a little more luck. They usually received a new suit of clothes and some extra change from the agent upon release. The few dollars from the state secured little more than transportation back to the prisoner's home community. Besides the lack of material resources, prisoners also experienced the social stigma of being convicted felons and the physical and mental effects of a stint in prison. Many struggled to find housing and employment. Still others returned to families often resentful of the financial and social strain that the convict's absence had put on them. Further, Hopper was convinced that many inmates emerged from the system "mostly debilitated in body and mind." Poverty, social isolation, and degradation thwarted many inmates' efforts to make good upon release. Hopper concluded that Christians must aid them so that they would not "resort to dishonest means to obtain a living."[16]

To alleviate these problems, Hopper marshaled the resources of local Protestants and networked with prison officials in charge of inmates before their release. Shortly after the NYPA organized, he set up an office in the city and began taking donations of money and clothing. Within a few months, he received correspondence from Sing Sing women's matron, asking Hopper to find a position for a soon-to-be-discharged inmate. He maintained a vast correspondence with prison officials across the country and other philanthropists and reformers. He offered material aid and assistance finding jobs. He began visiting inmates in their homes to check on their progress. Hopper believed that "evil associations and intemperance" led many to break the law. He hoped that inmates grounded in family life and decent jobs would avoid the things that had lured them into crime. After just three years work, Hopper reported that only 5 of the 273 men he assisted had returned to prison.[17]

Hopper kept detailed reports of his dealings with discharged convicts, including lists of the pieces of coal and spare dimes he distributed. He conversed with the ex-prisoners and recorded their life stories, including their place of birth and turn to trouble. He kept details about their family connections, job training, and religious affiliation. When he distributed relief to ex-convicts, he also recorded their testimonies. As reformers found themselves increasingly marginalized by the state, Hopper's work of ministering to released inmates and bearing witness to their experience became increasingly important. He wrote down details of prisoner abuse narrated by released convicts. He recorded visits with several inmates who complained about beatings that they or fellow inmates had suffered.

Written reports of abuse stretched back to 1846 when Hopper received a letter from George Andrews, a discharged convict from Auburn Prison. Andrews praised the NYPA for offering a "truly good and noble purpose" to the prisoner's "blank and dark soul." He wished Hopper well for his "disinterested goodness" and encouraged him in "rooting up the Prison Discipline of this State." While he cheered Hopper's work, he decried the situation at Auburn. He noted the "bloody administration" of the prison's staff. Andrews hoped that his letter would prompt further investigation, or at least encourage the NYPA in its current work.[18]

Accounts of abuse piled up. Beginning in 1848, Hopper's journal references numerous stories from discharged convicts. Hugh Quin, a native of Ireland, reported that he was flogged, strangled, and "put in the dungeon" at both Sing Sing and Auburn. Samuel Boyce said that he was beaten, clubbed, whipped, and showered at Sing Sing. By August, nearly every inmate Hopper aided had a tale of woe. Stories of abuse continued through 1848 and late into the next year. Edwin Smith said he was given "food not fit for dogs to eat." Mary Brown asserted that Sing Sing's new agent stopped the matron's reading and singing classes, beat some of the female inmates, and "cut off the hair of a colored woman." John Carrick reported that Sing Sing prisoners had scurvy.[19]

Hopper worked to assist ex-convicts making the transition to civilian life. He, too, quoted the prophet Isaiah. "The redemption of one individual," he wrote, "from a state of degradation and despair, to comfort and usefulness, is a work worthy of much Christian effort." To be sure, "comfort and usefulness" do not necessarily equal religious redemption. But given Hopper's overall approach to lawbreakers, it seems he had something in mind other than John Edmond's "machine-like prisoner." His career assisting inmates shows that Hopper focused on basic human needs like a comfortable environment and stable living that allowed the possibility of being useful to others. He wanted these things for ex-convicts who had experienced no comforts and had been of use only to state coffers.[20]

The NYPA not only praised Hopper's work but also held him up as a model of virtuous citizenship. They extolled his "lofty character of goodness." They claimed that his "forbearance and patience" made him stand out among the association's membership. His presence added a moral weight to the NYPA. His relationships with ex-inmates provided a window into New

York penal institutions. This access became increasingly important as the relationship between NYPA reformers and state officials began to sour. Suddenly, the quaint Quaker occupied a central spot in a dispute over prison discipline.[21]

As noted earlier, Sing Sing's agent denied NYPA members entry to the prison when they arrived for an 1847 inspection. Unable to visit prisoners, the NYPA looked to Hopper's notebooks filled with ex-convict stories as material for their annual reports. They acknowledged the problem with using "uncorroborated testimony" but insisted Hopper's notes were the "only clue" about potential abuses. In 1850 the NYPA presented thirty-four prisoner stories of harsh, often illegal punishments. The accounts detailed everything from a principal keeper's beating an inmate until "he wore the whip entirely out" to his assistants' throwing down another and "jump[ing] upon his breast and head until the blood run out his mouth and nose."[22]

Hopper's record of inmate stories gave the NYPA added leverage in its battles with prison agents and state officials. His benevolent work and obvious membership in the Society of Friends made him stand out among the lawyers and judges in the association. Sing Sing's agent also singled Hopper out. Though the official barred the NYPA's committee from Sing Sing for several years, he continued to welcome Hopper. On a June 1849 visit to the prison, Hopper initiated a silent service—with a bit of speaking and singing—for the men's and women's departments. The agent did not seem to think that Hopper's ministry threatened his regime, despite the fact that the NYPA cited his journals as evidence of the agent's cruelty. Hopper's exceptional status reveals the place that Protestant reformers occupied in the world of prison reform. According to the NYPA, Hopper's goodness and benevolence made him the proper head of the association's social services and its main liaison to the female branch of the organization. His personal interactions with prisoners gave them moral leverage and vital information with which to bargain with state officials. And while they respected him, the NYPA did not take his legal advocacy completely seriously. In a world of electoral politics, political favors, profits, and pragmatic policy decisions, Hopper's goodness and absolute claims against inmate brutality made him an exotic creature in the world of New York's prisons.[23]

Prisoners, too, pointed to Hopper's singular contribution. Former inmate Edwin C. Smith wrote Hopper to inform him that things were going well in his new carpentry job. Smith detailed his memories of Hopper's many visits to Sing Sing. He recalled his "countenance beaming with love" and "voice of encouragement." Smith appreciated these visits to such an "abode of ignominy." He also remembered Hopper's assistance upon his discharge. Smith wrote that the Quaker and others saved him from the "utter desolation, loneliness, and wretchedness" that was "natural" to the released criminal. But Smith's letter was not simply a trip down memory lane. Instead, he reported to Hopper his concern over the "inhumane proceedings of the Officers of the Prison." This problem was most acute for Smith as he worried that his brother, Joseph, might now also be incarcerated. Smith asked Hopper to inquire after his brother and continue his work against brutal prison officers.[24]

Others requested that Hopper support their appeals and pardon applications. Hopper often wrote to New York governors requesting pardons. In 1847 he contacted Governor John Young asking that a young man serving a twelve-year sentence for stealing a horse might be freed after serving eleven since his father was dying. Hopper noted that someone living under an "old dispensation" would refuse such a request. But those who accepted Christian faith, Hopper enjoined, practiced the "forgiveness of injuries."[25]

While Hopper noted instances of prisoner abuse and protested the state's use of such force, he firmly believed in the necessity of discipline. In his memoirs, he wrote of his relationship with young criminals. He urged at least one ex-convict to confess to his clergyman. Still another, he took to his Quaker meeting with the hope that she might join. While Hopper believed that discipline and the process of forgiveness and redemption mattered, he took exception to the way the state directed the process. His notebooks contain myriad stories in which inmates emerged from the prison worse than they entered it. On one occasion, Hopper recorded his sentiment that Sing Sing would be the best place for an offender. That particular criminal, Hopper commented in a letter to his wife, was marked by "incredible deception and extravagance."[26]

Almost without exception, Hopper found Sing Sing's conditions abominable and contrary to democratic society and Christian ethics. He certainly found prison practices at odds with the purported aim of inmate reformation. In turn, Christians had a duty to aid those who had experienced this hell on earth. He cringed that other believers did not live up to this calling. Even worse, ex-inmates reported that some prison chaplains contributed to the prison's harsh environment. In 1850 Hopper's journal included ex-convict accounts calling Sing Sing's new minister "lazy" and "negligent." A journal entry from the next year included James Ryno's story that "he has seen the Chaplain stand and look on and smile as the prisoners have been tortured." Hopper recognized that religion could still be invoked to underwrite violent regimes.[27]

Realizing that some clergymen, let alone the general public, seemed unfazed by increasingly brutal prison regimes, Hopper acknowledged that his sense of what was right did not necessarily cohere with the rest of the culture. An 1845 statement found among his records captured Hopper's willingness to push against the mainstream. "Benevolence and kindness" that proved unpopular required "more devotion to principle and more firmness than many possess," Hopper wrote. His notions of justice, however, compelled him to keep going. Those acts, he insisted, "lead to the enjoyment of that peace and consolation which the world can neither give nor take away." His particular approach distanced him from both state officials and his fellow reformers. Prison agents seemed unfazed that ex-convicts told their stories to him. The NYPA simply capitalized on his access to inmates' experiences in order to advance their disciplinary agenda. When Hopper died in 1852, the NYPA's work with discharged inmates stalled. No one stepped in to collect inmate stories or support ex-convicts in their post-prison lives.[28]

Ministering in Hell

Not long after Hopper's death, a veteran minister returned to Sing Sing. Shifts in Albany made his comeback possible. The Reverend John Luckey had been ousted from Sing Sing in 1848. In the meantime, he worked in the tumultuous Five Points neighborhood and at several parishes in upstate New York. Even as he ministered in other places, Sing Sing stayed on his mind. In 1853 he published *Prison Sketches*, a book about his earlier years at the prison. The book's content reflected his long-held concern for inmates' spiritual redemption. It included a couple of inmate conversion stories in which Luckey affirmed "the power of God to redeem those in prison." But the uplifting stories paled in comparison to the number Luckey included about bad prison staff, contaminating politics, insanity, false imprisonment, and despair. Like much cautionary literature of the time, *Prison Sketches* warned readers against crimes that resulted in prison sentences. Unlike his predecessors, Luckey did not hide his doubts about Sing Sing's reformative potential. Although God's grace was available in prison, many inmates failed to experience it. Convict life was awful, Luckey warned. Inmates were "overcome" by the prison's "dark realities."[29]

For Luckey, the possibility of a renewed prison ministry opened up in

1855 when statewide elections brought about partisan change. Although New York governors of the 1850s lacked strong opinions about prison discipline, changes in administration had some effects on life at Sing Sing and Auburn. Whig administrations supported the hiring of staff open to milder prison discipline. While they did not advocate legal transformation or detailed investigations of institutions, they ushered in staff with a different approach to corrections. When a Whig governor came to high office, Luckey found a way back into Sing Sing. His second tenure differed from the first. He spent less time trying to make the system better and focused instead on the way good Christians could minister within an awful situation.

Why come back to a place as dreadful as the one detailed in *Prison Sketches*? According to Luckey, Sing Sing was a hellish place. In *Prison Sketches*, he included only two stories of successful inmate conversion; the rest have dreadful endings. His text tells of an insane female inmate found, just weeks after her release, wandering New York streets with her Bible in one hand and shoes in the other. In another story, Luckey tried to find work for a discharged inmate hoping to lead a good life. His "vision and body were so greatly affected" by his beatings in prison that Luckey could find no work for him. The chaplain reluctantly left the man "penniless and broken in the streets." Another released convict featured in the book reported that employers refused his offers to work and that he felt "marked for life." And worst of all, to Luckey, inmates died in prison before they could be released or find hope of salvation. Luckey recounted the death of one impenitent convict, remarking that "the majority of the deaths in prison are characterized by similar hopelessness." While Luckey's stories can be read as classic warnings to the impenitent, they also can be seen as commentary on the slim possibilities of redemption in the prison as it was then administered.[30]

The details of the two hopeful stories provide the key for understanding Luckey's return. The accounts' successful outcomes rely on the intervention of benevolent Christians. A prisoner's redemption never resulted from regular prison routines. In one case, a clergyman offered forgiveness to a prisoner guilty of stabbing him. Another minister assisted the guilty man upon his release. In a second example, a "pious and humane" prison keeper offered a religious tract that prompted an inmate's reflection and conversion. Overall, the message was clear. The prison was a dreadful place of limited hope. God did not seem to be working through the system as the state administered it. Instead, change came when God worked though good Christians, such as ministers or pious keepers, who chose to intervene. Like

THE CHAPLAIN AND PRISONER.—P. 63.

Frontispiece from John Luckey, *Prison Sketches*. (American Antiquarian Society)

good Methodist class members, Christians were called to visit prisoners, admonish them for good, and support them on the path through humiliation and into the light of grace.[31]

Conditions at Sing Sing deteriorated throughout Luckey's second tenure. Punishments ranged from solitary confinement and whipping to showering and yoking. Prisoners responded to their experiences of abuse. In 1855 the *New York Times* reported back-to-back violent episodes at the prison. Inmates attacked a keeper they had lured into conversation. The very next day, a prisoner armed with a crowbar ran at guards. When the convict failed to stop after hearing a warning shot, the officers shot him dead. The episode proved even more dramatic when inmates responded in protest later in the evening. The *Times* quoted one observer of the mayhem, "The shaking of eight or nine hundred iron doors, and the unearthly groans of the men would be somewhat frightful were it not on the right side of substantial stone walls." Clearly, harsh conditions prompted inmate protest, and inmate protest prompted severe sanctions.[32]

Through the end of the decade, protests continued at Sing Sing and New York's other institutions. Sixty Auburn inmates took up hammers and tools as a threat to administrators when a fellow worker was put in the prison dungeon for misbehavior. Shortly after, convicts made two assassination attempts against the prison's agent. In 1857 Sing Sing convicts bolted from the line lockstepping to Sunday morning chapel. They brandished "slungshots, knives, hammers, and such other weapons" in an unsuccessful bid at escape. A year later, four inmates made a mad dash for the Hudson before being shot at and clubbed. Auburn's agent suppressed revolt by pulling out a revolver and shooting two inmates. Seven inmates escaped Dannemora after murdering a keeper in their workshop. Indeed, the 1850s witnessed the greatest number of riots and escape attempts of any in New York's prison history. Desperate inmates chose violent actions against staff and potential harm to themselves rather than remain in the prisons' overcrowded, overworked, and hellish environment.[33]

An 1858 article in *Harper's Weekly* detailed the instruments used by prison staff to keep order within an increasingly violent prison context. Referencing the 1846 death of Charles Plumb, an inmate at Auburn, the magazine sought to expose the prison's "tortures and punishments." The anonymous author wrote, "We need no longer, it seems, to travel to China or Japan for illustrations of torture." Indeed, the writer continued, "A visit to our own penitentiaries and prisons will furnish all the horrors that the most curious appetite can desire." The article included sketches of various instruments used at Auburn and other New York institutions. While an etching of Plumb being showered served as a centerpiece, the article also included depictions of inmates who were yoked, caged, and bucked.[34]

Chaplain Luckey acknowledged the grim conditions in which he worked. His memoir details the afflictions prisoners suffered that lay outside the boundaries of proper prison discipline. Hoping to overcome the hell of which he was a part, Luckey published story after story about Christians intervening within a broken prison system. And he also acknowledged that prison transformation required supernatural intervention. He wrote that God could sanctify prison afflictions, even if these hardships lay outside God's favor. In this way, Luckey's writing mirrored certain themes in antislavery literature. As literary critic Yolanda Pierce has observed, some enslaved persons wrote against the evils of slavery and at the same time insisted that God's power could work, even within unethical and dehumanizing situations. To be sure, Luckey's experience did not come close to the tortures of slavery. But the minister understood himself as speaking on behalf of prisoners who lived in a similarly degrading institution. Like some antebellum slave writers, Luckey condemned the system and simultaneously affirmed that something good could emerge from something bad. Good Christians acting on behalf of suffering inmates made such transformation possible.[35]

Luckey's final work, a memoir published in 1860, also focused on good Christians assisting inmates. In one story, Luckey's wife took in a prisoner's sister so that she could make regular visits to her lonely inmate brother. In another, kind prison staff recommended a convict for pardon even though such recommendations were against the rules. The pardoned inmate came back to lead a Sabbath service. In still another story, a prison inspector offered a mild punishment rather than a lash. The inmate responded to this kindness, changed his ways, and became a missionary to California. As with his earlier work, Luckey's memoir contained stories of prison success that hinged on Christian intervention in seemingly intractable circumstances. Indeed, stories of redemption usually involved breaking prison rules.[36]

Luckey's memoir also moved beyond individual stories to include an evaluative statement about New York prison discipline. After opening the book with a history of the Auburn system, he detailed the use of corporal punishments by various prison agents and reflected on his first term as Sing Sing's chaplain, recalling Agent Robert Wiltse's harsh regime. Luckey also noted the reforms undertaken by Governor Seward and the NYPA. Luckey hoped that his narrative of the prison's history would convince readers of

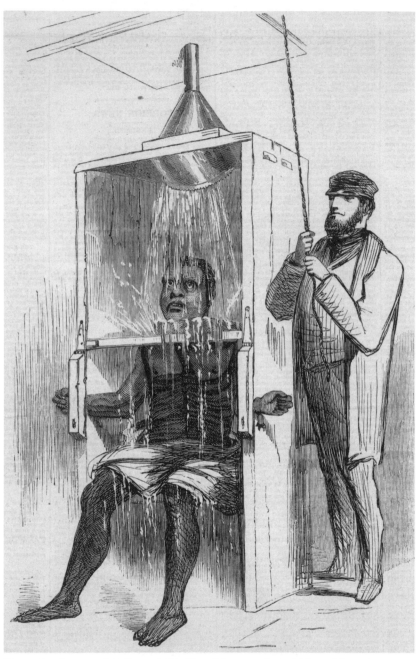

Illustration from an 1858 *Harper's Weekly* article on controversial punishments. (Picture Collection, The New York Public Library, Astor, Lenox and Tilden Foundations)

the necessity of a "mild, but firm discipline, intellectual culture, and religious education." Chaplains and good prison staff contributed to these efforts, but party politics and cruel administrators got in the way. Luckey insisted that political pressures and incompetent civil servants tried their best, but could not "fix the system they've put in place." Throughout the memoir, Luckey attempted an evenhanded account of affairs. As he wrote in his preface, he wanted not to be "critical" but, rather, "to provide information." Nevertheless, criticisms prevailed.[37]

In both *Prison Sketches* and his later memoir, Luckey depicted prisoners as fellow human beings who had done wrong. Convicts' lives started out like everyone else's. They were sinful and in need of redemption. Their prison experiences, however, made them undeniably worse. Without the intervention of concerned Christians, Sing Sing transformed wayward lawbreakers into a totally different class of people. State-directed discipline, even when determined by more liberal-minded officials, could not deliver a prisoner on the proper path of descent through suffering and ascent into redemption. The descent was too harsh and the ascent not high enough or for the right purposes. Rescue from this hell was available only through the help of benevolent Christians offering a tract, a dollar, some food, or a job. If the state would not allow for the prisons to have sufficient Christian character, believers needed to step in. They must, Luckey insisted, because "religion is the only efficient agent in moral improvement."[38]

While Christians could assist some prisoners in their current suffering, Luckey believed that God would someday act to comfort them all. At the end of his memoir, the chaplain included lines sent to him by a former inmate. The poem reflected on troubles both inside and outside prison. According to the convict, prison guards, potential employers, even old friends treated him cruelly. He looked, then, with "calm assurance" toward a future hope. "One thing's sure as fate itself," he wrote. "Heaven, at last the wrong will right." In using this inmate's words to close his memoir, Luckey confirmed his sense that the prison was indeed hellish. Merciful Christians could alleviate some of its horrors, but only God could overcome it all at the end of time.[39]

Winning Hearts and Minds

In their public statements, Hopper and Luckey argued that the New York prisons fell well below standards of humane treatment, lacked the necessary emphasis on reform, and left the aspirations for a Christian nation unfulfilled. They were, however, only two voices in a swirling debate. The conflict between NYPA inspectors and Sing Sing officials, as well as the furor caused by the *Harper's Weekly* exposé, speaks to antebellum Americans' deep disagreements about the course of prison discipline. The public questioned how much bodily force was necessary to maintain an orderly prison. It considered how a desire for a reformative institution could be balanced with security concerns. Once again, partisans invoked religion in support of various disciplinary regimes.

Louis Dwight continued his efforts to direct prison development. Dwight persisted in publishing voluminous reports about penal institutions across the nation. While he preferred the Auburn system as it was implemented in Massachusetts and Connecticut, he offered annual comments on New York institutions, hoping they would move closer to his Auburn ideal. He advocated "humane and Christian" prisons. These institutions, he argued, required a "system based upon reason and kindness, tending to inspire feelings of self-respect, hopefulness, and penitence." He did not see such a system in New York and argued that the shower bath and yoke be discontinued as legal punishments.[40]

Other Protestants seeking to influence the prison debate sometimes confounded the veterans intimately involved in the system. The widely read Protestant paper, *New York Evangelist*, published several articles on prison discipline. An anonymous article from 1851 detailed a visit to Sing Sing in which the writer witnessed the shower bath in use. The writer argued that the bath was a more humane punishment than whipping. Indeed, the writer believed it had the potential to boost good health. The shower bath was necessary, he reasoned, because officials needed some way to enforce the just sentences handed down by the state. If the state demanded a sentence of hard labor, agents and keepers required some way to compel it. The shower bath, the writer claimed, was not "barbarous and savage." It was, instead, more akin to popular "hydropathic" therapies. Beyond authorizing particular punishments, other interested Protestants offered reflections on New York prisons' reformative capacity. An 1855 *New York Evangelist* article attested to the redemptive power of state prison regimes. A visiting minister reported on a Sabbath he spent as the guest preacher in Sing Sing's pulpit. Not mentioning the labor done other days of the week or the punishments famously exacted on inmates, the minister detailed the convicts singing in chapel and the religious books filling inmate cells. He mused on the potential for prayers to waft up to Heaven. "Are souls converted here?" the writer asked. "Yes," he confidently replied. Confident of the prison's spiritual potential, the writer compared Sing Sing to the biblical Bethel, where Jacob wrestled an angel and then realized that he had an encounter with God.[41]

Trading One Hell for Another

The 1850s decline in prison conditions stopped only when the country turned its attention to another format for pain and suffering, the Civil War. Like so many pressing issues of the day, concerns about prison discipline naturally moved to the background as citizens prepared for and then participated in the most devastating conflict in the nation's history. The prisons, though, did not escape consideration during the conflict. In fact, the experience of Civil War prisoners of war—epitomized in the gruesome conditions as Andersonville—prompted a new reform movement that peaked in the 1870s.[42]

By that time, though, patterns for thinking about prisoners and prisons were firmly in place. Prisons were places that inmates did not want to be. Their actions within and their literary output once released attest to their collective experience of misery behind bars. Our surviving narratives resound with prisoner claims that Newgate, Auburn, and Sing Sing did not reform them. The prisons made them worse. The public remained both ambiguous and dissatisfied. It relied on prisons as the primary solution for getting criminals off the streets. It wanted firm discipline that deterred potential offenders. Most citizens, however, seemed uncomfortable with the idea that prisons simply warehoused criminals. They wanted institutions to reform offenders and believed religion was vital to any reformative program. Yet they never offered serious and sustained protest against episodes of inmate brutality. Politicians echoed these sentiments, with Democrats focusing on the need for institutional order and Whigs and Republicans emphasizing prison's reforming mandate.

While citizens sometimes registered displeasure at the most horrific cases of violence toward inmates, they generally accepted the institutions' presence and practices. They consented to the prisons, even though they did not reduce crime and even as recidivism rates went up. They tolerated prisons even when they became sites of awful violence. They embraced them and continued to build more. Indeed, the arguments that pitted mild and strict disciplines against each other only seemed to mask these failings. Partisans could keep tweaking the details of their prison projects, even as these institutions failed overall.

Historian Mark Kann has argued that the early prisons reveal the way citizens embraced the rhetoric of freedom and democracy but allowed only limited realization of the democratic ideal. To ensure the freedom of many, citizens required the enclosure and distancing of some, namely those on the margins of society. The early prisons coincided with the establishment of some of the first Native American reservations and the first organizations for African colonization. Historian Michael Meranze has also identified this paradox after the nation's founding. The prisons show that the democratic urge was complicated by the push for institutions that increased the state's capacity to intervene in people's lives.[43]

The Protestant reformers and ministers usually failed to see the way they participated in—indeed, encouraged and abetted—this undemocratic project. Even as the New York prisons became earthly hells, the reformers insisted that Christian prisons were still possible if the right people led them and the right practices were put in place. Hopper, Luckey, and Dwight saw themselves as going against the common impulse toward revenge. They believed their efforts to expose inmate suffering would prompt others to action. They sensed they were part of a massive campaign to change the hearts and minds of average Americans. In this way, they were classic antebellum reformers. But as literary critic Thomas Laqueur has observed, sometimes these humanitarian narratives worked and sometimes they did not. Simply exposing the public to the suffering of others was not enough. Americans clearly accepted and approved of some suffering imposed on their fellow citizens.[44]

To some degree, the Protestant prison activists made a distinctive claim against inmate suffering. They registered a particular voice affirming prisoners' reformative potential. They argued strenuously for the connection between democracy and humane punishment. But in other ways, they contributed to the prison's development in all its cruelty. They advocated an institution that enclosed people against their will, forced them to labor, separated them from all human comforts, and deprived them of every freedom. Despite all their experiences in which the prisons devolved into tyranny, they insisted that prisons could be "humane and Christian institutions." They argued for the continued cultural relevance of particular Protestant practices. They advocated Quaker silence, Presbyterian prayer, and

Methodist discipline. But their willingness to negotiate for public influence exacted a price. Their particular offerings were not only unwelcome but also unworkable. Their relevance lay only in their willingness to preach a religiosity of citizenship that invoked God's blessing on moral living, hard work, and obedience to secular authority.

The French observers of American prisons noticed this development, perhaps before the reformers and ministers recognized it themselves. Tocqueville and Beaumont visited a Sunday service at Sing Sing during their 1831 travels. Beaumont found the moment particularly illuminating as he pondered the connection between religion and American public life. Listening to the preacher, Beaumont's mind began to wander and his eyes glanced over to the inmates as they listened to the sermon. "Apparently it made no difference to the directors of the prison or to the prisoners themselves what branch of the Christian church the minister of the day belonged to. So long as he preached from the common body of Christian morality and abstained from pressing the dogmas peculiar to his sect." While Beaumont was convinced that the Sing Sing chapel service revealed the genius of American religious diversity, another reading is demanded. Restriction to a "common body of Christian morality" vexed Protestant prison reformers throughout the antebellum period. It troubled them not because they were unpatriotic or unwilling to ascent to the nation's religious pluralism. Rather, it signaled that religion held a central place in public life, but it was a religion increasingly unrecognizable for its traditionally Protestant components.[45]

While Protestant reformers may not have liked these developments, they participated in their creation. They did it in order to stay relevant, to have continued access to inmates and ex-convicts, and to remain a part of the nation's conversation about prison discipline. Because they stayed, interested politicians and the nation at large could claim that America's prisons had the spirit of religion. Indeed, they did have a religious spirit, but not one the reformers intended.

These developments haunted the Protestant prison activists. Most of them simply could not leave the prison alone. It always fell short of their wishes. It always changed just as they achieved even the smallest victory. Thomas Eddy died in 1827, claiming just the year before that New York's prisons never managed to secure inmate reformation. Stanford passed away in 1834 after a decades-long ministry at Newgate. Dwight died in 1857 while trying to finish yet another PDSB annual report. Chaplain Luckey's passing, though, attests to the way the prisons haunted the most ardent Protestant workers for reform. Upon retirement, Luckey moved to Missouri to enjoy a slower, rural life. Before his death, he made one request. When he died in 1876, his wife shipped his remains back to New York. His body is buried on Sing Sing's grounds.[46]

Epilogue

Americans incarcerate. State governments began this task in the early republic and continue it today. In recent years, the pace of incarceration has quickened. Indeed, the scope of American imprisonment sets the nation apart from its world neighbors. In April 2008 *New York Times* reporter Adam Liptak wrote that the "United States leads the world in producing prisoners, a reflection of a relatively recent and now entirely distinctive American approach to crime and punishment." More than two million people live behind bars in America. Or as a columnist in the *Guardian* has put it, the United States now has more prisoners than Lutherans, more inmates than farmers.[1]

Liptak's article focused on the recent turn toward longer prison sentences to account for the soaring statistics. Compared to their counterparts in other developed countries, American judges and juries dole out long terms. Criminologists point to this development, along with the nation's drug war, racial legacy, and absence of a strong social welfare system to account for the statistics, including their impact on racial minorities. While these specialists have typically concentrated on developments in the past forty years, a longer historical view focused on the development of the Auburn prison discipline—including the religious ideology that bolstered it— helps explain the roots of this phenomenon in our history and culture.

As this book makes clear, the Auburn system dominated antebellum disciplinary institutions in the American North. Most prisoners in America had their days organized by its routine of daytime labor and nighttime solitude. Inmates experienced corporal punishments for breaking prison rules. They received religious messages about suffering and redemption from the growing ranks of prison chaplains. Several key traits of the Auburn system continued to prevail and even intensified after the Civil War. To save money, prison officials made individual cells smaller and smaller. They sold prisoner labor to outside contractors. Living conditions continued to decline. Overcrowding became a perennial problem. Imagine housing more than one person in a cell at the Michigan State Prison at Jackson, a space that measured a scant three and a half feet wide, six and a half feet long, and seven feet high.[2]

Staff and administration also replicated problematic patterns from the antebellum period in order to win politicians' approval. Officials focused on prison order and profit. Many relied on keepers who meted out myriad corporal punishments to keep prisoners in line. As in the early years of the Auburn discipline, chaplains served at the pleasure of prison agents. Like Stanford, Barrett, and Luckey before them, these ministers offered the gospel as they understood it to inmates living within harsh, difficult regimes.

The continued use of prison chaplains after the Civil War testifies to the citizenry's persistent belief that prison ought to reform criminals. Even if administrations questioned the possibility of reform and fostered conditions that detracted from it, many Americans still thought prisons ought to improve lawbreakers. Indeed, cycles of reform activity centered on the prison's rehabilitative potential have marked prison history up to the present day. The 1870s witnessed a reformatory movement based in Elmira, New York. Elmira proponents wanted prisons to prepare convicts for successful life in the outside world through education and vocational training. Progressive Era reformers urged a therapeutic model that borrowed language and practices from behavioral science. In this period, reformers hoped that the prospect of probation and indeterminate sentencing—essentially time off for good behavior—would compel inmates toward reform. The 1950s also saw action to reform prisons, this time focused on treatment in a rehabilitative atmosphere. By the 1970s, prisoners themselves prompted a reform movement through the courts, filing lawsuits to protect their constitutional rights. In each of these movements, interested parties sought a prison environment that respected inmates' humanity and offered opportunities for convicts to better themselves.[3]

The periodic presence of reform movements testifies to the persistently woeful status quo. American prisons invariably have involved tough environments, strict guards, and severe punishments. Indeed, corporal punishments persisted for decades. While most states officially prohibited bodily sanctions by the Progressive Era, some administrators perpetrated them extralegally. In a few states, these punishments remained on the books. Colorado reaffirmed flogging as a legal punishment in 1925 and continued to use the ball and chain. Delaware witnessed its last public whipping in 1954. Most states, though, relied on solitary confinement that took on dramatically more punishing forms. Punishment in the "pit" or "hole" involved days on end in a pitch-black environment with little food and water. In some states, solitary cells were infested with vermin. In others, inmates were forced to stand all day and wear iron cuffs that bolted them to cell doors. Even for those inmates who avoided the whip or the solitary cell, prison life was grim. They lived in dirty, overcrowded institutions administered by officials whose actions bespoke a lack of interest in prisoner welfare. Reformers sometimes stopped the most brutal practices, but their activism rarely secured lasting change.[4]

This book argues that one reason for the prison's persistent brutality is that even the prisons' reformers have been committed to the notion that inmates must suffer for their wrongdoing. The disciplinary ideas of antebellum Protestant reformers were based on a theology of redemptive suffering. But even later reformers who embraced medical models and ideas from the behavioral sciences refused to speak out against the fundamentally punitive aim of American incarceration. They continued to assume that criminal offenders should be removed from the community. The prison's message has been clear: criminals are different from everybody else. They are worse than everybody else. They deserve to suffer.

Reformers have struggled to balance their sense of connection to prisoners with their desire to communicate to lawbreakers that their actions are unacceptable. Antebellum reformers such as Thomas Eddy hoped to make his prison a rehabilitative garden, an impulse mirrored by some twentieth-century reformers who took a therapeutic approach. Ministers such as John Stanford and Louis Dwight strove to create a furnace of affliction, a social space that allowed for God's painful, but saving, work on sinners. Contemporary evangelical ministries, particularly Prison Fellowship, have copied this model. Even as reformers just before the Civil War found the prison to be a hell on earth, they did not call for its abolition. Their acts of kindness registered as small instances of protest against the system's inertia. Indeed, most prison reformers, from the period this book covers until the present day, seem trapped by this tension between punitive and reformative impulses. They desire prisoners' redemption, but most Americans could not and cannot give up the notion that convicted criminals ought to suffer at least in some minimal way.

The movements that do question the necessity of suffering exist on the American margins, among some radical political and religious groups. Some groups calling for decarceration or prison abolition have anarchist connections. Interestingly, others point to Quakers as their inspiration.

A few religious and community groups, including the Mennonites, have advocated restorative justice practices that bring together victims and offenders in a process to facilitate forgiveness and reparation. This movement has found wider purchase in some criminal justice circles, but advocates fear that its radical renunciation of punitive measures could be diluted if applied more broadly. Muslim prison ministries, which offer messages of self-empowerment and community, have increased rapidly in the past few decades and draw in many prison converts. In states such as New York, Maryland, and Pennsylvania, Muslims make up 20 percent of the incarcerated male population.[5]

These movements on the margins affirm the human dignity of lawbreakers and assert the inhumanity of prison conditions in the United States. In short, they resist what some scholars have identified as the distinctively American traits exhibited in criminal justice. As legal theorist James Q. Whitman has argued, the American system is harsh, degrading, and rarely merciful because it "displays a resistance to considering the very personhood of offenders." To explain this impulse, Whitman looks to the long history of egalitarian social relations and the resistance to state power in the American cultural context. Essentially, American democracy has reinforced an impulse to treat criminals as lower-status, even nonhuman, beings. While Whitman does not claim that democratic leanings alone account for this movement, he persuasively uses comparisons with England, Germany, and France to show how the impulse to social equality can at the same time rely on the socially degrading treatment of criminals.[6]

Although it is not the focus of his study, Whitman notes that religion has contributed to this particular American approach to criminal justice. I argue that this examination of the roots of the Auburn system and its remarkable influence throughout the antebellum period offers us an account that both confirms Whitman's reading and complicates it. Indeed, the Protestant reformers profiled in this book preached a theology of redemptive suffering that contributed to an atmosphere that emphasized lawbreakers' chastisement. While they did not want to see inordinately harsh penalties, they certainly allowed for degrading practices ranging from social isolation and awful uniforms, to movement in the lockstep and limited use of corporal punishments. Whitman interprets such practices as ways in which the American system—and those trying to reform it—resisted acknowledging prisoners' humanity.

To push Whitman's thesis to more far-reaching implications, I argue that the reformers' theology of redemptive suffering not only allowed but actually demanded these degrading practices. To be sure, many of the reformers and ministers borrowed scriptural and philosophical language in their defense of inmates' humanity. But their theological notion of what it meant to be human necessarily involved a statement of degraded status: human beings are lower than God. While prisoners' humanity protected them from inordinate cruelty, it also demanded regimes designed to make them realize that they were less then God. Thomas Eddy affirmed the Inner Light within inmates. Isaac Hopper proclaimed that Jesus loved them. Indeed, even the ministers of Calvinist persuasions believed that God worked with those He longed to save. But these affirmations also demanded the painful acknowledgment that human beings are not God. For these reformers, prison was a training ground for lawbreakers—whether propelled into criminality by bad upbringing or hardened in it by personal iniquity—to understand every human being's degraded status before a God that governed the universe.

The reformers always exhibited astonishment when their efforts to communicate degraded status before God were easily translated into regimes dedicated to prisoners' degraded position in American society. While reformers cried out to protect lawbreakers' basic humanity, their theologies of redemptive suffering contributed to a prison environment dedicated to inmates' affliction and degradation. So their work inside prisons—and even some of their work to reform them from an outside vantage—contributed to the peculiar American system. Their theological understanding of inmates' humanity had a way of underwriting harsh and degrading regimes rather than challenging them. Religious reformers proved crucial players in the construction of what Liptak has called the "entirely distinctive American approach to crime and punishment."

While the antebellum Protestant reformers' stories tell us a great deal about the prison's eventual development, they also offer insight into the ambiguous history of American religious disestablishment. The reformers formed voluntary associations, designed prison disciplines, and pressed for public influence at a key moment in American history. They participated in a mostly united front to reform self, community, and nation. They argued for religion's vital place in public life, even as they wanted no single Christian group to secure government backing. As scholar of religion and literature Tracy Fessenden has written in her considerations of nineteenth-century public school controversies, these reformers "created the conditions for the dominance of an increasingly nonspecific Protestantism over nearly all aspects of American life." Fessenden has shown that the campaigns for "secular" public schooling actually allowed Protestants to push their own agendas to shape these institutions, especially in opposition to growing numbers of American Catholics. The New York prisons, however, reveal that a similar impulse to take Protestantism into the public sphere ended in an altogether different outcome. To secure religion's central place in the prisons, reformers found themselves stripping their programs of particular Protestant practices and replacing them with moralistic language about American citizenship. This is not to say—in the spirit of classic narratives of secularization—that religion began to have less impact. Rather, this book has shown that "religion" continued to have a central place in the prison discipline debate, even as its character was debated and transformed.[7]

As Fessenden observes, "simplified narratives" of secularization insist that religion no longer matters, a claim that strengthens conservative Christians' insistence that religion be allowed back into the public sphere. Convinced of secular dominance in America, officials at the InnerChange Freedom Initiative and Prison Fellowship can tell inmates and the courts that religion will help where secular institutions have fallen short. This sort of narrative, however, overlooks the impact of Protestant theologies of suffering and redemption on American prisons over the past two centuries. It also passes over the tumultuous experience of reformers' attempts to fashion "Christian" prisons in an era in which a religiosity of citizenship was taking shape. Their experiences show not that religion began to matter less but rather that interactions with the state and with people on society's margins required Protestant reformers to negotiate and change. Making religion central to state institutions that housed a diverse population meant that the reformers' particular Protestant practices—indeed, even their ecumenical Protestant reform platform—were necessarily altered. The Protestant reformers played an important role in giving us the institutions we have, prisons dedicated to punitive punishment, marked by a Protestant narrative of suffering and redemption, and pressed toward a religiosity of citizenship that holds adherence to law and obedience to state authority as its highest goals. These were not the prisons they wanted, but they were the hardly surprising result of their public aspirations in a disestablished and pluralistic society.[8]

Notes

Abbreviations

DA   *Documents of the Assembly of the State of New York*
DS   *Documents of the Senate of the State of New York*
JA   *Journal of the Assembly of the State of New York*
JS   *Journal of the Senate of the State of New York*
NYPA New York Prison Association (also called the Prison Association of New York)
PDSB Prison Discipline Society of Boston

Introduction

1. Adam Liptak, "Inmate Count in U.S. Dwarfs Other Nations,'" *New York Times*, 23 April 2008; Randal Archibold, "California, in Financial Crisis, Opens Prison Doors," *New York Times*, 23 March 2010.

2. California is one of the most striking examples of prison population expansion. As Glenda Gilmore has observed, between 1982 and 2000 the state's inmate population grew nearly 500 percent, despite the crime rate falling after a peak in the early 1980s. See Gilmore, *Golden Gulag*, 7.

3. N. Banerjee, "Court Bars State Effort Using Faith in Prisons," *New York Times*, 4 December 2007.

4. Sullivan, *Prison Religion*, 222, 224. For a survey of Protestant struggles to create political identities, see Hanley, *Beyond a Christian Commonwealth*. In his book about colonial and antebellum theology, Mark Noll noted evangelicals' insistence that civil magistrates not interfere on issues of internal "doctrine, discipline, and government." Evangelicals had in mind the sort of church-state alliances that marked European nations. Their resistance to state control over internal church matters, however, is not inconsistent with their interactions with state structures of authority, something Noll also notes. See Noll, *America's God*, 173. John Lardas Modern characterized the dynamic this way in his article on antebellum evangelical media: "[They] were wary of civil interference even as they insisted that religion should be a political force." See Lardas Modern, "Evangelical Secularism," 845. For another reading of the public school debates, see Fessenden, *Culture and Redemption*, chap. 3.

5. For examples of interpretations emphasizing Protestant influence, see Noll, *America's God*, 174–75, and Williams, *America's Religions*, 177–78.

6. This interpretation is especially common among historians writing on prisons and other antebellum disciplinary institutions. For examples, see Karen Halttunen's work on the transformation of murder narratives between the colonial and early republic periods. Halttunen's analysis is fascinating and helpful on many levels. She relies, however, on a narrative of religion's steeply declining significance. See Halttunen, "Early American Murder Narratives," 77–80. Historians of American religion have also made the argument for religion's, or at least the clergy's, declining significance. See Douglas, *The Feminization of American Culture*.

7. Beaumont and Tocqueville, *On the Penitentiary System*, 121.

8. In some respects, I am trying to ask questions about Tocqueville's understanding of how religion operates in culture in a similar vein to contemporary sociologists of religion who write about religion and civic participation in American life. Paul Lichterman and C. Brady Potts have contrasted those scholars who affirm Tocqueville's celebration of religion as a source for "trust and moral stability" in a democratic society with those who see religion waning in its public significance. They posit, instead, that religion continues to work in the public sphere, but in a much more complicated way than as a simple stabilizing and moralizing force. They pose a series of questions intended to get at the complex ways religions work to open and close opportunities, work in relationship to other civic commitments, and fit into wider cultural frameworks. See Lichterman and Potts, "Conclusion," 140–51.

9. For an extended consideration of the Christian nation ideal, see Cherry, *God's New Israel*. For the intersection of Christianity and republican values, see Noll, *America's God*, 73, 82, 85. For Protestant ambivalence about negotiating the political realm, see Hanley, *Beyond a Christian Commonwealth*, 14.

10. Smith, *The Prison and the American Imagination*, 13; Lardas Modern, "Evangelical Secularism," 868. Who are the Protestant evangelicals in this study? Scholars note the variety of people, persuasions, and theological affirmations that can be included under the antebellum evangelical tent. Scholars usually include some Congregationalists (formerly Puritans) and Presbyterians, as well as most Methodists and Baptists, along with some wings of Episcopal and German Pietist groups. This list includes Calvinists, Arminians, and those trying to strike a middle path between them. See Williams, *America's Religions*, 166–67. The Quakers, or Society of Friends, are the obvious group that played an important role in prison work but are not typically included in the evangelical classification. They exhibited important differences from their evangelical peers, but these should not obscure the similarities. Some American Quakers articulated their belief in tenets evangelicals cherished, such as the problem of sin, importance of faith in Jesus, and the possibility of redeemed living. For more on this, see chapter 1. For more on evangelicals' relationship with personal discipline and discipline mandated by law, see Howe, "The Evangelical Movement and Political Culture." For more on the united front animated by a variety of American Protestants, see the characterization of "Republican Religion" in Wood, *Empire of Liberty*, 582.

11. On the antebellum information revolution, see Hochfelder, "The Communications Revolution and Popular Culture," 314–15. Because the sources make the book,

authors must account for their choices. First, why focus on reformers and ministers' writings? Of course, these sources must be read critically. These folks not only came from the most privileged portions of society, but their published pieces also functioned as volleys in a rhetorical war. Nevertheless, their work provides some of the fullest accounts we have of antebellum prison conditions, especially when read in combination with state documents and inmate accounts. More important, these reformers had an undeniable effect on the prison's development, and no monograph has focused carefully and thoroughly on the nature of their influence. I take my example for critical reading of reformers' words from Thomas Laqueur. See Laqueur, "Bodies, Details, and the Humanitarian Narrative," 201–4. Second, whenever prisoner sources are available, I use them to the fullest. Unfortunately, the extant prisoner voices are limited. The first one I found comes from 1823. It is followed by a burst of activity as the New York prisons experienced low points of inmate cruelty in the late 1820s and into the 1830s. Only a handful of prisoner narratives serve as sources for this book. There has been interesting scholarship on critically reading them. See Glenn, "Troubled Manhood," and Fabian, *The Unvarnished Truth*, chap. 2. But prisoners' words are not the only resources for tapping into their worlds. I also rely on official documentation of inmate action. The legislative record and reports of voluntary societies include stories of prisoner compliance and defiance, labor and inactivity, reform and rule breaking. Only a few manuscript sources remain from the antebellum New York prisons. Unlike the cache of documents available from Philadelphia and used with such aplomb by historian Michael Meranze, there is little manuscript record from New York. While the state library has a few manuscript inmate registers on hand, it appears that much was lost, most likely in an archive fire early in the twentieth century.

12. For a discussion of the particulars of this debate, see Stout, *The New England Soul*, 222–26.

13. Marini, "Awakenings," 141. Several colonial groups published disciplines, including Baptist groups, Quaker yearly meetings, and eventually the Methodists. For studies of discipline in particular communities, see Nelson, *Dispute and Conflict Resolution in Plymouth County*, and Roth, *The Democratic Dilemma*. We have, however, no scholarship that synthesizes more local studies and analyzes larger disciplinary trends among colonial and antebellum Protestants.

14. Friedman, *Crime and Punishment in American History*, 22–24, 27–28; Hirsch, *The Rise of the Penitentiary*, 9; Greenberg, *Crime and Law Enforcement in the Colony of New York*, 33–34; Rothman, *Discovery of the Asylum*, 53. I discuss this context more fully in chapter 1.

15. Friedman, *Crime and Punishment in American History*, 37–40. For an overview of colonial criminal sanctions, see Preyer, "Penal Measures in the American Colonies."

16. Meranze, "Penality and the Colonial Project," 188; Boscoe, "Lectures at the Pillory"; Masur, *Rites of Execution*, 5–6. There is an extensive literature on colonial-era executions. Boscoe and Masur are key works. Others include Halttunen, "Early American Murder Narratives," and Cohen, *Pillars of Salt*. Again, I discuss this context more fully in chapter 1.

17. McLennan, *The Crisis of Imprisonment*, 3, 2. For older histories, see Klein, *Prison Methods in New York State*; O. Lewis, *The Development of American Prisons and Prison*

Customs; McKelvey, *American Prisons*; and Teeters, *The Cradle of the Penitentiary*. Scholarly trends in the 1960s made a new sort of inquiry possible. Most important was Michel Foucault's work on punishment in the early modern period. See Foucault, *Discipline and Punish*. David Rothman and Michael Ignatieff modeled this new form of inquiry in their studies of American and English institutions. See Rothman, *The Discovery of the Asylum*, and Ignatieff, *A Just Measure of Pain*. For an examination of prisons in light of emerging democracy and liberal values, see Meranze, *Laboratories of Virtue*. For an exploration of labor developments and the prison, see McLennan, *The Crisis of Imprisonment*. For the comparison to slavery, see Hindus, *Prison and Plantation*. The prisons, of course, were not the only unstable entities in the new republic. Carroll Smith Rosenberg details the tumult created by multiple political discourses—and the creation of many unwelcome Others—in the nation's earliest decades. See Smith-Rosenberg, *This Violent Empire*.

18. For an exploration of the way arguments against tyranny were key to continued American support of incarceration, see Kann, *Punishment, Prisons, and Patriarchy*, 6, 15, 17.

19. While I bring out inmate voices whenever there are texts available, there is much more to be explored. This book focuses on the Protestant reformers and their visions for inmates and prisons but does not offer as complete an account of the religious lives of the prisons' inhabitants. I welcome more work on these inmates, especially those who were Roman Catholic. More work is also needed on those inmates who made up the minority clusters among New York inmate populations, namely women and African Americans.

20. For the focus on denominational difference, see Adamson, "Wrath and Redemption," and Skotnicki, *Religion and the Development of the American Penal System*. For a thesis about religion's declining significance, see Halttunen, "Early American Murder Narrative," 76–80, and Douglas, *The Feminization of American Culture*.

21. For an analysis of this dynamic in a case study of two reformers, see Graber, "Quakers and Calvinists in the Making of New York Prison Discipline."

22. On the importance of cultivating virtuous citizens, see Noll, *America's God*, 203. On the population as object of "redemption and religious inquiry" as well as antebellum evangelical action to distinguish between true religion and corrupt political behavior, see Lardas Modern, "Evangelical Secularism," 802. Several synthetic histories of reform simply skip over prison activism. Morone's *Hellfire Nation* makes no mention of it. Abzug's *Cosmos Crumbling* refers to it only in discussions of Philadelphia reformer, Benjamin Rush. Other historians list it among various campaigns to deal with social problems such as poverty and unguided children. See Mintz, *Moralists and Modernizers*, 79–82, 86–90. Most fail to see the way in which prison reform was so difficult, and I would argue ultimately unsuccessful, because it demanded government partnership from the very beginning. It proved a much more difficult task than some of the other classic moral suasion campaigns did. A valuable comparison, though, can be made to the Federalist ministers in Harry Stout's work on the early republic. Stout argued that ministers had some overlapping values with the founders but others that were dramatically different. Even as these clergymen celebrated the Constitution, they maintained a vision of the new republic that, in Stout's words, was "corporate, coercive, providential,

deductive, and elitist." In the same way, the prison reformers and chaplains in this story appreciated many aspects of American government and society but sought to impose their more traditional sense of society's best organization onto a changing world. See Stout, "Rhetoric and Reality in the Early Republic," 65, 73. Scholars of social reform will notice that I skip over the endlessly recycled question of good intentions versus social control. For the historiography of this debate and the response of one scholar trying to take the conversation in new directions, see Howe, "The Evangelical Movement and Political Culture," 1216–20.

23. Lardas Modern, "Evangelical Secularism," 830; Noll, *America's God*, 85; Kann, *Punishment, Prisons, and Patriarchy*, 6.

24. For a helpful and succinct account of two trends in scholarly use of secularization theory, see Gilpin, "Secularism." Noll, *America's God*, 194, 205; Lardas Modern, "Evangelical Secularism," 824.

Chapter One

1. *JA*, 24th Session (January 1801), 66. While most people referred to the prison by its nickname, Newgate, it was formally known as the New York State Prison. Prison agents performed duties we now associate with prison wardens.

2. Knapp, *The Life of Thomas Eddy*, 50–51.

3. Rothman, "Perfecting the Prison," 101–2. Eddy's memoirist included his account of the stint in jail. See Knapp, *The Life of Thomas Eddy*; 50–51. Laqueur, "Bodies, Details, and the Humanitarian Narrative," 177–78, 201.

4. T. Eddy, *An Account of the State-Prison*, 5.

5. Spierenberg, "The Body and the State: Early Modern Europe," 46–48, 56–59.

6. McGowen, "The Well-Ordered Prison: England, 1780–1865," 72–73.

7. Ibid., 76; McLennan, *The Crisis of Imprisonment*, 18. To be sure, English authorities handed down many more death sentences in this period than they fulfilled. See Whitman, *Harsh Justice*, 164–65, and McKenzie, *Tyburn's Martyrs*, 3–4.

8. Spierenberg, "The Body and the State," 58–59; McGowen, "The Well-Ordered Prison," 73. For more on England's changing definition of poverty in this period—and the way in which religious bodies participated in this redefinition—see Landau, "The Regulation of Immigration." For information on this trend on the continent, see Lindberg, *Beyond Charity*.

9. McKenzie, *Tyburn's Martyrs*, 7–14. Of course, ministers also published these "condemned sermons" and gallows accounts. I go into more detail about these texts and the variety of ways they can be read later in the book. Further, European clergy's involvement with punishment generally and execution specifically was not limited to England. See Spierenberg on the role of ecclesiastical law and punishments in late medieval and early modern Europe. Spierenberg, "The Body and the State," 45, 49–52.

10. Friedman, *Crime and Punishment in American History*, 37–40, 6, 25; Boscoe, "Lectures at the Pillory," 156–76; Masur, *Rites of Execution*, 5–6.

11. Friedman, *Crime and Punishment in American History*, 48–50.

12. Halttunen, "Humanitarianism and the Pornography of Pain," 303, 318. Halttunen offers a fascinating argument about the way in which these instances of pain and torture

also had a titillating and erotic quality for eighteenth-century citizens who evidenced concern over them. Hunt, *Inventing Human Rights*, 30–34.

13. Masur, *Rites of Execution*, 50–54; Meranze, "The Penitential Ideal," 422–23.

14. McGowen, "The Well-Ordered Prison," 77–79; Ignatieff, *A Just Measure of Pain*, 44–79.

15. For more on the impulse to differentiate from England, see Davis, "The Movement to Abolish Capital Punishment." Gordon Wood provides a helpful overview of early republic organizing. See Wood, *Empire of Liberty*, 485–89. On early institutions, see Rothman, "Perfecting the Prison," 108–9.

16. Wood, *Empire of Liberty*, 491; Hirsch, *The Rise of the Penitentiary*, 11; Rothman, *The Discovery of the Asylum*, 61; Meranze, "The Penitential Ideal," 427, 441, 435, 447.

17. Teeters, *They Were in Prison*, 4–6. Historians have struggled to integrate some reformers' religious identities and their participation in broader reform movements. In this matter, I agree with Christopher Adamson that many Quakers involved in early prison reform were products of a "thorough intermingling of evangelical, Quaker, and republican values." See Adamson, "Evangelical Quakerism," 39.

18. Teeters, *They Were in Prison*, 122, 19–21; McGowen, "The Well-Ordered Prison," 78–80; Ignatieff, *A Just Measure of Pain*, 58–59; Teeters, *They Were in Prison*, 3–6. For more on the Quakers' campaign for a milder penal code during William Penn's career, see Thomas Dumm's article, "Friendly Persuasion." While experience of the Inner Light on the one hand and influence of church discipline on the other might seem dramatically different, the two cohere neatly in Quaker theology. Experiencing Christ demanded a change of living. An internal transformation demanded external verification in moral living. Church discipline was there—ostensibly—to ensure that one followed upon the other. Of course, Friends disagreed among themselves about how this system of discipline was to work.

19. Several older histories of the prisons connect Quaker prison work with their soteriology. See Teeters, *They Were in Prison*, and Barnes, *The Repression of Crime*.

20. For more on these varying tendencies in Quaker history, see Mullet, "Society of Friends"; Hamm, *The Quakers in America*, 30. Christopher Adamson makes a strong case for evangelical influence. See Adamson, "Evangelical Quakerism," 36–37.

21. Hamm, *The Transformation of American Quakerism*, 2; Barbour and Frost, *The Quakers*, 108.

22. Jack D. Marietta describes this transition, including its relation to Quaker political dealings and ideas about social reform. He argues that tightening community discipline was related. See *The Reformation of American Quakerism*. His thesis about Quaker particularism in the eighteenth century conflicts with Sidney V. James's assertion that Quaker interest in reform movements such as abolitionism reflected their move toward broader American values. See *A People among Peoples*. While many Friends used a discipline published by the Philadelphia Yearly Meeting for many years, other meetings began to publish their own. Thomas Eddy's community used one developed by the New York Yearly Meeting. See *Discipline of the Yearly Meeting of Friends*, 30, 36, 37.

23. Hamm, *The Quakers in America*, 34; Mullet, "Society of Friends," 782.

24. For the story of Pennsylvania's legal transformation, see Teeters, *They Were in Prison*, 9, 61, 75.

25. Greenberg, *Crime and Law Enforcement in the Colony of New York*, 25, 135–46, 125; Richmond, *New York and Its Institutions*, 512; T. Eddy, *An Account of the State-Prison*, 10–11; Rothman, *The Discovery of the Asylum*, 51.

26. Greenberg, *Crime and Law Enforcement in the Colony of New York*, 36, 71, 130.

27. T. Eddy, *Account of the State Prison*, 6, 64, 4.

28. Ibid., 5.

29. Ibid., 12; W. David Lewis, *From Newgate to Dannemora*, 22. For more on these reform impulses, see Mintz, *Moralists and Modernizers*, xiii–xxii.

30. T. Eddy, *An Account of the State-Prison*, 10; W. David Lewis, *From Newgate to Dannemora*, 1; T. Eddy, *An Account of the State-Prison*, 13–14. While the decision to build a prison was made by politicians at the state level, New York City partisans would also need to contribute to the effort. As historian Sean Wilentz has written, politics in the city took a conservative turn in the mid-1790s as some politicians searched for ways to rein in the lower classes. See Wilentz, *Chants Democratic*, 69.

31. Caleb Lownes to Thomas Eddy, 19 April 1796, box 37, reel 18, Philip Schuyler Papers. Eddy detailed Lownes's contribution in a letter to Schuyler. See Thomas Eddy to Philip Schuyler, 14 July 1796, letter no. 589, Philip Schuyler Papers.

32. T. Eddy, *An Account of the State-Prison*, 15–16.

33. Ibid., 16, 52, 69–70. In his influential book *The Discovery of the Asylum*, 58–64, Rothman argued that the first prisons were built more as storehouses for criminals. He wrote that the impulse for reformative incarceration did not emerge until the 1820s. This argument fits well with his thesis about the prisons as a particular manifestation of Jacksonian America. In his work on Philadelphia prisons, however, Michael Meranze identified the reforming impulse as early as the 1790s. See Meranze, *Laboratories of Virtue*, 139. In this work on New York, I find a similar impulse long before the age of Jackson. Eddy's writings on the New York prisons contain multiple references to his rehabilitative impulse.

34. Meranze provides a full discussion of Rush. See *Laboratories of Virtue*, 132–36. Rush sensed that any system, even one in which the prison served as a horrifying deterrent, constituted significant reform. As he wrote in an 1803 letter to Eddy, criminals needed an "idea of the mixture of divine mercy with divine justice" and that "we should found our laws wholly upon the mild religion and just precepts of Jesus Christ." See Rush to Eddy, 19 October 1803, in Butterfield, *Letters of Benjamin Rush*, 2:875.

35. The paternalism and naiveté of Eddy's position will become clear in the next section. I report Eddy's intentions, noting that he never acknowledged that inmates did not enjoy prison and his plans never proved successful.

36. Caleb Lownes to Thomas Eddy, 19 April 1796.

37. For more on Philadelphia's penal experiments, see Meranze, *Laboratories of Virtue*, 167–71.

38. For more on the "enclosed garden," see Barbour and Frost, *The Quakers*, 115. Eddy and other Quakers' environmentalism, or concentration on the social factors contributing to delinquency and criminality, is early. This perspective flourished among some reformers later. See Rothman, *The Discovery of the Asylum*, and Boyer, *Urban Masses and Moral Order in America*.

39. Finney, "Garden Paradigms in 19th Century Fiction," 21–22.

40. T. Eddy, *An Account of the State-Prison*, 54.

41. Ibid., 50. For a discussion of the timeline of reformative incarceration, see the introduction.

42. Ibid., 17–19.

43. Barbour and Frost, *The Quakers*, 116. To be sure, Quakers did not make too much of education. Lack of education did not keep one out of the ministry. At the same time, many Friends valued education and saw it as the path toward uplift for African Americans and Native Americans. See Woody, *Early Quaker Education in Pennsylvania*, 32–40, 262–65.

44. *JA*, 22nd Session (January 1799), 84.

45. T. Eddy, *An Account of the State-Prison*, 35; *JA*, 21st Session (January 1798), 84.

46. *JA*, 21st Session (January 1798), 83–84; T. Eddy, *An Account of the State-Prison*, 19, 38; *JA*, 22nd Session (January 1799), 84.

47. T. Eddy, *An Account of the State-Prison*, 39, 19.

48. Ibid., 47–49.

49. *JA*, 22nd Session (January 1799), 84; T. Eddy, *An Account of the State-Prison*, 53; Knapp, *The Life of Thomas Eddy*, 63; *JA*, 22nd Session (January 1799), 84; *JA*, 24th Session (January 1801), 65; Eddy, *An Account of the State-Prison*, 55; Knapp, *The Life of Thomas Eddy*, 95.

50. Stansell, *City of Women*, 4–10.

51. T. Eddy, *An Account of the State-Prison*, 20–24. At times, inspectors stepped in if they felt that a prisoner had been treated unjustly in the course of his arrest, trial, or sentencing. For instance, the inspectors reported to the legislature when offenders were tried for petty larceny by a panel of judges rather than a jury, a situation they considered illegal. *JA*, 22nd Session (February 1799), 85.

52. T. Eddy, *An Account of the State-Prison*, 52.

53. Eddy, Bowne, Franklin, and Murray are listed for various activities in the indexes of the New York Monthly Meeting. See *Abstracts of the Records of the Monthly Meetings of New York Yearly Meeting*, vol. 15, and *Abstracts of the Records of the Monthly Meetings of New York Yearly Meeting*, vol. 20. New York City directories from the period list Bowne, Franklin, and Murray as merchants. See *Longworth's American Almanac, 1804*. From the beginning, however, the Friends did not have total control over Newgate. In the prison's first years, Isaac Stoutenburgh, a New York civil servant, and Jotham Post, who eventually became a judge and U.S. congressman, joined the four Quaker inspectors. In 1798 the state legislature added a seventh member, George Warner. While little is known about these men, records underscore that a stint on the prison board lay at the beginning of their political careers as civil servants.

54. *JA*, 25th Session (February 1802), 79; T. Eddy, *An Account of the State-Prison*, 28, 21.

55. T. Eddy, *An Account of the State-Prison*, 27. For more on the relationship of the overseers and those under their care, see Barbour and Frost, *The Quakers*, 109.

56. *JA*, 22nd Session (January 1799), 86. The inmate statistics cover the 260 prisoners at Newgate on December 31, 1798. Records from the state show that violent crimes resulting in a death sentence also made up only a small percentage of convictions. New

York State executed only two people for murder in 1797 and 1798. See Hearn, *Legal Executions in New York State*, 28–29.

57. T. Eddy, *An Account of the State-Prison*, 31, 37.

58. Ibid., 19, 32; Knapp, *Life of Thomas Eddy*, 94; Hamm, *The Transformation of American Quakerism*, 2; Hamm, *The Quakers in America*, 30.

59. *JA*, 22nd Session (January 1799), 84–85; *JA*, 27th Session (February 1804), 87.

60. *JA*, 24th Session (January 1801), 66; *JA*, 25th Session (February 1802), 79; *JA*, 26th Session (February 1803), 97. For more on this broad-ranging effort, see Heale, "Humanitarianism in the Early Republic," 161–75.

61. T. Eddy, *Account of the State-Prison*, 38, 17.

62. *JA*, 22nd Session (January 1799), 83.

63. *JA*, 24th Session (January 1801), 66; *JA*, 25th Session (February 1802), 79.

64. *JA*, 22nd Session (January 1799), 84.

65. T. Eddy, *An Account of the State-Prison*, 62; *JA*, 24th Session (January 1801), 66; *JA*, 25th Session (February 1802), 80; Knapp, *The Life of Thomas Eddy*, 76.

66. *JA*, 22nd Session (January 1799), 85; *JA*, 25th Session (February 1802), 80; *JA*, 26th Session (February 1803), 97.

67. *JA*, 21st Session (January 1798), 84; *JA*, 24th Session (January 1801), 64; *JA*, 26th Session (February 1803), 97–98.

68. T. Eddy, *An Account of the State-Prison*, 5.

69. *JA*, 22nd Session (February 1799), 85; *JA*, 24th Session (January 1801), 66; *JA*, 25th Session (February 1802), 79; *JA*, 27th Session (February 1804), 87. The 1803 riot was also reported in the city papers. See *Weekly Museum* (New York), 9 April 1803.

70. Kass, *Politics in New York State*, 14, 21, 29. While some historians use the term Democratic-Republicans, scholars working on New York State refer to them as "Republicans." They then further distinguish these Republicans by noting whom they followed, usually Martin Van Buren or DeWitt Clinton. See Benson, *The Concept of Jacksonian Democracy*, 5, 9–10. For the impact of the 1800 election and growth of partisan politics in state governments, see McDonald, "Early National Politics and Power, 1800–1824," 10–11, 16.

71. Alvin Kass described this transition from active, bipartisan competition in late eighteenth-century New York State politics to the fierce partisanship exhibited by Federalists and various factions within the growing Republican Party (basically Jeffersonian Democratic-Republicans). See *Politics in New York State*, ix, 9, 14, 28–29. For more on how reformers confronted these political changes, see Heale, "From City Fathers to Social Critics," 26, 32–34.

72. *JA*, 26th Session (February 1803), 99; *JA*, 27th Session (February 1804), 87; *JA*, 28th Session (February 1805), 121. Historians have associated Eddy's resignation with the election of Republicans to the inspectors' board. See W. David Lewis, *From Newgate to Dannemora*, 34. Although Eddy had Federalist leanings, it seems that parts of the reforming community identified the board not politically as anti-Republican, but rather religiously as Quaker. As former New York assemblyman, senator, and New York City mayor, Cadwallader D. Colden, wrote in 1833, "The good order, comfort, cleanliness, industry, and devotion which prevailed, as long as the Friends had the management of

the [prison], were very remarkable." See Cadwallader D. Colden to Samuel L. Knapp, 23 June 1833, in Knapp, *The Life of Thomas Eddy*, 19.

73. Heale, "From City Fathers to Social Critics"; Sassi, *A Republic of Righteousness*, 185. Richard W. Pointer suggests that the problem of disestablishment, along with New York's diversity, allowed for unmatched religious-political partnerships. No group was strong enough to gain the powers formerly possible under establishment. See Pointer, *Protestant Pluralism and the New York Experience*, 139–40.

74. Many of the prison reformers expressed reservations about public assemblies. It makes their support for prisons—which were essentially assemblies of criminals—so strange. For more on the concern about the dangers of public crowds, see Frank, "Sympathy and Separation." Of course, the reformers thought the prisons, whether characterized by terror or nurture, served as a place to school the public that remained unregulated when in the public square. Eddy's optimism about the possibilities of escaping poverty reflects a broader mentality in the early republic. See J. M. Opal's biographical work *Beyond the Farm*, on rural Americans seeking greater self-fulfillment. See Marx, *The Machine in the Garden*, for a discussion of individuals who embraced both a pastoral ideal and technological possibility.

75. *JA*, 26th Session (February 1803), 98; T. Eddy, *An Account of the State Prison*, 32.

Chapter Two

1. *Sword of Justice*, 10, 4, 11.

2. Knapp, *The Life of Thomas Eddy*, 207.

3. Burrows and Wallace, *Gotham*, 349–52, 391–92, 401–6. For more on the question of afflictions experienced by veterans, see Resch's *Suffering Soldiers*. Students of prison history and the history of slavery have ample evidence of their braided development. It is no surprise, then, that the New York legislature took up discussion of penal reform and prison creation in the same year they countenanced the abolition of slavery. The year was 1796.

4. *JA*, 29th Session (January 1806), 136. Inmate statistics can be found in the inspectors' reports: see *JA*, 28th Session (November 1804), 122; *JA*, 29th Session (January 1806), 136; *JA*, 30th Session (January 1807), 89; *JA*, 31st Session (November 1808), 114; *JA*, 32nd Session (January 1809), 159; *JA*, 33rd Session (January 1810), 183–84; *JA*, 34th Session (January 1811), 105; *JA*, 35th Session (January 1812), 118; *JA*, 36th Session (November 1812), 237; *JA*, 38th Session (January 1815), 215; and *JA*, 39th Session (January 1816), 127. *JA*, 32nd Session (January 1809), 159. Similar to Newgate's earlier years, inmates were overwhelmingly convicted of property crimes. An analysis of the convictions of every prisoner held at Newgate between its opening in 1797 and 31 December 1814 found that less than 5 percent served time for violent crimes including manslaughter and assault and battery, whereas 92 percent had committed property crimes ranging from larceny and forgery to highway robbery and receiving stolen goods. See "A View of the New-York State Prison by a Member of the Institution," appendix p. 61. While the document is anonymous, Thomas Eddy likely wrote it. It repeats, nearly word for word, his 1801 *Account of the State-Prison*. Eddy was also a friend of Roscoe.

5. *Laws of the Legislature*, 16.

6. *JA*, 28th Session (November 1804), 123.

7. Deficits noted in *JA*, 28th Session (November 1804), 121; *JA*, 29th Session (January 1806), 134; *JA*, 30th Session (January 1807), 89; *JA*, 31st Session (November 1808), 113; *JA*, 32nd Session (January 1809), 159; *JA*, 33rd Session (January 1810), 189; *JA*, 34th Session (January 1811), 106; *JA*, 35th Session (January 1812), 119; *JA*, 36th Session (November 1812), 237; 38th Session (January 1815), 215; *JA*, 39th Session (January 1816), 125; and *JA*, 40th Session (November 1816), 284. *JA*, 37th Session (January 1814), 195–96.

8. *JA*, 28th Session (November 1804), 122.

9. *JA*, 37th Session (January 1814), 195, 197. See chapter 1 for Thomas Eddy's argument about pardons. In short, he claimed that pardons reduced an inmate's time in which to learn and master a skill to be used upon release.

10. *JA*, 33rd Session (January 1810), 183; *JA*, 35th Session (January 1812), 118; *JA*, 37th Session (January 1814), 197; *JA*, 38th Session (January 1815), 215.

11. *Rules and Regulations for the Internal Government of the New-York State Prison.*

12. *JA*, 34th Session (January 1811), 105; *Laws of the Legislature*, 17. Stanford noted the lackadaisical Sabbath schedule. See Stanford, "Report to the Prison Inspectors, 1822," in "State Prison Volume," John Stanford Papers.

13. *JA*, 28th Session (November 1804), 123; *JA*, 39th Session (January 1816), 123, 128.

14. At that time, six men—four Quakers, Jotham Post, and George Warner—served at least five-year terms. Between 1804 and 1816, however, change was frequent. Twenty-four men served thirty terms of two years or less on the board. Only five of those thirty inspectors held the post for five years or more. With regular turnover, the board lacked any semblance of continuity. Between 1811 and 1812, only two inspectors remained on the board from one year to the next. The transitions between 1813–14 and 1815–16 involved a total repopulation of the board.

15. *JA*, 37th Session (January 1814), 195; *JA*, 39th Session (January 1816), 123; *JA*, 32nd Session (January 1809), 161; *JA*, 34th Session (January 1811), 105; *Longworth's American Almanac, 1813*.

16. *JA*, 35th Session (January 1812), 119; *JA*, 38th Session (January 1815), 215; *JA*, 35th Session (January 1812), 118.

17. Stanford, "State Prison Volume"; Sommers, *Memoir of the Rev. John Stanford*, 113. Stanford interpreted physical suffering in Newgate through a religious lens. He was also, most certainly, affected by broader nineteenth-century claims about the natural and good aspects of pain as part of God's punishment for sin. See Pernick, *A Calculus of Suffering*. Pernick argues that the anesthesia debates reflected larger questions about individual circumstance and the rule of law that plagued other institutions trying to maintain social order (140). I agree, especially as prison reformers in later years considered the ethics of inflicting pain despite the environmental factors that contributed to criminality.

18. For more on the work of urban ministers, including Stanford, see Mohl. "The Urban Missionary Movement in New York City."

19. For an interesting reflection on mechanical metaphors among antebellum evangelicals, see Lardas Modern, "Evangelical Secularism," 816.

20. Bliss, *A Brief History of the American Tract Society*, 4; Sommers, *Memoir of the Rev. John Stanford*, 39, 43. Adult baptism notwithstanding, Particular Baptists affirmed

a confession with only a few changes to traditional Calvinism. They claimed that God elected the saved, making the atonement applicable only to the elect. Their counterparts, the General Baptists, took an Arminian position, claiming that Christ's atonement applied to all and that humans could act toward their salvation. While Particular Baptists were committed to election and predestination, many followed the lead of some Presbyterians and Congregationalists by moving toward a more evangelical Calvinism that chipped away at the doctrine of double predestination.

21. Stanford, *Directory on the Scriptures for Those under Confinement*, 8.

22. "The Philadelphia Confession of Faith," 64, 66.

23. Ibid., 78, 83.

24. Stanford's approach to the prisoner shares many aspects of Jonathan Edwards's ministry to native peoples in Massachusetts. See Wheeler, "Friends to Your Souls."

25. "The Philadelphia Confession of Faith," 86–87; "Covenant of First Baptist Church, Newport, Rhode Island," 196; "Covenant of Swansea Baptist Church, Rehoboth, Massachusetts," 194.

26. Stanford, "Sermon on Matthew 25:26," in "State Prison Volume"; Stanford, "Sermon on Psalm 79:11," in "State Prison Volume."

27. Sommers, *Memoir of the Rev. John Stanford*, 126, 178; Stanford, *The Prisoner's Companion*, 4.

28. Stanford, *The Prisoner's Companion*, 3; Stanford, "The State Prison of New York," in "State Prison Volume."

29. The nineteenth-century chaplaincy, though it functioned in many of the era's institutions, has received little attention from historians. For one work that lays out some of the basic issues and trends, see Budd, *Serving Two Masters*, chap. 1.

30. Stanford, *Directory on the Scriptures for Those under Confinement*, 5; Stanford, *A Catechism for the Improvement of Youth in the State Prison of New York*, 14; Stanford, "Sermon on Psalm 79:11."

31. Stanford, "Sermon on Psalm 79:11"; Stanford, *A Catechism for the Improvement of Youth in the State Prison of New York*, 11.

32. Stanford, *The Brand Plucked Out of the Fire*, 3; Hearn, *Legal Executions in New York State*, 36.

33. Stanford, *Discourse on the Death of an Unfortunate Youth*, 3–5.

34. Stanford, "State Prison Volume."

35. Stanford, *A Catechism for the Improvement of Youth in the State Prison of New York*, 16; Stanford, *The Prisoner's Companion*, 4–5.

36. Stanford, "Sermon on Genesis 39," in "State Prison Volume."

37. Sommers, *Memoir of the Rev. John Stanford*, 219, 227.

38. JA, 40th Session (November 1816), 8–9, 284.

39. JA, 39th Session (January 1816), 123, 128; *Laws of the Legislature*, 33.

40. JA, 40th Session (November 1816), 284; JA, 41st Session (January 1818), 278; JA, 47th Session (January 1824), 252.

41. Knapp, *The Life of Thomas Eddy*, 207, 215.

42. "To the Humane Society, the Committee Appointed to Produce Information on the Number of Licensed Taverns and Shops," John Jay Papers. The Humane Society was a benevolent organization focused on issues of urban poverty.

43. Knapp, *The Life of Thomas Eddy*, 244; "To the Humane Society."

44. Knapp, *The Life of Thomas Eddy*, 276.

45. Ibid., 244, 286.

46. Ibid., 275–77.

47. "Petition of the Rev. John Stanford, January 21, 1812," John Stanford Papers.

48. Interestingly, Stanford affirmed the state's recent decision to execute, rather than imprison for life, those guilty of arson. His support of a longer list of capital crimes can be easily explained. Stanford had a serious concern about prison arsonists, convicts damaging workshops, and endangering prison staff and residents in acts of defiance against the penal system. The state reinstated the death penalty for arsonists in its 1819 revamping of the penal code. Stanford affirmed the change. In his pamphlet, he described arson as a "diabolical act" and "worse than murder." Why? Because fire tended to spread beyond the intended target. Indeed, its "fatal consequences" extended to "persons unknown to the incendiary." Arsonists were a serious threat, particularly in the confined spaces of Newgate Prison. They disrupted workshops and threatened lives. Stanford believed that capital punishment provided an appropriate response to the crime's devastating potential. Stanford, *An Authentic Statement of the Case of Rose Butler*, 14–15.

49. Ibid., 6–8.

50. Ibid., 9–10.

51. Ibid., 10.

52. Ibid., 13.

53. "The Philadelphia Confession of Faith," 63.

54. McLennan, *The Crisis of Imprisonment*, 44.

55. Coffey, *Inside Out*, 51, 29.

56. Ibid., 236–38.

57. Ibid., 224, 230–31, 238.

58. Ibid., 224, 233, 220–21.

59. Ibid., 89, 50.

60. *Sword of Justice*, 3, 9, 4.

Chapter Three

1. PDSB, "Seventeenth Annual Report, Vol. 4, 1842," 115.

2. A. Eddy, *Black Jacob: A Monument of Grace*.

3. The issue of tension between officials and reformers, while important, does not get to another question, whether the partnership worked. It is very hard to tell from the surviving documents whether Powers and the Protestant reformers were able to put in place the system they desired in the mid-1820s.

4. Kurtz, *Auburn, N.Y.: Its Facilities and Resources*, 23. Kurtz referred to "Democratic" electoral victory in his 1884 history of Auburn. He did so because he identified the Jeffersonian Democratic-Republicans (often called Republicans in New York) with what eventually became a part of Jackson's Democratic Party, which competed with Henry Clay's Whigs.

5. Burrows and Wallace, *Gotham*, 478, 543–44.

6. Ibid., 546–47.

7. Ibid., 485, 532, 483, 486.

8. Kurtz, *Auburn, N.Y.: Its Facilities and Resources*, 43.

9. PDSB, "Second Annual Report, Vol. 1, 1827," 69, 100. Unlike Newgate, however, Auburn had no inmates from the West Indies at this time.

10. Ryan, *Cradle of the Middle Class*, chaps. 1 and 2; Johnson, *A Shopkeeper's Millennium*, 138.

11. PDSB, "Fourth Annual Report, Vol. 1, 1829," 320.

12. Thomas Eddy to Dewitt Clinton, 15 February 1817, microfilms vols. 7–10, reel 3, DeWitt Clinton Papers; Thomas Eddy, "Remarks on the Present State of Our Prisons," handwritten report to Dewitt Clinton, 17 November 1818, vol. 24, miscellaneous papers, reel 6, DeWitt Clinton Papers.

13. Knapp, *The Life of Thomas Eddy*, 275–77. Hopkins was a lawyer and represented New York in the U.S. Congress from 1813 to 1815. Tibbetts also served in Congress from 1803 to 1805. Just before joining the board of prison commissioners, he served in the New York State Senate. Allen was later elected mayor of New York.

14. W. David Lewis, *From Newgate to Dannemora*, 67; Kurtz, *Auburn, N.Y.: Its Facilities and Resources*, 44–45.

15. T. P., "Solitary Confinement," *United States Gazette*, 21 February 1829, 1; Kurtz, *Auburn, N.Y.: Its Facilities and Resources*, 44–45.

16. Society for the Prevention of Pauperism, *Report*, 19, 49–50, 67.

17. Ibid., 25, 45, 43.

18. Kurtz, *Auburn, N.Y.: Its Facilities and Resources*, 44.

19. W. David Lewis argued that Lynds resisted the presence of educational and religious services early on in his career at Auburn. While I certainly agree that Lynds eventually resisted such practices vehemently, I can find no evidence that he did so in the institution's earliest years. See Lewis, *From Newgate to Dannemora*, 101.

20. Ibid., 101; *JA*, 45th Session (January 1822), 220. Construction costs for institutions using the Pennsylvania discipline were higher because individual cells had to be larger. Inmates not only stayed in them twenty-four hours a day but also needed enough room to do some sort of manual labor. Eastern State Penitentiary in Philadelphia, which historians estimate to have been the most expensive building in America at the time of its construction, included fairly large individual cells with a separate, though small, outdoor recreation space.

21. Knapp, *The Life of Thomas Eddy*, 315.

22. *JA*, 48th Session (January 1825), 364; Kurtz, *Auburn, N.Y.: Its Facilities and Resources*, 44, 46.

23. Knapp, *The Life of Thomas Eddy*, 316–18.

24. Lynds was named the "late agent" as early as the January 1826 inspectors' report. See *JA*, 49th Session (January 1826), 429. Richard Goodell served as an interim agent until Powers was named in February. See *JA*, 50th Session (January 1827), 58.

25. Powers, *A Brief Account*, 34, 64.

26. Kurtz, *Auburn, N.Y.: Its Facilities and Resources*, 45–46.

27. Powers, *A Brief Account*, 33, 34, 4, 3.

28. Ibid., 18–19.

29. Ibid.

30. Ibid., 35; Knapp, *The Life of Thomas Eddy*, 94; Stanford, *Directory of the Scriptures for Those under Confinement*, 6.

31. Powers, *A Brief Account*, 19, 21.

32. Jenks, *A Memoir of the Rev. Louis Dwight*, 22.

33. North, *American Bible Society Historical Essay*, 121.

34. Laqueur, "Bodies, Details, and the Humanitarian Narrative," 177–78, 201; Jenks, *A Memoir of the Rev. Louis Dwight*, 23.

35. For an officer list, see PDSB, "First Annual Report, Vol. 1, 1826," 42. The list includes Andover professors, Rev. Leonard Woods and Rev. Ebenezer Porter; Williams's president, Rev. Edward D. Griffin; Amherst's president, Rev. Heman Humphrey; Brown's president, Rev. Justin Edwards; and American Board of Commissioners for Foreign Missions officers, Rev. B. B. Wisner and Rev. Rufus Anderson.

36. Dwight was a distant relation of Yale University's president, Timothy Dwight IV (1752–1817). Their common ancestor, Timothy Dwight (d. 1718), was Louis's great-great-grandfather and Timothy IV's great-grandfather. See Jenks, *A Memoir of the Rev. Louis Dwight*, 6–7.

37. Kling, "The New Divinity and the Origins of the American Board of Commissioners for Foreign Missions," 804, 802. The quotation comes from Leonard Woods, president of Andover Theological Seminary and later a board member of Dwight's prison society.

38. Sutton, "Benevolent Calvinism and the Moral Government of God," 24, 28, 26; Adamson, "Wrath and Redemption," 86–88. While Adamson gets much right about Dwight's evangelical Calvinism, his interpretation suffers from the strong connections he draws between Dwight and pro–capital punishment Calvinists. To be sure, Dwight supported capital punishment for murder. But he was not an active voice in the heated capital punishment debates of the 1840s. Similarly, the Calvinists who voiced strong opposition to reformers calling for capital punishment's abolition, particularly the Reverend George Cheever, did not play a part in prison reform. The prison reform Calvinists and Calvinists advocating capital punishment were two different groups. See Masur, *Rites of Execution*, and Mackey, *Hanging in the Balance*.

39. Kling, "The New Divinity," 803; Jenks, *A Memoir of the Rev. Louis Dwight*, 6.

40. Jenks, *A Memoir of the Rev. Louis Dwight*, 19; Minutes, Board of Managers, 4 November 1824, American Bible Society.

41. For more on Puritan understandings of the execution, see Boscoe, "Lectures at the Pillory."

42. Mary K. Cayton addresses the moderate Congregational and Presbyterian approach to reform and evangelization in "Social Reform through the Civil War." These efforts included the American Board of Commissioners for Foreign Missions, bible and tract societies, the American Sunday-School Union, and the American Education Society.

43. PDSB, "First Annual Report, Vol. 1, 1826," 39; Jenks, *A Memoir of the Rev. Louis Dwight*, 21.

44. Louis Dwight to John W. Taylor, published letter, 13 March 1826, Circular, New-York Historical Society Library.

45. PDSB, "First Annual Report, Vol. 1, 1826," 32–34; Gura, introduction, xxvi.

46. PDSB, "Second Annual Report, Vol. 1, 1827," 113, 118–19.

47. PDSB, "First Annual Report, Vol. 1, 1826," 32–33. Recall that the state prison in New York City housed serious offenders, the penitentiary (connected to the Almshouse) contained first-time and petty offenders, the bridewell functioned as a jail to hold vagrants and people awaiting trial, the debtor's jail held debtors, the hospital held those ill with both physical and mental ailments, and the almshouse held the perennially impoverished.

48. One might also ask why Dwight did not favor the emerging discipline in Philadelphia that relied on total solitary confinement. Some historians attribute this to Calvinist concerns about idleness or the financial cost. Both of these issues probably played a part. Dwight certainly acknowledged the latter. But in most of his public comments, he articulated the classic defense of New York proponents: the Philadelphia system was cruel because unceasing solitary confinement caused people to go mad.

49. Ibid., 37, 19, 18. While Dwight accepted the limited use of the lash, he understood it as acting in combination with other approaches to character formation. Literary historian Richard H. Brodhead has described these other methods as a kind of "disciplinary intimacy" or "discipline through love." For Brodhead, advocates of this nineteenth-century discipline opposed corporal punishment, modeled character formation, used training institutions, and supported a certain form of literacy. Above all, Brodhead argued, proponents of disciplinary intimacy abhorred slavery. Dwight provides a contrasting figure to the movement Brodhead illustrated. Dwight believed that the prison functioned to form character in the way Brodhead describes, except that he accepted some use of corporal punishment. This acceptance of the lash, however, did not equal his approval of slavery. Dwight witnessed the effects of the institution during his southern travels. While he was certainly no abolitionist, his PDSB reports contained many remarks on slavery's negative effects. If anything, he wanted lashing in the prisons to be used in a way that separated his institution from the unlimited cruelties visited on enslaved people. See Brodhead, *Cultures of Letters*, 15, 17–18.

50. For another reading of Horace Lane's life, this one concentrating on a range of life experiences and perceptions of masculinity in the early republic, see Glenn, "Troubled Manhood."

51. Lane, *Five Years in State's Prison*, 4, 11.

52. Ibid., 18.

53. Ibid., 1–15; Lane, *The Wandering Boy*, 191–92.

54. Lane, *The Wandering Boy*, 191–92; Fabian, *The Unvarnished Truth*, 54–56.

55. For biographical information on Curtis, see Gura, introduction, xxv–xxvi; Jared Curtis to M. A. Curtis, 11 November 1825, M. A. Curtis Papers.

56. PDSB, "Second Annual Report, Vol. 1, 1827," 91–92, 119.

57. Ibid., 91–92; J. Curtis to M. A. Curtis, 7 April 1826, M. A. Curtis Papers.

58. PDSB, "Second Annual Report, Vol. 1, 1827," 91–92; J. Curtis to M. A. Curtis, 21 November 1826, M. A. Curtis Papers; PDSB, "Second Annual Report, Vol. 1, 1827," 119.

59. Jared Curtis to M. A. Curtis, 11 November 1825. For Curtis's many references to revivals outside Auburn Prison, see letters from Jared Curtis to M. A. Curtis, 20 March 1826; 28 August 1826; 14 February 1827; and 21 March 1827, M. A. Curtis Papers.

60. Jared Curtis to M. A. Curtis, 14 June 1826; 7 April 1826; 1 November 1826; 23 September 1826, M. A. Curtis Papers.

61. T. Eddy, *Letters Addressed to the Commissioners*, 3, 19, 4.

62. Allen, *Remarks on the Stepping or Discipline Mill*, 15–16.

63. T. Eddy, *Communication to Stephen Allen*, 12, 4, 7.

64. Knapp, *The Life of Thomas Eddy*, 320.

65. Tooker, "Auburn State Prison," *Christian Advocate* 1:15 (16 December 1826): 57.

Chapter Four

1. Wiltse, "Report of the Agent of the Mount-Pleasant State Prison," 40–41. Sing Sing Prison was the frequently used name for the Mount Pleasant State Prison.

2. Rothman, "Perfecting the Prison," 107.

3. Burrows and Wallace, *Gotham*, 524. For discussion of these scholarly disagreements, see Lane, "Urban Police and Crime in Nineteenth-Century America." See also "Increase in Crime," *New York Evangelist* 2:42 (14 January 1832): 376.

4. Gilfoyle, *City of Eros*, 29; Cohen, *The Murder of Helen Jewett*, 64–68, 171–72, 195–99.

5. Burrows and Wallace, *Gotham*, 543.

6. On police reforms made in direct response to a growing urban underclass, see Johnson, *Policing the Urban Underworld*, 3–11. On New York criminal networks, see Gilfoyle, *A Pickpocket's Tale*, xiii. For more on the way Irish immigrants fell outside this category for full citizenship in the early republic, see Jacobsen, *Whiteness of a Different Color*, 1–38.

7. Beaumont and Tocqueville, *On the Penitentiary System*, 65; Smith, "Detention without Subjects."

8. Rothman, "Prisons and Penitentiaries," 621.

9. Rothman, "Perfecting the Prison," 106–7; Meranze, "A Criminal Is Being Beaten," 320.

10. PDSB, "First Annual Report, Vol. 1, 1826," 17, 36.

11. "Gerrish Barrett."

12. W. David Lewis, *From Newgate to Dannemora*, 139–40.

13. Ibid., 142–44; Dix, *Remarks on Prisons and Prison Discipline*, 16.

14. See chapters 1 and 2.

15. Clark, "The Sacred Rights of the Weak," 473.

16. For a concise survey of the religious elements of abolitionism, see Brown, "Abolition of Slavery." For the arguments about innocence in particular, see Clark, "Sacred Rights of the Weak," and Morone, *Hellfire Nation*.

17. Glenn, *Campaigns against Corporal Punishment*, 60; Morone, *Hellfire Nation*, 16–17.

18. PDSB, "Second Annual Report, Vol. 1, 1827," 115; PDSB, "Third Annual Report, Vol. 1, 1828," 162, 211.

19. PDSB, "Fourth Annual Report, Vol. 1, 1829," 258–59. For more on the singularity of Psalm 88, see Brueggemann, *The Psalms and the Life of Faith*, 13.

20. PDSB, "Fourth Annual Report, Vol. 1, 1829," 258–59.

21. Ibid., 258–59; Barrett, "Prison Discipline," *Boston Recorder and Religious Telegraph* 13:33 (15 August 1828): 129.

22. Beaumont and Tocqueville, *On the Penitentiary System*, 162–63.

23. Burr, *A Voice from Sing Sing*; Lane, *Five Years in State's Prison*; Brice, *Secrets of the Mount Pleasant State Prison*. Another narrative appeared in the 1830s, although it focused on Auburn rather than Sing Sing. The book, *A Peep into the State Prison at Auburn*, will be discussed later in the chapter. For more on the widespread use of physically detailed humanitarian narratives, see Halttunen, "Humanitarianism and the Pornography of Pain."

24. Burr, *A Voice from Sing-Sing*, preface, 17, 18, 23, 29, 20, 16.

25. Ibid., 15, 4; Fabien, *The Unvarnished Truth*, 64.

26. Lane, *Five Years in State's Prison*, 16, 12, 9.

27. Brice, *Secrets of the Mount-Pleasant State Prison*, 55, 60, 52, 69, 70.

28. PDSB, "Fifth Annual Report, Vol. 1, 1830," 340–42.

29. Ibid., 346–47.

30. W. David Lewis, *From Newgate to Dannemora*, 148.

31. PDSB, "Fifth Annual Report, Vol. 1, 1830," 341–43, 340, 347; PDSB, "Sixth Annual Report, Vol. 2, 1831," 483–84.

32. PDSB, "Fifth Annual Report, Vol. 1, 1830," 345.

33. For more on Lynds's refusal to comment, see Congressman Hopkins' report. PDSB, "Fifth Report, Vol. 1, 1830," 340–41.

34. Burr, *A Voice from Sing-Sing*, 14.

35. Lane, *Five Years in State's Prison*, 19–20.

36. Brice, *Secrets of the Mount-Pleasant State Prison*, 10, 12.

37. Ibid., 72.

38. W. David Lewis, *From Newgate to Dannemora*, 149–55.

39. Pierson, *Tocqueville in America*, 93–119, 206–13, 457–73.

40. Ibid., 706–9, 212–13.

41. Beaumont and Tocqueville, *On the Penitentiary System*, 88–89.

42. Ibid., 79; McLennan, *The Crisis of Imprisonment*, 81.

43. Beaumont and Tocqueville, *On the Penitentiary System*, 49, 82; Pierson, *Tocqueville in America*, 707.

44. Louis Dwight reprinted Hopkins's report. See PDSB, "Eighth Annual Report, Vol. 2, 1833," 680–81.

45. *DS*, 57th Session, vol. 1 (1834), 39, 43–44.

46. Ibid., 39–40, 42.

47. Ibid., 38.

48. Dickerson's choice to be a prison chaplain seems somewhat strange. What does make sense is that he took the job right out of seminary, kept it a short time, and then moved on to a church post. This pattern continues in hiring over the next several years. It might be that prison work offered decent work for young men recently trained who had not been called to parish ministry. "Jonathan Dickerson," in Hopper, *Biographical Catalogue of Princeton Theological Seminary*. For more on Hodge and the Princeton theologians, see Holifield, "'True Calvinism' Defended," in *Theology in America*, chap. 18.

49. *DS*, 54th Session, vol. 1 (1831), 11, 10.

50. PDSB, "Eighth Annual Report, Vol. 2, 1833, 686 87; DS, 56th Session, vol. 1, no. 27 (1833), 24.

51. *General Biographical Catalogue of Auburn Theological Seminary*; DS, 56th Session, vol. 1, no. 20 (January 1833), 168.

52. DS, 55th Session, vol. 1, no. 31 (January 1832), 8; DS, 56th Session, vol. 1, no. 20 (January 1833), 16; DS, 58th Session, vol. 1, no. 13 (December 1834), 16.

53. PDSB, "Sixth Annual Report, Vol. 2, 1831," 561–62; PDSB, "Eighth Annual Report, Vol. 2, 1833," 685; PDSB, "Tenth Annual Report, Vol. 2, 1835," 878; PDSB, "Fifth Annual Report, Vol. 1, 1830," 348–49. Smith published many such articles, for example, "Prison Discipline Society," *Christian Secretary* 9:49 (25 December 1830): 194; and "Conditions of the Prison at Auburn, NY," *Christian Register* 9:51 (18 December 1830): 204.

54. Smith's last salary is noted in PDSB, "Twelfth Annual Report, Vol. 3, 1837," 166. He is no longer listed in the treasurer's report in the 1838; see PDSB, "Thirteenth Annual Report, Vol. 3, 1838," 288. PDSB, "Thirteenth Annual Report, Vol. 3, 1838," 229, 296.

55. DS, 62nd Session, vol. 1, no. 11 (January 1838), 13–14, 16; DA, 63rd Session, vol. 1, no. 18 (1840), 13–14. 1840 is Smith's last report to the legislature.

56. *A Peep into the State Prison at Auburn*, 6, 27, 30, 41, 33, 48, 50, 12.

57. Ibid., 33, 26.

58. Ibid., 53–54, 63–65.

59. Ibid., 65, 74, 34.

60. Jonathan Dickerson, "Chaplain's Report," in DS, 54th Session (1831), 10–11.

61. PDSB, "Fourteenth Annual Report, Vol. 3, 1839," 339.

62. Ibid., 340–42.

63. Ibid., 343.

64. Ibid., 339.

65. James D. Bratt has argued that 1835 marked a major change in Protestant evangelicalism. He identifies cultural changes that demanded a move away from the revivals and reforms of the prior century and new formulations of piety that emphasized anything from sacred space, to ritual, to separation, and holiness. If we apply Bratt's argument to the prison reformers, their resistance to adapting their claims to a changing environment—especially around 1835—makes sense of their continued public losses. It also allows us to see how those willing to adapt toward a religiosity of citizenship continued to have a public voice, even if it was one they were not entirely comfortable with. See Bratt, "The Reorientation of American Protestantism."

66. "Gerrish Barrett"; Barrett, *The Boy in Prison*, 4–10, 12.

Chapter Five

1. Luckey, *Life in Sing Sing State Prison*, 160–63; W. David Lewis, *From Newgate to Dannemora*, 216–18.

2. The New York Prison Association was also sometimes called the Prison Association of New York. Historical records for the group can be found under both names.

3. W. David Lewis, *From Newgate to Dannemora*, 210; Luckey, *Life in Sing Sing State Prison*, 172–89, 236, 256–72; DS, 65th Session, vol. 2, no. 39 (1842), 25–27; DA, 64th Session, vol. 2, no. 42 (1841), 19.

4. Luckey, *Life in Sing Sing State Prison*, 172–89, 236, 256–72; *DS*, 65th Session, vol. 2, no. 39 (1842), 25–27; *DA*, 64th Session, vol. 2, no. 42 (1841), 19.

5. *American National Biography*, s.v. "William Seward"; Howe, *What Hath God Wrought*, 578–79.

6. Burrows and Wallace, *Gotham*, 619–23, 631–33, 737.

7. Ibid., 635; Kuntz, *Criminal Sentencing in Three Nineteenth-Century Cities*, 155; The Clinton facility, called Dannemora, was authorized in 1844. See W. David Lewis, *From Newgate to Dannemora*, 199–200.

8. Luckey, *Life in Sing Sing State Prison*, 110–12, 117.

9. Ibid., 172–89, 236, 256–72; *DS*, 65th Session, vol. 2, no. 39 (1842), 25–27; *DA*, 64th Session, vol. 2, no. 42 (1841), 19.

10. For an example of this treatment of Luckey, see Adamson, "Wrath and Redemption." For alternative approaches, see Wilentz, *Chants Democratic*, 80, and Howe, *What Hath God Wrought*, 179.

11. *The Doctrines and Discipline of the Methodist Episcopal Church*, 79, 13, 80.

12. Wigger, *Taking Heaven by Storm*, 87, 82, 84; *The Doctrines and Discipline of the Methodist Episcopal Church*, 78–79, 93.

13. Wigger, *Taking Heaven by Storm*, 102.

14. Luckey, *Life in Sing Sing State Prison*, 340–43.

15. "Who, on Earth, Should Despair?" *New York Evangelist* 11:46 (14 November 1840): 183; "Prison Discipline Society," *Boston Recorder* 27:6 (11 February 1842): 24; "Visit to Sing Sing Prison," *New York Evangelist* 13:37 (15 September 1842): 1.

16. PDSB, "Sixteenth Annual Report, Vol. 4, 1841," 33, 37–38.

17. Ibid., 39.

18. Ibid., 42–44.

19. Dwight's accolades can be found in PDSB, "Fifth Annual Report, Vol. 1, 1830," 5; PDSB, "Sixth Annual Report, Vol. 2, 1831," 23–24, 45–50; PDSB, "Seventh Annual Report, Vol. 2, 1832," 10, 62; PDSB, "Ninth Annual Report, Vol. 2, 1834," 48, 62–63. His criticisms can be found in PDSB, "Sixth Annual Report, Vol. 2, 1831," 80; PDSB, "Ninth Annual Report, Vol. 2, 1834," 67, 69; PDSB, "Thirteenth Annual Report, Vol. 3, 1838," 58; PDSB, "Fifteenth Annual Report, Vol. 3, 1840," 37.

20. W. David Lewis, *From Newgate to Dannemora*, 215–26; Luckey, *Life in Sing Sing State Prison*, 31; Mount Pleasant State Prison, "Inspectors' Report," quoted in Luckey, *Life in Sing Sing State Prison*, 30.

21. Luckey, *Life in Sing Sing State Prison*, 158, 181, 159–60.

22. PDSB, "Eighteenth Annual Report, Vol. 4, 1843," 260.

23. Luckey, *Life in Sing Sing State Prison*, 160–61, 32, 34; W. David Lewis, *From Newgate to Dannemora*, 216–19.

24. Heale, "The Formative Years of the New York Prison Association," 320–47.

25. NYPA, *First Report of the Prison Association of New-York*, 15–16; NYPA, *Third Report of the Prison Association of New-York*, 62.

26. NYPA, *First Report of the Prison Association of New-York*, 3, 6–7; Heale, "The Formative Years of the New York Prison Association," 339. Besides Edmonds, the early membership included financial expert Johann Tellkampf; lawyers William C. Russell, James Topham Brady, Pierre P. Irving, and Theodore Sedgewick (of *Amistad* fame); and

judges Charles Patrick Daly and Benjamin F. Butler. For information on the varying political and religious affiliations of NYPA members, see Heale, 321–31.

27. NYPA, *Second Report of the Prison Association of New-York*, 103–5.

28. NYPA, *Ninth Report of the Prison Association of New-York*, 52–53; NYPA, *First Report of the Prison Association of New-York*, 6.

29. NYPA, *Second Report of the Prison Association of New-York*, *103*; NYPA, *First Report of the Prison Association of New-York*, *58*.

30. NYPA, *Fifth Report of the Prison Association of New-York*, 144; NYPA, *Third Report of the Prison Association of New-York*, 34–35.

31. Floyd, "Dislocations of the Self," 311–25.

32. W. David Lewis, *From Newgate to Dannemora*, 242–45.

33. NYPA "Report of the Prison Discipline Committee," in *Third Report of the Prison Association of New-York*, 55–56, 51–52.

34. W. David Lewis, *From Newgate to Dannemora*, 245; "Mr. Luckey and the Sing Sing Prison," *New York Observer and Chronicle* 24:42 (17 October 1846): 166. The NYPA chronicled the Luckey-Farnham dispute in its annual reports. See NYPA, *Third Report of the Prison Association of New-York*, 49–50, 63–64.

35. NYPA, *Ninth Report of the Prison Association of New-York*, 45.

36. NYPA, *Third Report of the Prison Association of New-York*, 34.

37. NYPA, "Report of the Executive Committee," in *Fourth Report of the Prison Association of New-York*, 15; NYPA, "Report on Auburn Prison," in *Fourth Report of the Prison Association of New-York*, no page number available.

38. NYPA, *Fifth Report of the Prison Association of New-York*, 11.

39. A second trial that occurred soon after also dealt with moral insanity. For more on the case of William Freeman, see Arpey, *The William Freeman Murder Trial*.

40. *Report of the Trial of Henry Wyatt*, 11, 17, 23.

41. Ibid., 23.

42. Ibid., 27–28.

43. Ibid., 20; *DS*, 67th Session, vol. 1, no. 18 (1844), 88, 86; Morrill, "Green, the Reformed Gambler, at Auburn," *Prisoner's Friend* 1:5 (30 April 1845): 20.

44. "The Tragedies in Auburn, New-York," *Prisoner's Friend* 1:35 (2 September 1846): 137; Morrill, "Wyatt the Murderer," *Evangelical Magazine and Gospel Advocate* 16:33 (15 August 1845): 260. Morrill published similar defenses in the *Christian Advocate and Journal, Auburn Journal, Prisoner's Friend*, and *Cayuga Patriot*.

45. New York switched to two-year gubernatorial terms in 1821.

46. PDSB, "Twenty-seventh Annual Report, Vol. 6, 1852," 715–18.

47. Ibid., 718–19. W. David Lewis notes that the shower bath had been used earlier in the prisons. The difference was in its more mild application that reflected the popularity of water cures in the antebellum period. Lewis identifies the aggravated application of the shower bath after 1847. See Lewis, *From Newgate to Dannemora*, 269–72.

48. PDSB, "Twenty-first Annual Report, Vol. 5, 1846," 21–24, 17.

49. Ibid., 17.

50. W. David Lewis, *From Newgate to Dannemora*, 230.

51. NYPA, *Tenth Annual Report of the Prison Association of New-York*, 125; PDSB, "Sixteenth Annual Report, Vol. 4, 1841," 4; Luckey, *Life in Sing Sing State Prison*, 305.

52. Lardas Modern, "Ghosts of Sing Sing," 634, 643.

53. "The Office of Prison Chaplain, or Moral Instructor," *Pennsylvania Journal of Prison Discipline and Philanthropy* 3:1 (April 1847): 9.

Chapter Six

1. Bacon, *Lamb's Warrior*, 154–55. Given Quakers' long history of political advocacy, this story is somewhat surprising. As this chapter details, however, Hopper had similar experiences with state officials and legal reformers throughout his career.

2. Adamson, "Evangelical Quakerism," 51; NYPA, *Sixth Report of the Prison Association of New-York*, 49.

3. Indeed, New York led the young nation in prison inmate population. In 1850, for instance, New York incarcerated more than 1,100 people, a statistic that does not include the new penitentiary in Albany. Pennsylvania, on the other hand, had fewer than 400 state inmates and Massachusetts fewer than 300. See PDSB, "Twenty-fifth Annual Report, Vol. 6, 1850," 486.

4. Burrows and Wallace, *Gotham*, 736–37.

5. Ibid., 747–48, 754.

6. Ibid., 776, 778–80, 782–83; Gilfoyle, "Street-Rats and Gutter-Snipes," 855.

7. Burrows and Wallace, *Gotham*, 739, 756–57.

8. For statistics on the New York's prison population in the 1790s, see chapter 1. For statistics from this later period, see "Comparative View of the Statistics of Different Prisons," in NYPA, *Seventh Report of the Prison Association*.

9. W. David Lewis, *From Newgate to Dannemora*, 272; PDSB, "Twenty-second Annual Report, Vol. 5, 1847," 63; NYPA, *Third Report of the Prison Association of New York*, 45; NYPA, *Fifth Report of the Prison Association of New-York*, 133.

10. W. David Lewis, *From Newgate to Dannemora*, 268–69; "Torture and Homicide in an American Prison," *Harper's Weekly*, 18 December 1858, 808–9.

11. David, *Sing Sing Prison, Ossining, New York*; Herre, "The History of Auburn Prison." Elections prompted prison administrative changes at Auburn and Sing Sing in 1848, 1849, 1850, 1851, 1855, and 1856. When an inspectors' board at each prison was replaced with one committee serving the entire state in 1846, officials hoped that the transition might establish continuity. But these officials, too, were elected. With such quick turnover, even officials supportive of reforms often found themselves out of office before they could make a difference.

12. W. David Lewis, *From Newgate to Dannemora*, 263, 267. For a thorough study of the dynamics of prison labor in this period, see McClennan, *The Crisis of Imprisonment*, chap 2.

13. See chapter 1 for the Quaker backdrop to prison reform and the advent of the overseer. For a full biography of Hopper, see Bacon, *Lamb's Warrior*.

14. Meaders, *Kidnappers in Philadelphia*.

15. NYPA, *First Report of the Prison Association of New York*, 58–59.

16. Ibid., 15–16; NYPA, *Fourth Report of the Prison Association of New-York*, 171–72.

17. Isaac T. Hopper Journal, vol. 1, 27, 77, Prison Association of New York Records; NYPA, *Third Report of the Prison Association of New-York*, 89, 66. Much of Hopper's

correspondence was lost when his house was burned down during the New York draft riots.

18. Isaac T. Hopper Journal, vol. 2, 8–13, Prison Association of New York Records.

19. Ibid., 88–91, 113, 135, 154, 181.

20. NYPA, *Sixth Report of the Prison Association of New-York*, 48.

21. "Minutes of the Executive Committee of the New York Prison Association," 13 February 1852, box 5, Isaac Hopper folder, Women's Prison Association Records.

22. NYPA, *Fifth Report of the Prison Association of New-York*, 11, 14, 21.

23. Hopper's visit is recorded in a letter to his wife. See Isaac T. Hopper to Sarah H. Palmer, 27 June 1849, Sarah Hopper Palmer Family Papers.

24. Edwin C. Smith to Isaac T. Hopper, 31 January 1849, Sarah Hopper Palmer Family Papers.

25. Isaac T. Hopper to John Young, 2 February 1847, Sarah Hopper Palmer Family Papers.

26. Isaac T. Hopper to Sarah H. Palmer, 20 August 1857; Isaac T. Hopper to Sarah H. Palmer, 7 September 1847, handwritten letter, Sarah Hopper Palmer Family Papers.

27. Isaac T. Hopper Journal, vol. 2, 237, 240, 264.

28. Hopper, "Statement on the Requirements of Duty," Isaac T. Hopper Papers.

29. Luckey, *Prison Sketches*, 104. Luckey's words that the prison ought to be avoided echo Thomas Eddy's claims once the Quakers lost control of Newgate Prison in 1803. Before their removal, Eddy claimed that prison was just what any disorganized and problematic citizen needed. But as the institution came under state control, Eddy and later Luckey hoped to keep people out. See chapter 2 for Eddy's work with the Humane Society of the City of New York to keep people out of prison.

30. Luckey, *Prison Sketches*, 19, 29, 66, 70, 96.

31. *The Doctrines and Discipline of the Methodist Episcopal Church*, 79–83.

32. W. David Lewis, *From Newgate to Dannemora*, 273.

33. Ibid., 273–75.

34. "Homicide and Torture in an American Prison," *Harper's Weekly*, 18 December 1858, 808.

35. Pierce, *Hell without Fires*, introduction.

36. Luckey, *Life in Sing Sing State Prison*, 79, 91, 105–6, 161, 165.

37. Ibid., 41, 48, iv.

38. Ibid., 40.

39. Ibid., 346.

40. PDSB, "Twenty-fifth Annual Report, Vol. 6, 1850," 508; PDSB, "Twenty-seventh Annual Report, Vol. 6, 1952," 714–15.

41. *New York Evangelist* 22:31 (31 July 1851); *New York Evangelist*, 26:48 (29 November 1855).

42. Stout, *Upon the Altar of the Nation*.

43. Kann, *Punishment, Prisons, and Patriarchy*, 1–3; Meranze, *Laboratories of Virtue*, 4.

44. Laqueur, "Bodies, Details, and the Humanitarian Narrative," 201–4.

45. Pierson, *Tocqueville in America*, 107.

46. "Rev. John Luckey."

1. Adam Liptak, "Inmate Count in U.S. Dwarfs Other Nations,'" *New York Times*, 23 April 2008; K. Lofton, "The Question: What Good Is Prison," *Guardian*, ⟨http://www .guardian.co.uk/commentisfree/belief/2008/nov/19/justice-usa-prisons⟩.

2. Rotman, "The Failure of Reform," 152–53. For more on the particular developments in New York, see McClennan, *The Crisis of Imprisonment*, chaps. 3, 4, and 10.

3. Rotman, "The Failure of Reform," 155–60, 168–72.

4. Ibid., 164–65.

5. The Canadian Association of Elizabeth Fry Societies is one example of a decarceration movement that invokes historic Quaker involvement with prisons, in this case the British Friend and reformer, Elizabeth Fry. For more on restorative justice, see Zehr, *Changing Lens*. For the rise in Muslim converts in prison, see Lisa Miller, "Inside the Competitive World of Prison Ministries," *Wall Street Journal*, 7 September 1999, and Dannin, "Island in a Sea of Ignorance." It is important to note that this growth has been primarily among male inmates. See Dix-Richardson, "Resistance to Conversion to Islam among African American Women Inmates."

6. Whitman, *Harsh Justice*, 19, 9.

7. Fessenden, *Culture and Redemption*, 61.

8. Ibid., 3.

Bibliography

Manuscript Sources and Collections

Chapel Hill, North Carolina
    Southern Historical Collection, Wilson Library, University of North Carolina
        at Chapel Hill
        M. A. Curtis Papers (#199)
New York, New York
    Library and Archives, American Bible Society
        Minutes, Board of Managers, American Bible Society
    Manuscript Department, New-York Historical Society Library
        Louis Dwight to Honorable Mr. Taylor, Washington, D.C., 13 March 1826,
            published letter
        John Jay Papers
        John Stanford Papers (BV Stanford, John)
    Manuscripts and Archives Division, Astor, Lenox and Tilden Foundations,
        New York Public Library
        Philip Schuyler Papers
        Prison Association of New York Records
        Women's Prison Association Records
    Rare Book and Manuscript Library, Columbia University
        DeWitt Clinton Papers
Swarthmore, Pennsylvania
    Friends Historical Library, Swarthmore College
        Isaac T. Hopper Papers, 1833–1902 (SC/058)
        Sarah Hopper Palmer Family Papers, 1705–1883 (RG5/115)

Government Documents

Documents of the Assembly of the State of New York. Albany, N.Y.: E. Croswell,
    1830–48.
Documents of the Senate of the State of New York. Albany, N.Y.: E. Croswell, 1831–48.
Journal of the Assembly of the State of New York. Albany: n.p., 1798–1828.
Journal of the Senate of the State of New York. Albany: n.p., 1823–29.

Laws of the Legislature of the State of New-York for the Government of the New-York State Prison. New York: Broderick and Ritter, 1819.

Rules and Regulations for the Internal Government of the New-York State Prison. New York: n.p., 23 February 1804.

Newspaper and Periodical Sources

Boston Recorder and Religious Telegraph (also called *Boston Recorder*)
Christian Advocate (also called *Christian Advocate and Journal*)
Christian Register
Christian Secretary
Evangelical Magazine and Gospel Advocate
Guardian
Harper's Weekly
New York Evangelist
New York Observer and Chronicle
New York Sun
New York Times
Pennsylvania Journal of Prison Discipline and Philanthropy
Prisoner's Friend
United States Gazette
Wall Street Journal
Weekly Museum

Published Primary Sources

Abstracts of the Records of the Monthly Meetings of New York Yearly Meeting. Vol. 15, Quaker Records: Monthly Meeting of New York (Pre-Separation). Swarthmore, Pa.: Friends Historical Library, 2003.

Abstracts of the Records of the Monthly Meetings of New York Yearly Meeting. Vol. 20, Quaker Records: New York Monthly Meeting (Hicksite). Swarthmore, Pa.: Friends Historical Library, 2003.

Allen, Stephen. *Remarks on the Stepping or Discipline Mill at the New-York Penitentiary.* New York: Van Pelt and Spear, 1823.

Barrett, Gerrish. *The Boy in Prison.* Philadelphia: American Sunday-School Union, 1839.

Beaumont, Gustave de, and Alexis de Tocqueville. *On the Penitentiary System in the United States and Its Application in France.* Philadelphia: Carey, Lea & Blanchard, 1833. Reprint, Carbondale: Southern Illinois University Press, 1964.

Bliss, Seth. *A Brief History of the American Tract Society, Instituted at Boston, 1814, and Its Relations to the American Tract Society at New York, Instituted in 1825.* Boston: T. R. Marvin, 1857.

Brice, James R. *Secrets of the Mount-Pleasant State Prison, Revealed and Exposed.* N.p., 1839.

Burr, Levi S. *A Voice from Sing-Sing. Giving a General Description of the State Prison. A Short and Comprehensive Geological History of the Quality of the Stone of the Quarries; and a Synopsis of the Horrid Treatment of the Convicts in that Prison.* Albany: n.p., 1833.

Butterfield, L. H., ed. *Letters of Benjamin Rush.* Vol. 2. Philadelphia: American Philosophical Society, 1951.

Coffey, W. A. *Inside Out; or, An Interior View of the New-York State Prison; Together with Biographical Sketches of the Lives of Several of the Convicts.* New York: James Costigan, 1823.

"Covenant of First Baptist Church, Newport, Rhode Island." In *Baptist Confessions, Covenants, and Catechisms,* edited by Timothy George and Denise George, 195–98. Nashville, Tenn.: Broadman & Holman Publishers, 1996.

"Covenant of Swansea Baptist Church, Rehoboth, Massachusetts." In *Baptist Confessions, Covenants, and Catechisms,* edited by Timothy George and Denise George, 193–94. Nashville, Tenn.: Broadman & Holman Publishers, 1996.

Discipline of the Yearly Meeting of Friends, Held in New-York, and Parts Adjacent, as Revised and Adopted, in the Sixth Month, 1810. New York: Mahlon Day, 1836.

Dix, Dorothea. *Remarks on Prisons and Prison Discipline in the United States.* Philadelphia: Joseph Kite & Co., 1845.

The Doctrines and Discipline of the Methodist Episcopal Church. New York: T. Mason and G. Lane, 1840.

Eddy, Ansel D. *Black Jacob: A Monument of Grace; The Life of Jacob Hodges, an African Negro Who Died at Canandaigua, N.Y., February 1842.* Philadelphia: American Sunday-School Union, 1842.

Eddy, Thomas. *An Account of the State-Prison or Penitentiary House in the City of New York by One of the Inspectors of the Prison.* New York: Isaac Collins, 1801.

———. *Communication to Stephen Allen, Esquire and Mayor of the City of New-York, from Thomas Eddy.* New York: P. & H. Van Pelt, 1823.

———. *Letters Addressed to the Commissioners Appointed by the Legislature of New York to Examine and Report on Certain Questions Relating to the State Prison.* New York: Mahlon Day, 1825.

———. *To the Senate of the State of New-York. The Memorial of the Subscribers Respectfully Sheweth, That Your Memorialists Were Appointed by the Inspectors of the State Prison.* Broadside. Albany, N.Y.: n.p., 1801.

General Biographical Catalogue of Auburn Theological Seminary. Auburn, N.Y.: Auburn Seminary Press, 1918.

"Gerrish Barrett." In *Genealogy—Descendants of Thomas Barrett, Senior,* edited by William Barrett. Saint Paul, Minn.: D. Ramaley & Son, 1888.

"Homicide and Torture in an American Prison." *Harper's Weekly,* 18 December 1858, 808–10.

Hopper, Orien Cornelius. *Biographical Catalogue of Princeton Theological Seminary, 1815–1954: Biographies, 1865–1954.* Princeton, N.J.: Theological Seminary of the Presbyterian Church, 1955.

Jenks, William. *A Memoir of the Rev. Louis Dwight, Late Secretary of the Boston Prison Discipline Society, Prepared at the Request of the Society.* Boston: T. R. Marvin, 1856.

Knapp, Samuel L. *The Life of Thomas Eddy; Comprising an Extensive Correspondence with Many of the Most Distinguished Philosophers and Philanthropists of This and Other Countries*. New York: Conner & Cooke, 1834. Reprint, New York: Arno Press, 1976.

Kurtz, D. Morris. *Auburn, N.Y.: Its Facilities and Resources*. Auburn, N.Y.: Kurtz Publishing Co., 1884.

Lane, Horace. *Five Years in State's Prison; or, Interesting Truths, Showing the Manner of Discipline in the State Prison at Sing Sing and Auburn, Exhibiting the Great Contrast between the Two Institutions, in the Treatment of the Unhappy Inmates; Represented in a Dialogue between Sing Sing and Auburn*. New York: Luther Pratt & Sons, 1835.

———. *The Wandering Boy, Careless Sailor, and Result of Inconsideration: A True Narrative*. Skaneateles, N.Y.: L. A. Pratt, 1839.

Longworth's American Almanac, New-York Register, and City Directory, for the Thirty-eighth Year of American Independence. New York: D. Longworth, 1813.

Longworth's American Almanac, New-York Register, and City Directory, for the Twenty-ninth Year of American Independence. New York: D. Longworth, 1804.

Luckey, John. *Life in Sing Sing State Prison, as Seen in a Twelve Years' Chaplaincy*. New York: N. Tibbals & Co., 1860.

———. *Prison Sketches*. New York: Carlton & Phillips, 1853.

New York Prison Association. *First Report of the Prison Association of New-York*. New York: The Association, 1845.

———. *Second Report of the Prison Association of New-York*. New York: Doggett's, 1846.

———. *Third Report of the Prison Association of New-York*. New York: Burns & Baner, 1847.

———. *Fourth Report of the Prison Association of New-York*. Albany, N.Y.: Weed, Parsons, & Co., 1849.

———. *Fifth Report of the Prison Association of New-York*. Albany, N.Y.: Weed, Parsons, & Co., 1850.

———. *Sixth Report of the Prison Association of New-York*. Albany: Van Benthuysen, 1851.

———. *Seventh Report of the Prison Association of New-York*. Albany: Van Benthuysen, 1852.

———. *Eighth Annual Report of the New-York Prison Association*. Albany, N.Y.: Van Benthuysen, 1853.

———. *Ninth Report of the Prison Association of New-York*. Albany: Van Benthuysen, 1854.

———. *Tenth Report of the Prison Association of New-York*. Albany: Van Benthuysen, 1855.

———. *A Peep into the State Prison at Auburn, NY, with an Appendix, by One Who Knows*. Auburn, N.Y.: n.p., 1839.

"The Philadelphia Confession of Faith." In *Baptist Confessions, Covenants, and Catechisms*, edited by Timothy George and Denise George, 56–93. Nashville, Tenn.: Broadman & Holman, 1996.

Powers, Gershom. *A Brief Account of the Construction, Management, and Discipline of the New-York State Prison at Auburn, Together with a Compendium on Criminal*

Law. Also a Report of the Trial of an Officer of Said Prison for Whipping a Convict. Auburn, N.Y.: U. F. Doubleday, 1826.

Prison Association of New York. See New York Prison Association

Prison Discipline Society of Boston. *Reports of the Prison Discipline Society of Boston, the Twenty-nine Annual Reports of the Board of Managers, 1826–1854, with a Memoir of Louis Dwight*. Vol. 1. Boston: Perkins and Marvin, 1855. Reprint, Montclair, N.J.: Patterson Smith, 1972.

———. *Reports of the Prison Discipline Society of Boston, the Twenty-nine Annual Reports of the Board of Managers, 1826–1854, with a Memoir of Louis Dwight*. Vol. 2. Boston: Perkins and Marvin, 1855. Reprint, Montclair, N.J.: Patterson Smith, 1972.

———. *Reports of the Prison Discipline Society of Boston, the Twenty-nine Annual Reports of the Board of Managers, 1826–1854, with a Memoir of Louis Dwight*. Vol. 3. Boston: Perkins and Marvin, 1855. Reprint, Montclair, N.J.: Patterson Smith, 1972.

———. *Reports of the Prison Discipline Society of Boston, the Twenty-nine Annual Reports of the Board of Managers, 1826–1854, with a Memoir of Louis Dwight*. Vol. 4. Boston: Perkins and Marvin, 1855. Reprint, Montclair, N.J.: Patterson Smith, 1972.

———. *Reports of the Prison Discipline Society of Boston, the Twenty-nine Annual Reports of the Board of Managers, 1826–1854, with a Memoir of Louis Dwight*. Vol. 5. Boston: Perkins and Marvin, 1855. Reprint, Montclair, N.J.: Patterson Smith, 1972.

———. *Reports of the Prison Discipline Society of Boston, the Twenty-nine Annual Reports of the Board of Managers, 1826–1854, with a Memoir of Louis Dwight*. Vol. 6. Boston: Perkins and Marvin, 1855. Reprint, Montclair, N.J.: Patterson Smith, 1972.

Report of the Trial of Henry Wyatt, a Convict in the State Prison at Auburn Indicted for the Murder of James Gordon, Another Convict within the Prison, before the Court of Oyer and Terminer Held at Auburn, N.Y., Commencing Wednesday, February 11, 1846. Auburn, N.Y.: J. C. Derby & Co., 1846.

"Rev. John Luckey." In *Minutes of the New York Conference of the Methodist Episcopal Church*. New York: Nelson & Phillips, 1876.

Richmond, J. F. *New York and Its Institutions, 1609–1871*. New York: E.B. Trent, 1871.

Society for the Prevention of Pauperism. *Report on the Penitentiary System in the United States*. New York: Mahlon Day, 1822. Reprint, New York: Arno Press, 1974.

Sommers, Charles George. *Memoir of the Rev. John Stanford, D.D., Late Chaplain to the Humane and Criminal Institutions in the City of New-York*. New York: Swords, Stanford & Co., 1835.

Stanford, John. *An Authentic Statement of the Case and Conduct of Rose Butler*. New York: Broderick and Ritter, 1819.

———. *The Brand Plucked Out of the Fire*. New York: T. & J. Swords, 1821.

———. *A Catechism for the Improvement of Youth in the State Prison of New York*. New York: James Oram, 1814.

———. *Directory on the Scriptures for Those under Confinement*. N.p., n.p.

———. *A Discourse on the Death of an Unfortunate Youth, Aged 18 Years*. New York: J. Gray, 1815.

———. *The Prisoner's Companion*. New York: American Tract Society, 1827.

Sword of Justice, Wielded by Mercy: A Dialogue between the Inspectors of the State Prison, in New-York, and a Convict on the Day of His Liberation. New York: Office of the Gospel Herald, 1822.

"A View of the New-York State Prison by a Member of the Institution." In *Observations on Penal Jurisprudence and the Reformation of Criminals with an Appendix Containing the Latest Reports of the State-Prisons or Penitentiaries of Philadelphia, New-York, and Massachusetts; and Other Documents*, edited by William Roscoe. London: T. Cadell and W. Davies, 1819.

Wiltse, Robert. "Report of the Agent of the Mount-Pleasant State Prison." In *Documents of the Senate of the State of New York*, 57th Session, vol. 2, no. 92 (1834).

Secondary Sources

Abzug, Robert H. *Cosmos Crumbling: American Reform and the Religious Imagination.* New York: Oxford University Press, 1994.

Adamson, Christopher. "Evangelical Quakerism and the Early American Penitentiary Revisited: The Contributions of Thomas Eddy, Roberts Vaux, John Griscom, Stephen Grellet, Elisha Bates, and Isaac Hopper." *Quaker History* 90, no. 2 (Fall 2001): 35–57.

———. "Wrath and Redemption: Protestant Theology and Penal Practice in the Early American Republic." *Criminal Justice History* 13 (1992): 75–111.

Arpey, Andrew W. *The William Freeman Murder Trial: Insanity, Politics, and Race.* Syracuse, N.Y.: Syracuse University Press, 2004.

Bacon, Margaret Hope. *Lamb's Warrior: The Life of Isaac T. Hopper.* New York: Thomas Y. Cromwell, 1970.

Barbour, Hugh, et al. *Quaker Crosscurrents: Three Hundred Years of the Friends in the New York Yearly Meetings.* Syracuse, N.Y.: Syracuse University Press, 1995.

Barbour, Hugh, and J. William Frost. *The Quakers.* New York: Greenwood Press, 1988.

Barnes, Harry Elmer. *The Repression of Crime: Studies in Historical Penology.* 1926. Reprint, Montclair, N.J.: Patterson Smith, 1969.

Benson, Lee. *The Concept of Jacksonian Democracy: New York as Test Case.* Princeton, N.J.: Princeton University Press, 1961.

Boscoe, Ronald A. "Lectures at the Pillory: The Puritan Execution Sermon." *American Quarterly* 30, no. 2 (Summer 1978): 156–76.

Boyer, Paul. *Urban Masses and Moral Order in America, 1820–1920.* Cambridge, Mass.: Harvard University Press, 1978.

Bratt, James D. "The Reorientation of American Protestantism, 1835–1845." *Church History* 67, no. 1 (March 1998): 52–82.

Brodhead, Richard H. *Cultures of Letters: Scenes of Reading and Writing in Nineteenth-Century America.* Chicago: University of Chicago Press, 1993.

Brown, Candy Gunther. "Abolition of Slavery." In *The Encyclopedia of Protestantism*, edited by Hans Hillerbrand, 1740–45. New York: Routledge Press, 2004.

Brueggemann, Walter. *The Psalms and the Life of Faith.* Minneapolis: Fortress Press, 1995.

Budd, Richard M. *Serving Two Masters: The Development of the American Military Chaplaincy, 1860–1920.* Lincoln: University of Nebraska Press, 2002.

Burrows, Edwin G., and Mike Wallace. *Gotham: A History of New York City to 1898.* New York: Oxford University Press, 1999.

Cayton, Mary K. "Social Reform through the Civil War." In *The Encyclopedia of the American Religious Experience: Studies of Traditions and Movements,* vol. 3, edited by Charles H. Libby and Peter W. Williams, 1429–40. New York: Scribner, 1988.

Cherry, Conrad. *God's New Israel: Religious Interpretations of American Destiny.* Chapel Hill: University of North Carolina Press, 1998.

Clark, Elizabeth A. "'The Sacred Rights of the Weak': Pain, Sympathy, and the Culture of Individual Rights in Antebellum America." *Journal of American History* 82, no. 2 (September 1995): 463–93.

Cohen, Daniel A. *Pillars of Salt, Monuments of Grace: New England Crime Literature and the Origins of American Popular Culture, 1674–1860.* New York: Oxford University Press, 1993.

Cohen, Patricia Cline. *The Murder of Helen Jewett: The Life and Death of a Prostitute in Nineteenth-Century New York.* New York: Knopf, 1998.

Colvin, Mark. *Penitentiaries, Reformatories, and Chain Gangs: Social Theory and the History of Punishment in Nineteenth-Century America.* New York: St. Martin's Press, 1997.

Cross, Whitney. *The Burned-Over District: The Social and Intellectual History of Enthusiastic Religion in Western New York, 1800–1850.* Ithaca, N.Y.: Cornell University Press, 1950.

Dannin, Robert. "Island in a Sea of Ignorance: Dimensions of a Prison Mosque." In *Making Muslim Space in North America and Europe,* edited by Barbara Daly Metcalf, 131–46. Berkeley: University of California Press, 1996.

David, Joseph F., Jr., ed. *Sing Sing Prison, Ossining, New York: Its History, Purpose, Makeup, and Program.* New York: New York State Department of Correction, 1953.

Davis, David Brion. Introduction to *Antebellum American Culture: An Interpretative Anthology,* edited by David Bryon Davis, xix–xxiii. University Park: Pennsylvania State University Press, 1979.

———. "The Movement to Abolish Capital Punishment in America, 1787–1861." *American Historical Review* 63, no. 1 (October 1957): 23–46.

Dix-Richardson, Felecia. "Resistance to Conversion to Islam among African American Women Inmates." *Journal of Offender Rehabilitation* 35, nos. 3 and 4 (December 2002): 107–24.

Douglas, Ann. *The Feminization of American Culture.* New York: Farrar, Straus and Giroux, 1998.

Dumm, Thomas L. "Friendly Persuasion: Quakers, Liberal Toleration, and the Birth of the Prison." *Political Theory* 13, no. 3 (August 1985): 387–407.

Fabian, Ann. *The Unvarnished Truth: Personal Narratives in Nineteenth-Century America.* Berkeley: University of California Press, 2000.

Fessenden, Tracy. *Culture and Redemption: Religion, the Secular, and American Literature.* Princeton, N.J.: Princeton University Press, 2007.

Finney, Gail. "Garden Paradigms in 19th Century Fiction." *Comparative Literature* 36, no. 1 (Winter 1984): 20–33.

Floyd, Janet. "Dislocations of the Self: Eliza Farnham at Sing Sing Prison." *Journal of American Studies* 40, no. 2 (2006): 311–25.

Foucault, Michel. *Discipline and Punish: The Birth of the Prison*. New York: Vintage, 1977.

Frank, Jason. "Sympathy and Separation: Benjamin Rush and the Contagious Public." *Modern Intellectual History* 6, no. 1 (2009): 27–57.

Freedman, Estelle B. *Their Sisters' Keepers: Women's Prison Reform in America, 1830–1930*. Ann Arbor: University of Michigan Press, 1984.

Friedman, Lawrence M. *Crime and Punishment in American History*. New York: Basic Books, 1993.

Garland, David. *Punishment and Modern Society: A Study in Social Theory*. Chicago: University of Chicago Press, 1990.

Gilfoyle, Timothy. *City of Eros: New York City, Prostitution, and the Commercialization of Sex, 1790–1920*. New York: Norton, 1992.

———. *A Pickpocket's Tale: The Underworld of Nineteenth-Century New York*. New York: W. W. Norton, 2006.

———. "Street-Rats and Gutter-Snipes: Child Pickpockets and Street Culture in New York City, 1850–1900." *Journal of Social History* 37, no. 4 (Summer 2004): 853–82.

Gilmore, Ruth Wilson. *Golden Gulag: Prisons, Surplus, Crisis, and Opposition in Globalizing California*. Berkeley: University of California Press, 2007.

Gilpin, W. Clark. "Secularism: Religious, Irreligious, and Areligious." Marty Center Religion and Culture Web Forum, March 2007. ⟨http://divinity.uchicago.edu/martycenter/publications/webforum/032007/⟩, 1 July 2009.

Glenn, Myra C. *Campaigns against Corporal Punishment: Prisoners, Sailors, Women, and Children in Antebellum America*. Albany: State University of New York Press, 1984.

———. "Troubled Manhood in the Early Republic: The Life and Manhood of Sailor Horace Lane." *Journal of the Early Republic* 26, no. 1 (2006): 59–93.

Graber, Jennifer. "'When Friends Had the Management It Was Entirely Different': Quakers and Calvinists in the Making of New York Prison Discipline." *Quaker History* 97, no. 2 (Fall 2008): 19–40.

Greenberg, Douglas. *Crime and Law Enforcement in the Colony of New York*. Ithaca, N.Y.: Cornell University Press, 1976.

Gura, Philip F. Introduction to *Buried from the World: Inside the Massachusetts State Prison, 1829–1831; The Memorandum Books of the Rev. Jared Curtis*, edited by Philip F. Gura, ix–lxxii. Boston: Massachusetts Historical Society, 2001.

Halttunen, Karen. "Early American Murder Narratives: The Birth of Horror." In *The Power of Culture: Critical Essays in American History*, edited by Richard Wightman Fox and T. J. Jackson Lears, 67–102. Chicago: University of Chicago Press, 1993.

———. "Humanitarianism and the Pornography of Pain in Anglo-American Culture." *American Historical Review* 100, no. 2 (April 1995): 303–34.

Hamm, Thomas D. *The Quakers in America*. New York: Columbia University Press, 2003.

─────. *The Transformation of American Quakerism: Orthodox Friends, 1800–1907*. Bloomington: Indiana University Press, 1988.

Hanley, Mark Y. *Beyond a Christian Commonwealth: The Protestant Quarrel with the American Republic, 1830–1860*. Chapel Hill: University of North Carolina Press, 1994.

Hatch, Nathan O. *The Democratization of American Christianity*. New Haven, Conn.: Yale University Press, 1989.

Heale, M. J. "The Formative Years of the New York Prison Association, 1844–1862: A Case Study in Antebellum Reform." *New-York Historical Society Quarterly* 59, no. 4 (1975): 320–47.

─────. "From City Fathers to Social Critics: Humanitarianism and Government in New York, 1790–1860." *Journal of American History* 63, no. 1 (June 1976): 21–41.

─────. "Humanitarianism in the Early Republic: The Moral Reformers of New York, 1776–1825." *Journal of American Studies* 2 (1968): 161–75.

Hearn, Daniel Allen. *Legal Executions in New York State: A Comprehensive Reference, 1639–1963*. Jefferson, N.C.: McFarland, 1997.

Herre, Ralph S. "The History of Auburn Prison from the Beginning to about 1867." Ph.D. diss., Pennsylvania State University, 1950.

Hindus, Michael Stephen. *Prison and Plantation: Crime, Justice, and Authority in Massachusetts and South Carolina, 1767–1878*. Chapel Hill: University of North Carolina Press, 1980.

Hirsch, Adam Jay. *The Rise of the Penitentiary: Prisons and Punishment in Early America*. New Haven, Conn.: Yale University Press, 1992.

Hochfelder, David. "The Communications Revolution and Popular Culture." In *A Companion to 19th-Century America*, edited by William L. Barney, 303–16. Malden, Mass: Blackwell, 2001.

Holifield, E. Brooks. *Theology in America: Christian Thought from the Age of the Puritans to the Civil War*. New Haven, Conn.: Yale University Press, 2003.

Howe, Daniel Walker. "The Evangelical Movement and Political Culture in the North during the Second Party System." *Journal of American History* 77, no. 4 (March 1991): 1216–39.

─────. "Religion and Politics in the Antebellum North." In *Religion and American Politics from the Colonial Period to the 1980s*, edited by Mark A. Noll, 121–45. New York: Oxford University Press, 1990.

─────. *What Hath God Wrought: The Transformation of America, 1815–1848*. New York: Oxford University Press, 2007.

Hunt, Lynn. *Inventing Human Rights: A History*. New York: W. W. Norton, 2007.

Ignatieff, Michael. *A Just Measure of Pain: The Penitentiary in the Industrial Revolution, 1750–1850*. New York: Pantheon, 1978.

Ingle, H. Larry. *Quakers in Conflict: The Hicksite Reformation*. Knoxville: University of Tennessee Press, 1986.

Jacobsen, Matthew Frye. *Whiteness of a Different Color: European Immigrants and the Alchemy of Race*. Cambridge, Mass.: Harvard University Press, 1999.

James, Sidney V. *A People among Peoples: Quaker Benevolence in Eighteenth-Century America*. Cambridge, Mass.: Harvard University Press, 1963.

Johnson, David R. *Policing the Urban Underworld: The Impact of Crime on the Development of the American Police, 1800–1887.* Philadelphia: Temple University Press, 1979.

Johnson, Paul E. *A Shopkeeper's Millennium: Society and Revivals in Rochester, New York, 1815–1837.* New York: Hill and Wang, 1978.

Kann, Mark E. *Punishment, Prisons, and Patriarchy: Liberty and Power in the Early American Republic.* New York: New York University Press, 2005.

Kass, Alvin. *Politics in New York State, 1800–1830.* New York: Syracuse University Press, 1965.

Klein, Philip. *Prison Methods in New York State.* New York: Columbia University, 1920.

Kling, David W. "The New Divinity and the Origins of the American Board of Commissioners for Foreign Missions." *Church History* 72, no. 4 (December 2003): 791–819.

Kuntz, William Francis. *Criminal Sentencing in Three Nineteenth-Century Cities: Social History of Punishment in New York, Boston, and Philadelphia, 1830–1880.* New York: Garland, 1988.

Landau, Norma. "The Regulation of Immigration, Economic Structures, and Definitions of the Poor in Eighteenth-Century England." *Historical Journal* 33, no. 3 (1990): 541–72.

Lane, Roger. "Urban Police and Crime in Nineteenth-Century America." *Crime and Justice* 2 (1980): 1–43.

Laqueur, Thomas W. "Bodies, Details, and the Humanitarian Narrative." In *The New Cultural History*, edited by Lynn Hunt, 176–204. Berkeley: University of California Press, 1989.

Lardas Modern, John. "Evangelical Secularism and the Measure of Leviathan." *Church History* 77, no. 4 (December 2008): 801–76.

———. "Ghosts of Sing Sing, or the Metaphysics of Secularism." *Journal of the American Academy of Religion* 75, no. 3 (September 2007): 615–50.

Lewis, Orlando F. *The Development of American Prisons and Prison Customs, 1776–1845, with Special Reference to Early Institutions in the State of New York.* Albany: Prison Association of New York, 1922.

Lewis, W. David. *From Newgate to Dannemora: The Rise of the Penitentiary in New York, 1797–1848.* Ithaca, N.Y.: Cornell University Press, 1965.

Lichterman, Paul, and C. Brady Potts. "Conclusion: Rethinking Religion's Civic Life." In *The Civic Life of American Religion*, edited by Paul Lichterman and C. Brady Potts, 140–56. Stanford, Calif.: Stanford University Press, 2009.

Lindberg, Carter H. *Beyond Charity: Reformation Initiatives for the Poor.* Minneapolis: Augsburg Fortress Press, 1993.

Mackey, Philip English. *Hanging in the Balance: The Anti-Capital Punishment Movement in New York State, 1776–1861.* New York: Garland, 1982.

Marietta, Jack D. *The Reformation of American Quakerism.* Philadelphia: University of Pennsylvania Press, 1984.

Marini, Stephen. "Awakenings." In *The Encyclopedia of Protestantism*, edited by Hans Hillerbrand, 139–50. New York: Routledge Press, 2004.

Marsden, George M. *The Evangelical Mind and the New School Presbyterian Experience: A Case Study of Thought and Theology in Nineteenth-Century America*. New Haven, Conn.: Yale University Press, 1970.

Marx, Leo. *The Machine in the Garden: Technology and the Pastoral Ideal in America*. New York: Oxford University Press, 1964.

Masur, Louis. *Rites of Execution: Capital Punishment and the Transformation of American Culture, 1776–1865*. New York: Oxford University Press, 1989.

McDonald, Robert M. S. "Early National Politics and Power, 1800–1824." In *A Companion to 19th-Century America*, edited by William L. Barney, 5–18. Malden, Mass: Blackwell, 2001.

McGowen, Randall. "The Well-Ordered Prison: England, 1780–1865." In *The Oxford History of the Prison: The Practice of Punishment in Western Society*, edited by Norval Morris and David J. Rothman, 71–99. New York: Oxford University Press, 1998.

McKelvey, Blake. *American Prisons: A Study in American Social History Prior to 1915*. Chicago: University of Chicago Press, 1936.

McKenzie, Andrea. *Tyburn's Martyrs: Execution in England, 1675–1775*. London: Hambledon Continuum, 2007.

McLennan, Rebecca M. *The Crisis of Imprisonment: Protest, Politics, and the Making of the American Penal State, 1776–1941*. New York: Cambridge University Press, 2008.

Meaders, Daniel E. *Kidnappers in Philadelphia: Isaac Hopper's Tales of Oppression, 1780–1843*. New York: Garland, 1994.

Meranze, Michael. "A Criminal Is Being Beaten: The Politics of Punishment and the History of the Body." In *Possible Pasts: Becoming Colonial in Early America*, edited by Robert Blair St. George, 304–21. Ithaca, N.Y.: Cornell University Press, 2000.

———. *Laboratories of Virtue: Punishment, Revolution, and Authority in Philadelphia, 1760–1835*. Chapel Hill: University of North Carolina Press, 1996.

———. "Penality and the Colonial Project: Crime, Punishment, and the Regulation of Morals in Early America." In *The Cambridge History of Law in America*, vol. 1, *Early America (1580–1815)*, edited by Christopher Tomlins and Michael Grossberg, 178–210. Cambridge: Cambridge University Press, 2008.

———. "The Penitential Ideal in Late Eighteenth-Century Philadelphia." *Pennsylvania Magazine of History and Biography* 108 (1984): 419–50.

Mintz, Steven. *Moralists and Modernizers: America's Pre–Civil War Reformers*. Baltimore: Johns Hopkins University Press, 1995.

Miskell, John N. *Chronicles of Auburn State Prison: A Collection of Facts and Anecdotes*. Auburn, N.Y.: John N. Miskell, 1999.

Mohl, Raymond A. "The Humane Society and Urban Reform in Early New York." *New-York Historical Society Quarterly* 54, no. 1 (January 1970): 30–52.

———. "Humanitarianism in the Preindustrial City: The New York Society for the Prevention of Pauperism, 1817–1823." *Journal of American History* 57, no. 3 (1970): 576–99.

———. *Poverty in New York, 1783–1825*. New York: Oxford University Press, 1971.

———. "The Urban Missionary Movement in New York City, 1800–1825." *Journal of Religious History* 7 (December 1972): 110–28.

Morone, James A. *Hellfire Nation: The Politics of Sin in American History*. New Haven, Conn.: Yale University Press, 2003.

Mullet, Michael A. A. "Society of Friends." In *The Encyclopedia of Protestantism*, edited by Hans Hillerbrand, 779–84. New York: Routledge Press, 2004.

Nelson, William E. *Dispute and Conflict Resolution in Plymouth County, Massachusetts, 1725–1825*. Chapel Hill: University of North Carolina Press, 1981.

Noll, Mark A. *America's God: From Jonathan Edwards to Abraham Lincoln*. New York: Oxford University Press, 2002.

North, Eric M. *American Bible Society Historical Essay #14, Part II*. New York: American Bible Society, 1964.

Opal, J. M. *Beyond the Farm: National Ambitions in Rural New England*. Philadelphia: University of Pennsylvania Press, 2008.

Pernick, Martin S. *A Calculus of Suffering: Pain, Professionalism, and Anesthesia in Nineteenth-Century America*. New York: Columbia University Press, 1985.

Pierce, Yolanda. *Hell without Fires: Slavery, Christianity, and the Antebellum Spiritual Narrative*. Gainesville: University Press of Florida, 2005.

Pierson, George Wilson. *Tocqueville in America*. New York: Oxford University Press, 1938. Reprint, Baltimore: Johns Hopkins University Press, 1996.

Pointer, Richard W. *Protestant Pluralism and the New York Experience*. Bloomington: Indiana University Press, 1988.

Pratt, John Webb. *Religion, Politics, and Diversity: The Church-State Theme in New York History*. Ithaca, N.Y.: Cornell University Press, 1967.

Preyer, Kathryn. "Penal Measures in the American Colonies, an Overview." *American Journal of Legal History* 26 (1982): 326–53.

Rabinow, Paul, and Nikolas S. Rose. "Introduction: Foucault Today." In *The Essential Foucault: Selections from Essential Works of Foucault, 1954–1984*, vii–xxxv. New York: New Press, 2003.

Rafter, Nicole Hahn. *Partial Justice: Women in State Prisons, 1800–1935*. Boston: Northeastern University Press, 1985.

Resch, John. *Suffering Soldiers: Revolutionary War Veterans, Moral Sentiment, and Political Culture in the Early Republic*. Amherst: University of Massachusetts Press, 1999.

Roth, Randolph A. *The Democratic Dilemma: Religion, Reform, and the Social Order in the Connecticut River Valley of Vermont, 1791–1850*. Cambridge: Cambridge University Press, 2003.

Rothman, David J. *The Discovery of the Asylum: Social Order and Disorder in the New Republic*. Boston: Little, Brown, 1971.

———. "Perfecting the Prison, United States, 1789–1865." In *The Oxford History of the Prison: The Practice of Punishment in Western Society*, edited by Norval Morris and David J. Rothman, 100–116. New York: Oxford University Press, 1998.

———. "Prisons and Penitentiaries." In *The Oxford Companion to United States History*, edited by Paul S. Boyer, 620–21. New York: Oxford University Press, 2001.

Rotman, Edgardo. "The Failure of Reform: United States, 1865–1965." In *The Oxford History of the Prison: The Practice of Punishment in Western Society*, edited by

Norval Morris and David J. Rothman, 151–77. New York: Oxford University Press, 1998.

Ryan, Mary P. *Cradle of the Middle Class: The Family in Oneida County, New York, 1790–1865*. New York: Cambridge University Press, 1981.

Sassi, Jonathan D. *A Republic of Righteousness: The Public Christianity of the Post-Revolutionary New England Clergy*. New York: Oxford University Press, 2001.

Skotnicki, Andrew. *Religion and the Development of the American Penal System*. Lanham, Md.: University Press of America, 2000.

Smith, Caleb. "Detention without Subjects: Prisons and the Poetics of Living Death." *Texas Studies in Literature and Language* 50, no. 3 (Fall 2008): 243–67.

———. *The Prison and the American Imagination*. New Haven, Conn.: Yale University Press, 2009.

Smith-Rosenberg, Carroll. *This Violent Empire: The Birth of an American National Identity*. Chapel Hill: University of North Carolina Press, 2010.

Spierenberg, Pieter. "The Body and the State: Early Modern Europe." In *The Oxford History of the Prison: The Practice of Punishment in Western Society*, edited by Norval Morris and David J. Rothman, 44–70. New York: Oxford University Press, 1998.

Stansell, Christine. *City of Women: Sex and Class in New York, 1789–1860*. Urbana: University of Illinois, 1987.

Stout, Harry S. *The New England Soul: Preaching and Religious Culture in Colonial New England*. New York: Oxford University Press, 1988.

———. "Rhetoric and Reality in the Early Republic: The Case of the Federalist Clergy." In *Religion and American Politics from the Colonial Period to the 1980s*, edited Mark A. Noll, 62–76. New York: Oxford University Press, 1990.

———. *Upon the Altar of the Nation: A Moral History of the Civil War*. New York: Viking, 2006.

Sullivan, Winnifred Fallers. *Prison Religion: Faith-Based Reform and the Constitution*. Princeton, N.J.: Princeton University Press, 2009.

Sutton, William R. "Benevolent Calvinism and the Moral Government of God: The Influence of Nathaniel W. Taylor on Revivalism in the Second Great Awakening." *Religion and American Culture* 2, no. 1 (Winter 1992): 23–47.

Teeters, Negley K. *The Cradle of the Penitentiary: The Walnut Street Jail at Philadelphia, 1773–1835*. Philadelphia: Temple University Press, 1955.

———. *They Were in Prison: A History of the Pennsylvania Prison Society, 1787–1937, Formerly the Philadelphia Society for Alleviating the Miseries of the Public Prisons*. Philadelphia: John C. Winston, 1937.

Wheeler, Rachel. "'Friends to Your Souls': Jonathan Edwards' Indian Pastorate and the Doctrine of Original Sin." *Church History: Studies in Christianity and Culture* 72, no. 4 (December 2003): 736–65.

Whitman, James Q. *Harsh Justice: Criminal Punishment and the Widening Divide between America and Europe*. New York: Oxford University Press, 2005.

Wigger, John H. *Taking Heaven by Storm: Methodism and the Rise of Popular Christianity in America*. Urbana: University of Illinois Press, 2001.

Wilentz, Sean. *Chants Democratic: New York City and the Rise of the American Working Class, 1788–1850*. New York: Oxford University Press, 2004.

Williams, Peter W. *America's Religions: Traditions and Cultures*. Urbana: University of Illinois Press, 1998.

Wood, Gordon S. *Empire of Liberty: A History of the Early Republic, 1789–1815*. New York: Oxford University Press, 2009.

Woody, Thomas. *Early Quaker Education in Pennsylvania*. New York: Arno Press, 1969.

Youngs, J. William T. *The Congregationalists*. Westport, Conn.: Greenwood Press, 1990.

Zehr, Howard. *Changing Lenses: A New Focus for Crime and Justice*. Scottdale, Pa.: Herald Press, 1990.

Index

Adamson, Christopher, 90, 190 (n. 17), 199 (n. 38)

African Americans: and social practices, 29; Stanford's tract on, 65–66; colonization organizations, 176; and Quakers' view of education, 192 (n. 43). *See also* Free blacks; Slavery

Alcohol consumption, 11–12, 28, 32, 38, 64, 77, 79, 163

Allen, Stephen, 80, 198 (n. 13)

Allen, William, 65

American Bible Society, 88, 91

American Board of Commissioners for Foreign Missions, 90, 199 (n. 42)

American Education Society, 90, 199 (n. 42)

American Sunday-School Union, 73, 133, 199 (n. 42)

American Tract Society, 58, 90

Anderson, Rufus, 199 (n. 35)

Andersonville Prison, 175

Andover Theological Seminary, 89–90, 108, 123

Andrews, George, 164

Arch Street Prison, 24

Auburn Prison: discipline system of, 73–74, 75, 80–86, 89, 93, 94, 95–96, 100, 101, 103, 104, 106, 120, 121, 124–29, 130, 179, 182; and inmate reformation, 74, 75, 83, 97–98, 99, 100, 104, 116, 122, 125, 126, 127–28, 142; budget of, 74, 75, 83–84, 120, 126, 130; and inmate statistics, 74, 78, 79; corporal punishment in, 74, 79, 80, 83, 84–86, 94, 95, 99, 107, 120, 125–30, 142, 149, 151, 164, 179; staff of, 74, 80, 95–96, 125, 128, 164;
and religious services, 74, 83, 87, 93, 96, 97, 100, 104, 125, 127, 130, 141, 143, 150, 198 (n. 19); scandals of, 74, 85, 96, 99; and administrators/prison chaplains partnership, 74, 86–88, 100, 101, 116, 125–26, 127, 129, 143, 197 (n. 3); common night rooms, 75, 76, 79, 83, 126; keepers of, 75, 76, 86, 95, 130, 150, 151; and silence, 75, 80, 82–83, 86, 142; design of, 75–76; construction of, 76, 78; workshops of, 76, 79, 86; board of prison inspectors, 76, 89, 125, 126, 131, 152; and politics, 76, 168, 197 (n. 4), 206 (n. 11); immigrants as inmates in, 78, 79, 198 (n. 9); riots in, 79; and lockstep, 82, 86, 94, 142, 150; chaplains of, 83, 84, 86–88, 92, 94, 96–98, 99, 100, 122, 124–25, 129, 131, 143, 147, 151–52, 179, 180; and educational services, 83, 86, 99, 125, 127, 130, 198 (n. 19); and violence, 84, 85, 107, 128, 129, 170–71; female inmates of, 84, 106, 126, 127; and inmate classification, 93; recidivism rate of, 93, 97, 100; and inmate resistance, 94, 170; tensions at, 95–100; and inmate writings, 114, 117, 127–28, 202 (n. 23); mentally ill inmates of, 127, 150–52; fraud in, 149; and insanity defenses, 150–52; release of inmates, 163

Baptists: Particular Baptists, 55, 56, 57, 195–96 (n. 55); and Calvinism, 55–56, 57, 195–96 (n. 20); Philadelphia Confession, 56, 57, 67–68; discipline of, 57–58

Barbour, Hugh, 22

Barclay, Robert, 22

Barrett, Gerrish: as chaplain at Sing Sing
Prison, 108, 111–13, 115–16, 117, 122, 129,
180; and inmate suffering, 111–13, 131,
139; Lynds's removal of, 115–16, 117; and
hell-on-earth model, 132–33; writings of,
133–34
Baxter, Richard: *Call to the Unconverted*,
118, 155
Beach, John H., 76, 79
Beaumont, Gustave de, 3–4, 5, 9, 119–21,
122, 177
Beccaria, Cesare, 19, 25
Behavioral sciences, 180, 181
Bellevue Hospital, 159
Benezet, Anthony, 29
Bentham, Jeremy, 19, 20
Black Jacob (American Sunday-School
Union), 73
Blackwell's Island, 159
Boston Recorder and Religious Telegraph,
112, 141
Bowne, Robert H., 34, 192 (n. 53)
Boyce, Samuel, 164
Brady, James Topham, 204 (n. 26)
Bratt, James D., 203 (n. 65)
Brice, James, 115, 117–18, 129
Britten, William, 76, 78, 79, 80
Brodhead, Richard H., 200 (n. 49)
Brown, Mary, 164
Burr, Levi S., 113–14, 117, 129
Burrows, Edwin G., 77
Butler, Benjamin F., 205 (n. 26)
Butler, Rose, 66–67, 71

California, 1, 185 (n. 2)
Calvinist New Divinity movement, 89–90,
96, 108
Calvinist reformers: and disciplinary
routines, 6; and particularity, 22; and
Dwight, 89–90, 108, 199 (n. 38); mission
field of, 92, 108; and common experience, 109; and prison experiments, 131;
and grace, 139; and inmate reformation,
183; and death penalty, 199 (n. 38)
Canadian Association of Elizabeth Fry
Societies, 208 (n. 5)
Capital punishment. *See* Death penalty

Carrick, John, 164
Castle Island, prison experiment in, 20–21
Catholics: and immigrants, 3, 76–77, 105;
and conversion of Catholic inmates to
Protestantism, 147; Protestant opposition
to, 184
Cayton, Mary K., 199 (n. 42)
Cheever, George, 199 (n. 38)
Christian Register, 126
Christian Secretary, 126
Church of England, 55, 56
Church/state separation, 43, 58. *See also*
Disestablishment of religion
Citizenship: religiosity of, 5, 12, 13, 104, 132,
134, 136, 155, 177, 184, 203 (n. 65); and
New York Prison Association, 149, 155,
158; virtuous citizens, 156, 164, 188 (n. 2).
See also Marginal citizens
Civil War, 175, 179, 180
Clark, Elizabeth A., 110
Clay, Henry, 197 (n. 4)
Clinton, DeWitt, 62, 79, 193 (n. 70)
Coffey, William, 68–70
Cohen, Patricia Cline, 105
Colden, Cadwallader D., 193–94 (n. 72)
Collins, Isaac, 99
Colonial-era justice, 8–9, 16, 17–19, 22, 25,
27, 41, 122
Colorado, 180
Colquhoun, Patrick, 63
Combe, George, 148
Connecticut, 143, 153, 174
Connecticut State Prison at Wethersfield,
122, 133
Coolman, Jacob, 68–69
Corporal punishment: and prison history,
10, 41; in New York, 25, 26, 28, 47; in
Newgate Prison, 35, 47–48, 49, 63, 68,
70, 71; religion used in defense of, 48; in
Auburn Prison, 74, 79, 80, 83, 84–86, 94,
95, 99, 107, 120, 125–30, 142, 149, 151, 164,
179; and Dwight, 94, 101, 142, 153, 200
(n. 49); in Sing Sing Prison, 101, 103, 106,
107, 108, 109, 113–16, 119, 121, 122, 130, 137,
139, 142, 143, 144, 149, 153, 164; debates
on, 109–11, 180–81
Covenant, language of, 91

Crime: relationship to sin, 7, 8–9, 151, 152; capital crimes, 18, 19, 66, 154, 197 (n. 48); as civil and religious offense, 19, 149; violent, 24, 36, 160, 192–93 (n. 56); vice leading to, 40; and poverty, 69, 70; as civil offense, 149; and insanity defenses, 150–52; organized, 160; and cautionary literature, 167, 168; and socially degrading treatment of criminals, 182, 183

Crime prevention: and Eddy, 17, 207 (n. 29); Beccaria on, 19; and deterrence, 27–28, 132–33, 167, 168, 207 (n. 29); and penitentiary system, 30, 103

Crime rates: in New York, 24, 25, 38, 41, 47–48, 49, 62, 138; public concerns about, 104–5, 108, 110, 118; and policing, 137, 138; and urban conditions, 158, 159–60; effect of prisons on, 175

Criminal justice reform: role of religion in, 3, 4, 5–6; and Quakers, 16, 17, 21, 24, 190 (n. 17); and Europe, 19, 20, 21, 25; and punishment, 19, 27, 28, 30; and Eddy, 25–27; and Stanford, 59; and New York State legislature, 130, 131; and Seward, 130, 131, 137–38, 141–42, 143, 147, 150, 161, 171; and New York Prison Association, 145–46, 157; and politics, 152, 161; periodic presence of, 180–81; and Quakers as inspiration for prison reformers, 181, 208 (n. 5); and abolition of slavery, 194 (n. 3). *See also* Protestant reformers; Reformative prison programs

Curtis, Jared, as chaplain of Auburn Prison, 73, 96–98, 100, 117, 118, 139

Daly, Charles Patrick, 205 (n. 26)

Dannemora Prison, 160, 170, 204 (n. 7)

Death penalty: and doctrine of original sin, 11; and colonial-era justice, 16; and capital crimes, 18, 19, 66, 154, 197 (n. 48); and condemned sermons, 18, 189 (n. 9); and English punishment, 18, 189 (n. 7); in New York, 25, 26; and Dwight, 199 (n. 38)

Delaware, 180

Democratic Party, 106, 135–36, 138, 143–45, 149, 161, 175, 197 (n. 4)

Dickens, Charles, 148, 155

Dickerson, Jonathan, 123, 129, 202 (n. 48)

Disciplinary routines: prison enforcement of, 2; and labor, 4, 10, 21; and Protestant reformers, 4–5, 11, 71, 75, 158, 174; and Calvinist reformers, 6; religion used to promote, 10, 11, 47, 48, 68, 74, 75, 86, 87–88, 100, 152, 158, 174, 179, 184; Pennsylvania model of, 21, 24, 26, 28, 84, 85, 104, 106, 107, 120, 121, 198 (n. 20), 200 (n. 48); and Eddy, 28, 29–30, 31, 42, 74, 79–81, 84–85, 98–99, 100, 131, 183; in Newgate Prison, 48, 49, 50, 51, 52, 53–54, 59–60, 63–64, 65, 70, 80, 98–99, 131; in Auburn Prison, 73–74, 75, 80–86, 89, 93, 94, 95–96, 100, 101, 103, 104, 106, 120, 121, 124–29, 130, 179, 182; in Sing Sing Prison, 104, 106, 107, 108, 116, 118, 119, 122–24, 130, 135, 137, 141, 144, 160, 166–67, 173, 174; debates on, 106–7, 119–20, 123, 154–56, 158, 174, 175–76, 184; and fear to transgress approach, 122–24, 131–32; and New York Prison Association, 136, 145, 146, 147, 149, 157, 161–62, 167; and shower bath, 153, 160, 161, 164, 170, 171, 174, 205 (n. 47); and yoke, 153, 160, 170, 171, 174; and pulley, 160; and bucking, 161, 171; and Hopper, 163–65, 166; and Luckey, 171, 173; and Civil War, 175; disciplinary intimacy, 200 (n. 49). *See also* Labor; Solitary confinement

Discipline: and sin, 8, 9, 187 (n. 13); of Quakers, 22, 23, 24, 29–30, 31, 33, 34, 37, 42, 57, 190 (n. 18, 22); of Baptists, 57–58

Disestablishment of religion: and reformative prison programs, 2, 43; and Protestants' desire to shape culture, 3, 12, 101, 184; ambiguities of, 4, 183; and Christian identity of nation, 5, 11, 13; and religious-political partnerships, 194 (n. 73). *See also* Church/state separation

Dix, Dorothea, 109

Dwight, Louis: and furnace-of-affliction model, 74, 88, 92, 95, 96, 100, 107, 116, 127, 132, 143, 153–54, 181; tour of southern prisons, 88–89, 91, 92–93; and Auburn discipline system, 89, 92, 93, 94, 95, 97, 100, 107–8, 111, 124–27, 129, 130, 131, 141,

Garden model: and Quakers, 6, 7; and Eddy, 28–33, 43, 44, 48, 181; and Newgate Prison, 29, 30, 32, 35–42

Gardens: as symbol of ethical character, 29; as symbol of pastoral ideal, 44

German immigrants, 105, 138, 159

Gilfoyle, Timothy, 105

Gilmore, Glenda, 185 (n. 2)

Glenn, Myra, 110–11

Goodell, Richard, 198 (n. 24)

Gordon, Henry, 150, 151, 152

Grace: and sin, 8, 56; role in virtuous living, 13; and Quakers, 22; and Baptists, 56, 57; and Calvinist New Divinity movement, 90, 139; and Protestant evangelicals, 109; and Barrett, 112; and Dickerson, 123; and Methodists, 140

Greenberg, Douglas, 25

Grellet, Stephen, 99

Griffin, Edward D., 199 (n. 35)

Guardian, 179

Halttunen, Karen, 19, 186 (n. 6), 189–90 (n. 12)

Harper's Weekly, 161, 170, 174

Heale, M. J., 145–46

Hell-on-earth model: and Protestant reformers, 6, 7, 134, 156, 158, 176, 181; state officials' disagreement with, 7; and Barrett, 132–33; and Hopper, 166, 176; and Luckey, 167, 168, 170, 171, 173, 176, 207 (n. 29)

Hills, Horace, 89

Hodge, Charles, 123

Hodges, Jack, 73

Hopkins, Samuel, 80, 198 (n. 13)

Hopper, Isaac: and New York Prison Association's aid to released inmates, 145, 149, 157–58, 162, 163–67; and runaway slaves, 157, 162, 163; and politics, 157, 206 (n. 1); and pardons, 162, 166; and inmates' life stories, 163–67; and inmate reformation, 166, 183; and inhumane treatment of inmates, 173–74

House of Refuge, 71

Howard, John, 20, 25, 26, 32, 35, 79, 80, 83

Howe, Daniel Walker, 139

Humane Society of the City of New York, 64, 65, 196 (n. 42)

Humanitarianism: and humane treatment of inmates, 4, 11, 21, 30, 41, 45, 95, 107, 110, 113, 117, 124–25, 127, 136, 137, 141–42, 145–46, 152, 174, 176, 180, 182, 183; of Eddy, 26, 30, 99; and inhumane treatment of inmates, 84, 95, 115–16, 121–24, 128–29, 139, 142, 143–45, 149–53, 158, 160–61, 164–67, 170, 173–75, 181

Humphrey, Heman, 199 (n. 35)

Hunt, Lynn, 19

Ignatieff, Michael, 188 (n. 17)

Immigrants and immigration: Protestant fears of, 3; immigrants as inmates, 38, 44, 77, 78, 79, 106, 108, 109, 111, 116, 198 (n. 9); in New York City, 46, 76, 105, 158–59; and competition for jobs, 49, 105, 110, 138, 159–60; Irish, 76–77, 105, 106, 110, 138, 159; English, 105, 138, 159; German, 105, 138, 159; rise in, 118, 138, 158–60; city agencies and voluntary agencies responding to, 137; and humanitarianism, 137; and ethnic tensions, 159

Inmate reformation: religious influence on, 4, 5, 13, 136, 146, 148, 154, 155–56, 175; and Protestant reformers, 4, 5–6, 73, 136, 146–48, 182; as prison's primary purpose, 4, 181; and Quakers' separation and silence, 21; and solitary confinement, 21, 24, 36, 40; and Eddy, 26, 27, 33–35, 37–38, 41, 44, 56, 58, 82, 84, 86, 98, 99–100, 177; and incarceration as deterrence, 27–28; and garden model, 28, 29, 30; and corporal punishment, 49; and Newgate Prison, 50–53, 54, 62–63, 82, 86; and Stanford, 54, 55, 56, 58, 61–62, 65, 67, 71, 84, 86; inmate writings on, 68–70; debates on, 70–71, 154, 180; and Auburn Prison, 74, 75, 83, 97–98, 99, 100, 104, 116, 122, 125, 126, 127–28, 142; and Prison Discipline Society of Boston, 91–92, 93, 112, 118, 132, 155; and Dwight, 93, 94, 111, 112, 118, 131, 132, 142, 155; and Sing Sing Prison, 103, 104, 107, 108, 111–19, 120, 121–24, 126, 129, 132, 136, 141, 144; and New York Prison Association, 136, 146–49, 154–55; and Farnham, 147–48; emergence of, 191 (n. 33)

Inmates: humane treatment of, 4, 11, 21, 30, 41, 45, 95, 107, 110, 113, 117, 124–25, 127, 136, 137, 141–42, 145–46, 152, 174, 176, 180, 182, 183; reactions to Protestant piety, 5, 7, 118; conversion of, 6, 91, 92, 96, 98, 100, 101, 141, 147, 152, 158, 167, 168; writings of, 7, 11, 68–70, 95–96, 97, 100, 113–14, 115, 117–18, 127–29, 155, 175, 187 (n. 11), 188 (n. 19), 202 (n. 23); reactions to religious elements of prison discipline, 11, 152; immigrants as, 38, 44, 77, 78, 79, 106, 108, 109, 111, 116, 198 (n. 9); mentally ill as, 38, 55, 127, 130, 137, 139, 144, 150–52, 154; inhumane treatment of, 84, 95, 115–16, 121–24, 128–29, 139, 142, 143–45, 149–53, 158, 160–61, 164–67, 170, 173–75, 181; New York Prison Association's interviews with, 149; constitutional rights of, 180. *See also* Released inmates

Inmate suffering: and theology of redemptive suffering, 5, 48, 54–56, 58, 65, 68, 71, 74, 92, 96, 108, 111–13, 117–20, 122, 124, 127–29, 131, 136, 146, 149, 152, 155, 164, 166, 173, 179, 181, 182–83, 184; and furnace-of-affliction model, 7, 54, 68, 74, 152; and Stanford, 54, 56, 58, 60, 62, 65, 67, 87, 195 (n. 17); and Powers, 87; as end in itself, 131; and New York Prison Association, 146, 149; exposure of public to, 176; and inhumane treatment, 181; and inmate reformation, 182

InnerChange Freedom Initiative (IFI), 2, 184

Insanity defenses, 150–52, 205 (n. 39)

Iowa, 2, 3, 13

Irish immigrants, 76–77, 105, 106, 110, 138, 159

Irving, Pierre P., 204 (n. 26)

Jackson, Andrew, 106, 191 (n. 33), 197 (n. 4)

James, Sidney V., 190 (n. 22)

Jefferson, Thomas, 21

Johnson, Paul, 78, 79

Juveniles, houses of refuge for, 154, 159

Kann, Mark E., 12, 176

Kass, Alvin, 193 (n. 71)

Kentucky, 143

Kling, David W., 89

Kurtz, D. Morris, 197 (n. 4)

Labor: and disciplinary routines, 4, 10, 21; and Protestant reformers, 12; and workhouse, 17; and criminal justice reform, 20, 21, 26, 32; and garden model, 28, 30; and Newgate Prison, 30, 31–32, 34, 36, 38, 39, 41, 43, 47–53, 62, 65, 70, 77; and Auburn Prison, 75, 78, 80, 82, 83, 84, 86, 93, 94, 120, 127, 142, 153, 179; and Sing Sing Prison, 106, 108, 114, 115, 119, 121, 135, 48, 160

Lane, Horace, 95–96, 100, 114, 117, 129, 200 (n. 50)

Laqueur, Thomas, 16, 88, 176, 187 (n. 11)

Lardas Modern, John, 5, 155, 185 (n. 4)

Lewis, W. David, 108, 109, 119, 154, 160, 198 (n. 19), 205 (n. 47)

Lichterman, Paul, 186 (n. 8)

Liptak, Adam, 179, 183

Louisiana, 104, 121

Lownes, Caleb, 24, 26–27, 28

Luckey, Dinah, 147, 148

Luckey, John: as chaplain of Sing Sing Prison, 131, 136, 138–41, 143–44, 147–49, 167–68, 170, 171, 180; and Edmonds, 135–36, 147–48, 155; dismissal of, 136, 149, 167; writings of, 155, 167, 168, 170, 171, 173; and hell-on-earth model, 167, 168, 170, 171, 173, 176, 207 (n. 29); burial at Sing Sing Prison, 177–78

Lynds, Elam: and Auburn discipline system, 80–85, 86, 94, 106, 107, 108, 143, 161, 198 (n. 19); relieved of duties at Auburn Prison, 84, 85, 96, 106, 198 (n. 24); and Sing Sing Prison, 101, 106, 107, 108, 113, 114, 115–17, 119, 132–33, 135, 143, 144; Tocqueville's and Beaumont's interview with, 119–20; return to Auburn Prison, 126, 130, 134; firing from Sing Sing Prison, 145; New York Prison Association disagreeing with, 146, 147

Magdalene Society, 105

Magdalen house, 84

Maine, 143

Marginal citizens: and Protestant reformers, 3, 5, 184; and criminal justice reform, 17; and social practices, 29; and Quakers, 42; criminals treated as, 110, 182, 183; enclosure and distancing of, 176

Marietta, Jack D., 190 (n. 22)

Marx, Leo, 44

Maryland, 104

Massachusetts: and criminal justice reform, 20; prisons built in, 104; Dwight's support of prisons in, 143, 153, 174; prison population of, 206 (n. 3)

McGowen, Randall, 17

McLennan, Rebecca, 10, 68, 120

Mennonites, 182

Meranze, Michael, 9, 21, 107, 176, 191 (nn. 33, 34)

Methodists, 12, 100, 139–40, 170, 177, 186 (n. 10), 187 (n. 13)

Michigan, 104

Michigan State Prison, 180

Missionaries, 90, 199 (n. 42)

Mississippi, 104

Missouri, 104

Monroe, James, 62

Montesquieu, Charles Louis de Secondat de, 19, 25

Morality: and Protestant reform movements, 3, 12; and sin, 8; and Quaker administration of Newgate Prison, 16; God's moral law, 56; decline in after serving in prison, 69–70; and personal accountability, 90; and crime rates, 105; and prostitution, 105; and disciplinary routines, 123–24; and inmate reformation, 147, 148; and civic life, 155; role of religion in, 173, 177

Morrill, O. E., 151–52

Mount Pleasant State Prison. See Sing Sing Prison

Movies, 1

Murder narratives, transformation of, 186 (n. 6)

Murray, John, Jr., 34–35, 192 (n. 53)

Muslim prison ministries, 182, 208 (n. 5)

Native Americans: and social practices, 29; and Murray, 35; and reservations, 176; and Quakers' view of education, 192 (n. 43)

Nativism, 138

Newgate Prison: conflict over armed guard ordered for, 15, 16, 41, 45; escape in 1800, 15, 41; Quaker administration of, 15–16, 26, 33–35, 65, 131, 192 (n. 53); construction of, 26–28, 30, 38; and garden model, 29, 30, 32, 35–42; and spiritual needs, 29, 33, 35, 37, 45, 54, 82; and Quaker discipline, 31, 33, 37; Board of Prison Inspectors, 32, 33, 34, 36, 39, 43, 45, 47, 50, 52, 53–54, 56, 61, 62, 63, 68, 70, 71, 192 (n. 51, 53), 195 (n. 14); and cleanliness, 32, 34, 36, 43; diet in, 32, 43; workshops of, 32, 36, 39, 47, 48, 49, 50, 51, 63, 77, 197 (n. 48); religious meetings in, 33, 38, 48, 86; and inmate guidance, 33–35, 53, 61; and individual needs of inmates, 34; keepers of, 35, 36, 39, 52, 70; corporal punishment in, 35, 47–48, 49, 63, 68, 70, 71; staff of, 35, 36, 47–48, 63, 64, 70; female inmates of, 36, 60; and inmate statistics, 36, 78, 192–93 (n. 56), 194 (n. 4), 200 (n. 47); immigrants as inmates in, 38, 44, 77, 198 (n. 9); and mentally ill inmates, 38, 55; common night rooms of, 39, 41, 48, 49, 51, 64, 77, 85; and inmate classification, 39–40, 44, 51–52, 54, 79; Eddy's reports to legislature on, 40–41; riots in, 41, 48, 54, 63, 68, 85; and inmate dissatisfaction, 41–42, 44; and Protestant piety, 42; and profits, 45, 47, 49, 50, 51, 53, 54, 63, 70, 71; chaplain of, 45, 48, 52–56, 58–62, 71, 86, 93, 94; and pardons, 47, 51, 52, 60, 69; and discipline, 48, 49, 50, 51, 52, 53–54, 59–60, 63–64, 65, 70, 80, 98–99, 131; overcrowding in, 48, 49, 50, 51, 56, 62, 65, 70, 75, 77, 104, 105, 107; civil servants' administration of, 48, 49, 51–53, 63; and inmate resistance, 48, 52, 61, 63, 68, 69, 77, 197 (n. 48); and rival gang members, 49; and inmate reformation, 50–53, 54, 62–63, 82, 86; and sentencing rules, 51; and transport of inmates, 51, 75; and silence, 52, 54, 56, 62; Sabbath schedule of, 52–53, 60, 195 (n. 10); and inmate writings, 68–70; failures of, 75; recidivism rate of, 93

New Hampshire, 143

New Jersey, 104

New York: Quakers in, 24; criminal justice reform in, 24–28, 75; county jails of, 25, 36, 40, 65, 78; social disruption in upstate villages, 78–79; prison population of, 160, 206 (n. 3)

New York City: criminal population of, 29, 76; and Newgate Prison inmates, 36, 38, 39; Eddy's reform ideas for vice, 40, 64; jail of, 40, 67, 200 (n. 47); unemployment in, 48–49; immigrants in, 49, 76, 105, 158–59; Five Points slum, 49, 77, 138, 167; former inmates as gangs in, 51; free blacks in, 77; sex industry in, 77, 105; increase in vice, 77, 105, 159; police force of, 105, 159; Bowery, 138; social disorder in, 138; gangs of, 138, 159, 160; released inmates in, 145; and criminal justice reform, 191 (n. 30)

New York Evangelist, 105, 141, 174

New York Observer and Chronicle, 148

New York Prison Association (NYPA): and disciplinary routines, 136, 145, 146, 147, 149, 157, 161–62, 167; formation of, 136, 145, 147; and inmate reformation, 136, 145–49, 154–55; inspections of prisons, 145, 148, 162, 165; aid to released inmates, 145, 149, 157–58, 162, 163–67; legal reforms of, 145, 157, 161–62, 171; and chaplains, 146–47; reports to legislature, 149–50, 165

New York State legislature: relationship with Quaker prison administrators, 15, 16, 45; Wiltse's report to, 121–22; and Auburn Prison, 126; and prison reform, 130, 131; and New York Prison Association reports, 149–50, 165

New York State Prison. *See* Newgate Prison

New York Sun, 105, 148

New York Times, 179

Noll, Mark, 12, 185 (n. 4)

Ohio, 104, 143

Organized crime, 160

Panopticon, 20

Particular Baptists, 55, 56, 57, 195–96 (n. 55)

Penal codes: and criminal justice reform, 26, 27, 28, 38; and New York Prison Association, 145

Pennsylvania: and criminal justice reform, 20–22, 26, 27–28; Quakers in, 21, 23, 24, 26–27, 28; disciplinary model of, 21, 24, 26, 28, 84, 85, 104, 106, 107, 120, 121, 198 (n. 20), 200 (n. 48); prison population of, 206 (n. 3)

Pernick, Martin S., 195 (n. 17)

Philadelphia Society for Alleviating the Miseries of the Public Prisons (PSAMPP), 21, 24

Phillips Academy, 108

Physical health programs, 4, 32–33, 38, 82

Pierce, Yolanda, 171

Plumb, Charles, 170–71

Pointer, Richard W., 43, 194 (n. 73)

Politics: and Eddy, 42–43, 45, 79–80, 100, 193–94 (n. 72); and Protestant reformers, 42–43, 54, 118, 124, 144; and Newgate Prison, 53; and Stanford, 54–55, 71; and Auburn Prison, 76, 168, 197 (n. 4), 206 (n. 11); and Dwight, 92–93, 137, 138; and Lynds, 106, 116–17, 130, 143, 161; and Sing Sing Prison, 116, 143, 145, 168, 206 (n. 11); and prison disciplinary routines, 145, 168, 173; and criminal justice reform, 152, 161; and Hopper, 157, 206 (n. 1); and Luckey, 167–68; growth of partisanship, 193 (n. 70, 71)

Porter, Ebenezer, 199 (n. 35)

Post, Jotham, 192 (n. 53), 195 (n. 14)

Potts, C. Brady, 186 (n. 8)

Poverty and the poor: and English punishment, 18; and Protestant reformers, 20; and criminal justice reform, 26, 28; Eddy's view of problems of, 29, 38, 64,

70, 194 (n. 74); Murray's work with, 34–35; and competition for jobs, 49, 105; and Stanford, 55; and crime, 69, 70; and free blacks, 77; and immigrants, 77; and prostitution, 105; relief for, 138; and Hopper, 162, 163

Powers, Gershom: and Auburn's disciplinary system, 74, 85–87, 94, 95–96, 97, 99–100, 125, 198 (n. 24); and educational programs, 86; and chaplains, 86–88, 92, 93, 95, 97; and inmate suffering, 87; and Dwight, 94–95, 142

Pratt, Robert, 2

Princeton Theological Seminary, 108, 123

Prison Association of New York. *See* New York Prison Association

Prison Discipline Society of Boston: disciplinary programs of, 6, 88, 92, 94, 97, 101; officers of, 89, 199 (n. 35); and inmate reformation, 91–92, 93, 112, 118, 132, 155; and inmate statistics, 92; and prison conditions, 92; and prison inspections, 92, 133; and religious instruction in prisons, 93–94; chaplains of, 96; and Sing Sing Prison, 107, 108, 116, 119, 123, 130, 141, 142–43, 144, 147–48; and Auburn Prison, 107–8, 125–26, 141, 144, 152

Prisoner's Friend, 152

Prison Fellowship Ministries, 2, 181, 184

Prison inspectors: and Newgate Prison, 32, 33, 34, 36, 39, 43, 45, 47, 50, 52, 53–54, 56, 61, 62, 63, 68, 70, 71, 192 (n. 51, 53), 195 (n. 14); and Auburn Prison, 76, 89, 125, 126, 131, 152; Dwight on, 88; and Sing Sing Prison, 115, 116, 117, 119, 130, 131, 135, 136, 143–44, 147–48; and politics, 206 (n. 11)

Prisons: economic and human costs of, 1; retributive programs, 1–2, 6; purpose of, 1–2, 10, 19, 27, 48, 191 (n. 33), 194 (n. 74); rehabilitative programs, 3, 30, 180, 181; Tocqueville's and Beaumont's study of, 3–4, 101, 119–21, 122, 177; colonial history of, 8–10, 19, 191 (n. 33); Dwight's tour of southern, 88–89, 91, 92–93; rise in construction of, 104–5; effect of crime rates on, 175. *See also* Auburn Prison; Furnace-

of-affliction model; Garden model; Hell-on-earth model; Newgate Prison; Reformative prison programs; Sing Sing Prison; *and other specific prisons*

Probation, 180

Progressive Era, 180

Prostitution, 105

Protestant evangelicals: and reformative prison programs, 2, 5; and church-state alliances, 3, 5, 7, 12, 185 (n. 4), 188 (n. 22); and redefinition of Protestant piety, 12, 13, 109–10, 118, 132, 203 (n. 65); and perfectionism, 22; and Irish immigrants, 76–77; and upstate New York, 78–79; prison as mission field for, 91, 92, 93; and individual responsibility, 109–10, 118; and revivalism, 109–10, 118, 123; missions in New York City, 159; classification of, 186 (n. 10)

Protestant reformers: and marginal citizens, 3, 5, 184; and inmate reformation, 4, 5–6, 73, 136, 146–48, 182; and prison experiments, 4, 6, 20–21, 131; and disciplinary routines, 4–5, 11, 71, 75, 158, 174; theology of redemptive suffering, 5, 48, 54–56, 58, 65, 68, 71, 74, 92, 96, 108, 111–13, 117–20, 122, 124, 127–29, 131, 136, 146, 149, 152, 155, 164, 166, 173, 179, 181, 182–83, 184; and hell-on-earth model, 6, 7, 134, 156, 158, 176, 181; partnerships among, 7, 11, 136, 138; writings of, 7, 133–34, 186–87 (n. 11); disagreements among, 10, 27–28, 136, 139, 154, 174; and social order, 20, 105, 194 (n. 74); and politics, 42–43, 54, 124, 138, 144; cooperation with state officials, 74, 92–93, 94, 95, 101, 103–4, 124, 184, 197 (n. 3); cooperation with prison officials, 74, 135; role in prison system, 123, 165; changes in approach, 133–34, 136, 156, 184; New York Prison Association's shared goals with, 136, 155; New York Prison Association contrasted with, 146, 147–49; and insanity defenses, 152; and social work, 156; and urban conditions, 159. *See also specific reformers*

Protestants: power of, 2–3; and desire to shape culture, 3, 12, 90, 95, 101, 176–77,

and inmate suffering, 54, 56, 58, 60, 62, 65, 67, 87, 195 (n. 17); as Newgate Prison chaplain, 54, 56, 58–62, 71, 88, 93, 94, 111, 117, 118, 131, 139, 177, 180; sermons of, 54, 58, 60–62, 71; and furnace-of-affliction model, 54–62, 68, 71, 134, 181; family background of, 55; and evangelism, 57; tracts written by, 58, 60, 61, 65–67, 71, 134, 197 (n. 48); and inmate guidance, 61; and submission, 61–62; hosting touring dignitaries, 62; and Auburn Prison, 84, 94; Sabbath schedule of Newgate Prison, 195 (n. 10); Edwards compared to, 196 (n. 24); and capital crimes, 197 (n. 48)

Stansell, Christine, 33

State officials: reactions to Protestant piety, 5, 7; relationship with Quaker administrators of Newgate Prison, 15–16; and Stanford, 57; cooperation with Protestant reformers, 74, 92–93, 94, 95, 101, 103–4, 124, 184, 197 (n. 3); and Eddy's report to, 98–99; and New York Prison Association, 149–50, 165, 174

Stout, Harry, 188–89 (n. 22)

Stoutenburgh, Isaac, 192 (n. 53)

Stowe, Harriet Beecher, 110

Sullivan, Winnifred, 2–3

Sutton, William, 90

Sword of Justice, Wielded by Mercy (anonymous pamphlet), 47–48, 71

Technology, potential of, 44

Television shows, 1

Tellkampf, Johann, 204 (n. 26)

Tibbetts, George, 80, 198 (n. 13)

Tocqueville, Alexis de, 3–4, 5, 9, 101, 119–21, 122, 177, 186 (n. 8)

Townsend, Thomas, 131

Underground Railroad, 162

Unitarians, 89

United States, incarceration rate of, 1, 179

Urban conditions: and criminal justice reform, 28; Eddy on, 41; and Stanford, 54; and crime rates, 158, 159–60; and Protestant reformers, 159

Van Buren, Martin, 106, 193 (n. 70)

Vanderpool, George, 60–61

Vermont, 104, 143

Vice: Eddy's reform ideas for, 40, 64; increase in, 77, 159

Violence: Protestant reformers' protesting, 6; and criminal justice reform, 21; and Quakers' antislavery campaigns, 23; violent crime, 24, 36, 160, 192–93 (n. 56); and Auburn Prison, 84, 85, 107, 128, 129, 170–71; abolitionist's arguments against, 110; and Sing Sing Prison, 113–15, 122, 128, 129, 170; and colonial-era justice, 122

Virginia, 21

Wadler, Ezekiel, 70

Wallace, Mike, 77

Walnut Street Jail, 21, 24, 26, 27, 28, 36, 93, 162

Warner, George, 192 (n. 53), 195 (n. 14)

War of 1812, 47, 49

Wendover, Peter, 53

Wesley, John, 140

Whig Party, 130, 137, 138, 143, 152, 161, 168, 175

White, James, 69

White, William, 162

Whitman, James Q., 182

Wigger, John, 140

Wilentz, Sean, 191 (n. 30)

Wiltse, Robert: and Sing Sing Prison, 103–4, 119, 121–24, 129, 130, 131–32, 134, 137–39, 171; disciplinary regime of, 119, 121–24, 129, 130, 131–32, 134, 161; Seward's firing of, 137; investigation of, 138; New York Prison Association disagreeing with, 146, 147

Wisner, B. B., 199 (n. 35)

Wood, Gordon, 20

Woodhull, S. S., 88

Woods, Leonard, 199 (n. 35, 37)

Woolman, John, 24

Workhouse, and social order, 17

Wyatt, Henry, 150–51

Yellow fever, 48–49

Young, John, 166